ZEW Economic Studies
Volume 45

Publication Series of the Centre for European Economic Research (ZEW), Mannheim, Germany

For further volumes:
http://www.springer.com/series/4041

Marcus Kappler · Andreas Sachs
Editors

Business Cycle Synchronisation and Economic Integration

New Evidence from the EU

Physica-Verlag
A Springer Company

ZEW
Zentrum für Europäische Wirtschaftsforschung GmbH
Centre for European Economic Research

Series Editor
Prof. Dr. Dr. h.c. mult. Wolfgang Franz

Editors
Dr. Marcus Kappler
Centre for European Economic Research
Mannheim
Germany

Dipl.Oec. Andreas Sachs
Centre for European Economic Research
Mannheim
Germany

ISSN 1615-6781 ISSN 1867-2027 (electronic)
ISBN 978-3-7908-2854-2 ISBN 978-3-7908-2855-9 (eBook)
DOI 10.1007/978-3-7908-2855-9
Springer Heidelberg New York Dordrecht London

Library of Congress Control Number: 2012936665

Printed on acid-free paper

Physica is a brand of Springer
Springer is part of Springer Science+Business Media (www.springer.com)

Table of Contents

1 Introduction

This book establishes facts about business cycle synchronisation and convergence in the euro area and beyond as well as examines determinants of cyclical correlation. The identification of factors that are robustly linked to business cycle synchronisation and that are amenable to economic intervention may improve the formulation of policies that foster cyclical convergence. Synchronicity of business cycles is often regarded as an important prerequisite for a well-functioning common currency. In the absence of a certain degree of synchronicity, a common monetary policy may not satisfy the needs of all member countries and may even contribute to cyclical divergence. The extent of business cycle convergence in a monetary union is determined by a number of factors, including the degree of symmetry between macroeconomic shocks, transmission channels and institutional features – including fiscal policy – as well as the level of economic integration between member countries. All of these aspects play an important role in optimal currency area (OCA) theory, which seeks to determine the costs and benefits of a common currency and which received a great deal of attention in the discussion about the introduction of the euro. According to the seminal work by Mundell (1963) and the subsequent rich literature on OCA theory, the benefits of a currency union outweigh the cost of a foregone independent monetary policy if (i) the countries share similar business cycles, (ii) labour mobility across the region is high, (iii) the economies are open with capital mobility and price and wage flexibility across and region, and (iv) a risk-sharing system such as an automatic fiscal transfer mechanism is in place. The financial and economic crisis of 2008/09 has indicated that the traditional OCA indicators pay too little attention to financial markets. After the collapse of the US investment bank *Lehman Brothers* in September 2008, the inter-bank money market dried up completely as commercial banks lost confidence in the solvency of their counterparties. As a result, non-financial corporations had problems obtaining financing. These financial problems were a main reason for the drastic decline in world trade as well as the sharp recession that struck industrialised nations and many emerging markets almost simultaneously. In this way, tight financial market linkages and disruptions contributed significantly to a synchronous economic downturn. Thus, an analysis of financial markets is important for the investigation and understanding of business cycle synchronisation.

A common monetary policy may even contribute to a de-coupling of business cycles, as the experience of some countries at the periphery of the euro area (Greece, Spain, Portugal and also Ireland) has shown. Particularly the southern euro area countries experienced a significant drop in their interest rates after the founding of the euro area. At the same time, wage-induced inflation was high in these countries, leading to low or even negative real interest rates. These low interest rates contributed to rising domestic demand and further wage increases. As a consequence, the international competitiveness of these countries deteriorated markedly, resulting in rising current account deficits. On the other hand, core euro area countries with lower internal demand and wage pressures gained international competitiveness, and the current account of these countries improved considerably. Hence, the common monetary policy contributed to the build-up of external imbalances within the euro area, making a long-lasting and for some countries painful adjustment process necessary.

The second chapter of this book provides a summary of the latest findings in the *empirical literature* in order to address the key objectives of the study. Section 2 summarises the recent literature on business cycle synchronisation and convergence, which can be subdivided into several groups: studies that investigate these issues with a particular focus on the euro area and the New Member States (sub-section 2.1.1), studies that look at the cyclical conformity between the G7 and OECD countries (sub-section 2.1.2), and literature that compares the developments within the euro area with the global business cycle (sub-section 2.1.3). This is followed by a review of papers and reports that identify clusters of countries for which cyclical similarity is particularly pronounced (sub-section 2.1.4) as well as a summary of the findings for regional business cycle cohesion between US states and between Canadian provinces (sub-section 2.1.5). In sub-section 2.1.6, the role of idiosyncratic and common shocks as well as the role of shock propagation mechanisms are assessed by a review of the relevant literature. If there is risk sharing, i.e. if there are inter-state fiscal and market institutions that help smooth income between states and countries, a looser connection between individual countries' cycles may be less problematic since such equalisation mechanisms can partly substitute for the loss of an independent national monetary policy when it comes to stabilising asymmetric shocks and asymmetric business cycle fluctuations within a monetary union. Therefore, the latest findings regarding the degree of risk sharing between the Member States of the euro area and between US states are summarised in sub-section 2.1.7.

Section 2.2 reviews the literature dealing with the *determinants* of business cycle synchronisation and convergence. We first provide a detailed overview of recent studies and their main findings; the different approaches considered are then delineated. More specifically, sub-sections 2.2.1 to 2.2.6 examine determinants of business cycle synchronisation such as trade integration, membership in currency unions, monetary integration, fiscal policy, sectorial structure and financial market integration. This literature survey provides an overview of the existing evidence and serves as a guide for the empirical analysis that is conducted in chapter 1.

The remaining chapters of the book deal with empirical examinations. Chapter 1 starts off with addressing and discussing key methodological concepts for estimating business cycles, their similarity and convergence. The business cycle itself cannot be observed; assumptions therefore have to be made about its characteristics in order to estimate it. Section 3.1 presents and discusses several methods for disentangling the cycle and trend from observed data. In this section, we demonstrate how one's view of the business cycle and its synchronicity depends on the methodology chosen (section 3.2). Furthermore, we discuss how convergence may be assessed by means of statistical measures and tests, allowing us to draw conclusions regarding the significance of the obtained findings (section 3.3). Then, a set of *stylised facts* concerning the characteristics of business cycles and synchronisation in the euro area and elsewhere are presented (sections 3.4 and 3.5). This part of the book also provides a descriptive overview on the question of whether *convergence or divergence* patterns between the euro area countries changed after the introduction of the euro. In addition, we take a look at the degree of business cycle synchronisation between other countries and the euro area average. The analysis is complemented by a frequency domain approach which allows us to characterise *coherence, dynamic correlation* and the *lead and lag relationship* between the business cycles of the euro area on the one hand and the US, UK and Japan on the other (section 3.6). In this part of the book, the main focus lies on convergence with respect to the cyclical component of output. However, both real and nominal convergence is needed for a common monetary policy to be efficient for all participants. For this purpose, section 3.7 looks beyond output gaps by also analysing convergence of *budget balances*, *inflation rates* and *real long-term interest rates*. Next, with the aid of a *cluster analysis,* groups of euro area and OECD countries sharing common business cycles are identified (section 3.8). In section 3.9, business cycle similarities between the US states are studied so as to facilitate a conclusive comparison between the euro area and the US, a mature currency union that is characterised by a larger amount of risk sharing through financial markets and federal fiscal instruments. Finally, in chapter 3.10 some conclusions are drawn.

The empirical work in chapter 4 is devoted to two aspects which have not received much attention in the literature so far: first, the significance of financial market integration and second, the influence of structural reforms and institutional determinants of business cycle synchronisation. The close financial links between European economies can be seen as a channel for the transmission of shocks between countries. Financial market integration thus functions as a catalyser for shocks. However, the integration of international financial markets also helps to insulate the domestic economy to a certain degree against idiosyncratic shocks and also facilitates specialisation. An analysis of the overall impact of these countervailing partial effects is the focus of section 4.1. Structural reforms may serve to increase flexibility and thereby improving resilience to macroeconomic shocks. In this way, as emphasised by the OCA literature, it can partly substitute for the loss of monetary and exchange rate adjustments in a monetary union. After presenting the key contents of the European reform agenda and their likely effects on the cyclical conformity of Member States, the effects of structural reforms on business cycle synchronisation, particularly in the field of labour markets, are analysed in section 4.2. In these sections, we employ panel data regressions that build on and extend the recent empirical literature on both factors in important ways.

Analyses of cyclical co-movement by correlation measures do not answer the question whether (a)symmetries in business cycles are caused by different responses to common shocks or by differences in idiosyncratic, country-specific shocks. Such reactions to different sorts of macroeconomic disturbances are central to the understanding of co-movements in economic activity which is not revealed by basic correlation analyses. Chapter 5 provides analyses of shock propagation mechanisms and international business cycles based on structural vector autoregression (SVAR) models. Results from two different empirical models are presented. The first model (section 5.2) includes the G7 countries. The subjects of interest are the properties of output cycles and changes in inflation rates. In this regard, the role of common and structural (supply, demand and nominal) shocks is established. The second model (section 5.3) covers a shorter sample period and has less theoretical structure, but deals with more countries than the first model. It allows us to investigate whether differences in the aforementioned variables between the euro area average and its 12 Member States are mainly due to common or country-specific shocks.

The empirical analyses in this book cover a period ending in 2007, i.e. before the culmination of the financial and subsequent to the real economic crisis. It is conceivable that business cycle synchronicity has increased during the crisis since it hit nearly almost all industrialised countries and many emerging market economies more or less simultaneously. On the other hand, the cyclical upswing observed in 2009/10 was concentrated in emerging markets, particularly in Asia. Among the industrialised countries, Germany could benefit most from this recovery. While these stylised facts could be observed in the recent business cycle, it is too early to assess whether the long-run business cycle relationships have changed during the crisis and subsequent recovery. As this book focuses on these longer term patterns, it seemed appropriate to exclude the recent episode from our empirical investigations.

The last chapter of the book summarises the main findings and illuminates their policy implications.

This book is based on the research project "Study on economic integration and business cycle synchronisation", carried out by the Centre for European Economic Research (ZEW)in Mannheim and the Institute for Advanced Studies (HIS)in Vienna, commissioned and financed by the Bureau of European Policy Advisers (BEPA) of the European Commission in the context of "10 years EMU".

2 Literature Review

By Bas van Aarle, Marcus Kappler, Jonas Keil, Atilim Seymen, and Klaus Weyerstrass

2.1 Business Cycle Synchronisation and Convergence

A tabulated overview of the literature on business cycle convergence and its determinants is provided at the end of this section. In the following paragraphs, we will summarise the main findings of the many-faceted contributions to this strand of research.

2.1.1 Literature on the Euro Area and New Member States

In recent years a substantial literature has developed on business cycle synchronisation within the euro area and between the euro area and the countries that entered the EU in 2004 and 2007 (New Member States, NMS) in view of the pending euro area enlargement. The situation in Sweden, Denmark and the UK and their relation to the euro area have also been analysed in a number of studies. The literature on business cycle convergence between the euro area countries and other, non-EU countries is obviously much smaller.

Important contributions regarding the euro area have been made by Artis and Zhang (1999), who find that correlation has increased substantially over time in the euro area. They show that the European Exchange Rate Mechanism (ERM) period (1979-1993) influenced homogeneity positively and identify the clear emergence of a European business cycle during this time frame. A recent study by Gayer (2007) observes a significant harmonisation of output growth since the early 1990s, albeit with a short interruption in 2003/2004. The recovery in 2004 showed that the decline was probably just a transitory phenomenon due to increased uncertainty as a result of the war in Iraq, terrorism, etc. Interestingly, Gayer (2007) finds a recurrent pattern in the history of business cycle synchronisation in the euro area which implies that synchronisation typically decreases in the recovery phases of the cycle and that it rises again as the cycle continues. Using correlation-based measures of business cycle synchronisation, Gayer (2007) finds no evidence of higher correlation after the launch of the euro in 1999. Furthermore, by comparing the patterns of a "world cycle" and the euro area cycle, he observes continuous evidence for a distinct euro area business cycle. He concludes that the increased correlation in the euro area may not be regarded as a *"mere by-product of globalisation"*. However, de Haan et al. (2005) observe that we cannot speak of a *"monotone movement towards the emergence of a 'European' business cycle"*.

The literature is also conflicting with regard to the effects of European Monetary Union (EMU) on synchronisation in the euro area. While Afonso and Furceri (2007) find evidence that, since the introduction of the euro, the degree of synchronisation has increased remarkably for all countries except Germany – where it has remained similar – de Haan et al. (2002) are unable to provide a definite answer as to whether the currency union has a positive impact on synchronisation. Massmann and Mitchell (2004) find a long-run trend of rising correlations among euro area business cycles, a finding that stands in contrast to Mink et al. (2007), who conclude that synchronicity and co-movement in the euro area exhibit no clear upward tendency. In terms of country-specific patterns, Gayer (2007) shows that Greece in particular – but also Finland, Belgium and Ireland – has had business cycles that are uncoupled from the cycles shared in general by the larger European countries. The case of Greece can be mainly interpreted as a structural phenomenon, whereas Finland, for instance, had to deal with the breakup of the Soviet Union.

Business cycle synchronisation between the NMS and the euro area – as measured, say, by correlations between de-trended industrial output in NMS and the euro area – is generally found to be present, but at a lower average level than for individual euro area countries. A similar conclusion emerges concerning inflation. The literature on business cycle synchronisation is restricted by the relatively short sample of data for the NMS. Furthermore, the wide variety of business cycle methods and indicators used lead to considerable differences in the outcomes and conclusions reached in studies on this topic. Moreover, the results differ across countries as the NMS are quite heterogeneous, and general conclusions are hard to draw. Another drawback has been the frequent practice of using Germany as a reference country instead of using the euro area business cycle itself. Finally, many studies concentrate on industrial production since the corresponding data are often more reliable. On the other hand, a robustness check concerning results, using, say, GDP data, seems desirable since industrial production represents only a certain share of the total economy. Basing conclusions entirely on this variable is thus a precarious proposition.

Darvas and Szapary (2005) provide a relatively detailed analysis of business cycle synchronisation between the NMS and the euro area. Thanks to the use of a larger set of variables and more countries (similar to the countries in our analysis), more sub-periods and more measures of synchronisation than in most studies, more robust results on business cycle synchronisation between the NMS and euro area are achieved. The authors find that Hungary, Poland and Slovenia are the most synchronised of the NMS when compared to the countries in the euro area periphery (Portugal, Ireland and Finland). The other NMS are less synchronised with the euro area, raising doubts about the suitability of adopting the euro as soon as the countries with a higher degree of synchronisation. The authors also calculate impulse responses from a VAR model in order to analyse the impact of shocks in the euro area on the NMS. Slovenia and Poland are found to be most sensitive to euro area shocks.

In a meta study, Fidrmuc and Korhonen (2006) provide a very good overview of the literature on business cycle synchronisation between the NMS and the euro area as well as of the literature on the degree of symmetry of macroeconomic shocks between the NMS and euro area. Thirty-five studies are analysed concerning (i) the NMS countries included, (ii) methodology used, (iii) frequency of the data and (iv) the reference country used. On average the highest average estimates of business cycle correlation with the euro area are found in the case of Hungary (0.36), followed by Slovenia (0.26) and Poland (0.25). In several studies, one or more of the NMS are found to have higher business cycle correlations with the euro area than one or more peripheral euro area economies (Greece, Portugal and Ireland).

Concerning euro area enlargement, the discussion has not only considered business cycle synchronisation of the NMS with the euro area but also OCA questions such as the following: For which countries is accession profitable in the sense that the likely benefits exceed the likely costs? In this complicated question, shocks play a particularly important role, in addition to the appropriateness of the current monetary and fiscal policy framework in the euro area and the current amount of business cycle convergence. Another aspect that has received attention is the role of the entry conditions (convergence criteria) laid down in the Maastricht Treaty and the choice of the concrete entry date and conversion rate. In general, it is suggested that due to a general catching up process and a larger amount of idiosyncrasies in macroeconomic shocks and macroeconomic structures, the NMS as a group are not as similar and homogenous as the current Member States. As a consequence, accession to the euro area is a process that should be carefully undertaken and supervised to avoid serious problems later on.

Empirical evidence on the degree of shock symmetry between the NMS and the euro area is provided by Fidrmuc et al. (2003), among others. Using a structural VAR model that is based on Blanchard and Quah (1989), demand and supply shocks are identified and their correlation with euro area demand and supply shocks is determined. Correlation of demand shocks with the euro area appears to be lower than the correlation of supply shocks for most NMS. The majority of NMS show a lower degree of macroeconomic shock correlation than the current euro area countries in relation to the euro area aggregate. This could reflect diverging macroeconomic conditions, different institutions and structures, and differences in macroeconomic policies (monetary policy, including exchange rate and fiscal policy). Clearly, a monetary union will leave most of these asymmetries unaffected; it will first and foremost reduce asymmetries resulting from independent monetary and exchange rate management. On the other hand, the introduction of a common monetary policy could lead to a new source of macroeconomic shocks and to uncertainty on the part of an acceding country, in the sense that it no longer has any influence on interest and exchange rates.

Babetskii (2005) finds that higher trade integration and lower exchange rate volatility induces a higher degree of demand shock symmetry in the NMS and that the effects on supply shocks vary from country to country. This partly confirms the "endogenous OCA" hypothesis and the EU Commission's view on economic integration and the synchronisation of shocks. The results concerning supply shocks, on the other hand, do not rule out Krugman's hypothesis that due to increased specialisation, monetary unions can be subject to increased shock asymmetries. This possibility, when one also takes into account the greater structural and institutional heterogeneity of the NMS, could imply that euro accession of the NMS will aggravate the "core-periphery" dichotomy in the euro area, leading to potential risks for macroeconomic stability and convergence.

Taken altogether this literature leaves some doubt as to whether most of the NMS are natural candidates at present for the adoption of the euro. On the other hand, there is clearly a potential the prospect of euro area accession to induce a further and swift increase in synchronisation, in accordance with the logic of the endogenous OCA hypothesis. In particular, several studies have pointed to the importance of intra-industry trade in increasing business cycle synchronisation rather than bilateral trade integration per se.

2.1.2 Literature on the G7 and OECD Countries

Studies that focus on business cycles in the G7 countries typically find no evidence for an overall increase in synchronicity over the last decades. For instance, Stock and Watson (2005) find no signs of rising business cycle synchronisation in the G7 countries from 1960 to 2002, but observe an emergence of a European cycle and of one between English-speaking countries. They also find evidence for falling output volatility and explain this lower volatility with the absence of common shocks propagating through the G7. The synchronisation of the Japanese business cycle in particular with the rest of the G7 was low over the period under examination, as Japan had a very distinct cyclical development. Doyle and Faust (2002) find a slow though insignificant fall in the synchronisation of the G7 countries over the period from 1970 to 2002, a finding that stands in contrast to observed downtrend in the volatility of output fluctuations. This fall in the standard deviation of output volatility would imply a rise in business cycle correlation. The reason for this is that a decline in the prominence of idiosyncratic shocks in a country lowers the standard deviation of the country's economic growth. If, at the same time, common variation, measured by covariance, remains unchanged, then correlation rises. Moreover, Stock and Watson observe that co-movements are generally higher during recessions than in recovery phases. This is the same pattern that Gayer (2007) and others find for the euro area countries.

Kose et al. (2005) observe a notable increase in the synchronicity of business cycles among the G7 countries. They distinguish between three factors – common (G7), country-specific and idiosyncratic – that drive an economy and estimate their relative importance. First, they find that common and country-specific factors play different roles at different points in time in different countries. Second, the G7 factor is found to play a crucial role in explaining variations in GDP, implying that worldwide events are of sizable importance. Third, by dividing the full sample from 1960 to 2003 into three sub-periods – 1960-72 (Bretton Woods), 1973-86

(Common shocks) and 1987-2003 (Globalisation period) – the authors show that the common factor was most important in the second period and less important in the first. Finally, Kose et al. find that the G7 factor has less explanative power for variation in output among the G7 countries during the globalisation period. A study by Bordo and Helbling (2003), which builds on evidence from 16 countries, documents evidence of a rise in business cycle synchronisation over the past century. Furthermore, the authors find that global shocks are the dominant influence across different periods and that these shocks have gained increasing importance over time. This finding would appear to be a product of increasing globalisation, particularly the integration of goods and services through international trade and integration of financial markets. Taken together, the literature suggests that the synchronisation of business cycles among industrialised nations has undergone a change during the last three to four decades; however, mixed results are obtained regarding the question of whether country-specific or global impacts have gained in importance.

Additional insights from studies with broader country samples suggest, among other things, that English-speaking country pairs have a much higher correlation than other country pairs. Furthermore, a very low symmetry between New Zealand and Japan, which is attributable to several idiosyncratic shocks (Voss, 2000), can be identified. Akin (2007) observes that the co-movement of cycles is stronger among industrialised nations in comparison to emerging and developing countries. But while convergence tendencies can be observed in emerging economies, synchronisation has been rather stable in developed countries. Otto et al. (2001), who consider 17 OECD countries, show that the mean correlation of GDP growth has shrunk, although they do find evidence for greater cross-country economic integration. Akin (2007) analyses 47 countries from 1970 to 2003 and divides the full sample into three subsamples: the oil shock period, debt crisis period and globalisation period. He concludes that there is no significant change in the symmetry of business cycles, yet uncovers significant alternation in the various periods: for instance, increasing co-movement of output in Asian countries during the debt crisis period (1980-89) and an EU cycle in the globalisation period (1990-2003).

2.1.3 Literature on the Euro Area Versus Global Convergence

The last decades have seen a significant increase in trade and financial globalisation. Accordingly, cross-country output spillovers and financial linkages – e.g. regarding commodity and asset prices as well as volatility swings in the global financial system – are ever more important for the developed and developing countries. The recent experience with the collapse of the US subprime mortgage market and attendant impacts to the global financial system illustrate the new risks and vulnerabilities associated with financial globalisation.

In the euro area, business cycles are not only driven by domestic factors and euro area/EU wide adjustments, but also by global factors. The European Commission (2008) observes that while there have been no major further synchronisation gains since the single currency was introduced, the synchronisation between the euro area and the rest of the world has increased in the last decade. This suggests that the euro area has been moving more in line with the global business cycle.

This implies that an analysis of euro area business cycles must include a country-specific part relating to country-specific developments and asymmetric shocks, an euro area-wide part reflecting euro area-wide adjustments – including the common monetary policy and symmetric euro area-wide shocks – and a global part that measures the impact of the global business cycle and global shocks. Kose et al. (2008) use such a decomposition of output into country-specific, group-specific, global and idiosyncratic factors to analyse business cycle convergence and decoupling for a panel of 106 countries over the period 1960-2005. Three groups are distinguished: 23 industrial countries, 24 emerging markets and 59 developing countries. For industrial countries, the global factor explains 27 per cent of output fluctuations, the group-specific factor 17 per cent, the country-specific factor 33 per cent and a residual factor 21 per cent. For Western Europe these factors are similar (23 per cent, 22 per cent, 34 per cent and 21 per cent, respectively). Over time, the group-specific factors tend to increase while the global and country-specific factors decrease as a result. This might be interpreted as the influence of phases of 'recoupling and decoupling' in the global economy where global and group/regional factors fluctuate in importance in explaining the business cycles of individual countries. In particular, a recent decoupling of emerging countries could explain why these countries have not been strongly affected by the slowdown in the US economy, which was caused mostly by developments specific to the US.

The increasing global integration is also manifested in two stylised facts that have been observed: (i) the volatility of the business cycle of the global economy and of the developed and developing countries has, on average, declined since the end of the 1970s, and (ii) the synchronisation of business cycles has increased globally. A number of explanations for the observed decline in volatility have been proposed: improved institutional quality contributing to political stability, improved quality of monetary and fiscal management, changes in structural features – such as financial deepening, improved inventory management, the information technology revolution and more flexible labour and product markets – lower terms-of-trade volatility and an overall decline of the size of supply shocks, particularly oil-supply disruptions (a so-called 'good-luck' factor). Explanations for the rise in business cycle co-movement are in particular linked to the observed increase in trade and financial linkages in the global economy and the increase in the symmetry of macroeconomic shocks across countries.

2.1.4 Literature on Country Clusters

Drawing on industrial production data, Camacho et al. (2005a) analyse business cycle co-movement as quantified by a combination of different synchronisation measures. Using data for the 27 EU countries (except Malta and Bulgaria), Canada, the US, Norway, Japan and Turkey, the authors identify three clusters. The first cluster includes the euro area countries (except Finland) plus Denmark, Sweden, Cyprus, Lithuania, Slovenia and Hungary. The second group consists of the US, Canada, the UK, Japan and Finland. The remaining countries, i.e. Latvia, Estonia, Slovakia, the Czech Republic, Romania, Turkey, Norway and Poland form the third group.

In a related study, the same authors (Camacho et al., 2005b) measure the similarity of business cycles by considering the duration, amplitude and so-called 'excess' of expansions and contractions. Excess is defined as the departure of the actual growth path from a hypothetical path that would have been witnessed if the transition between the two consecutive turning points in the series had been linear. The analysis is again based on industrial production data for the same sample of countries examined in the previously mentioned study. In this paper, the authors identify four clusters. The first cluster is composed of Cyprus, Estonia, Latvia, Lithuania, Romania and Turkey. The second group consists of Slovakia, the Czech Republic, Denmark, Spain, Sweden, Finland, Luxembourg, Austria, the US and Canada. In the third cluster, Slovenia, Japan, Norway, the UK, Portugal, the Netherlands, Italy, France, Greece, Germany and Belgium are grouped together. Finally, Poland, Hungary and Ireland form the fourth cluster, as they exhibit business cycle characteristics that are most distinct from the other countries.

Graff (2006) estimates the business cycle position on the basis of the deviation between the actual and trend capital coefficient over the period from 1970 to 2000. The sample comprises the 15 EU countries prior to the enlargements of 2004 and 2007 (EU15), plus Argentina, Australia, Chile, Hong Kong, Iceland, Israel, Japan, Canada, New Zealand, Norway, Switzerland, Singapore, Korea, Uruguay and the US. Based on a hierarchical cluster analysis, the author identifies two main business cycle clusters. The first one consists of Belgium, Germany, France, Greece, Ireland, Iceland, Israel, Italy, Japan, Luxembourg, Austria, Portugal, Switzerland and Spain. The second main group is made up of Denmark, Finland, Australia, New Zealand, the US, Canada, the UK, the Netherlands, Norway and Sweden. The remaining countries in the sample exhibit business cycle characteristics that are quite different from these two main country groups.

In an earlier study, Artis and Zhang (1997) measure the business cycle synchronisation of 18 countries, using Germany as a benchmark. The sample comprises the EU15 (except Luxembourg), the US, Japan, Switzerland, Norway and Canada. Three clusters are identified: the "US group", consisting of the US, Canada, Sweden and Finland; the "European group" with Italy, Ireland, the UK, Denmark, Portugal, Norway, Greece and Spain; and the "core group" with France, Austria, the Netherlands and Belgium. Switzerland and Japan do not belong to any of these groups.

2.1.5 Literature on Canada and the US: Lessons for the Euro Area

The literature on business cycle convergence and synchronisation between the provinces and states of Canada and the US as common-currency areas is summarised in table 2. Partridge and Rickman (2005) exclusively analyse the evolution of US state cycles and observe a decline in their co-movement over time despite a high degree of overall synchronisation. They find the decline of overall US volatility to be the primary source of this result, and point to an important methodological problem regarding the assessment of optimal currency areas. According to the authors, a common monetary policy can still be beneficial despite an increase in asymmetry, provided the magnitude of nation and region-specific shocks declines sufficiently.

In Clark and van Wincoop (2001), de Haan et al. (2002) and Wynne and Koo (2000), the cycles of US states are used as a benchmark in order to evaluate the effects of European monetary integration on business cycle synchronisation. Clark and van Wincoop (2001) compare the degree of synchronisation across US census regions with that across European countries by defining a border dummy that describes the difference between cross-region and cross-country correlations of the considered business cycle variable. Although this border dummy is found to decline over time, a significantly lower degree of business cycle synchronisation across European countries compared to that of US regions is observed throughout. The lower level of trade between European countries seems to play the crucial role in this border effect. As the effect of a common monetary policy on business cycle synchronisation is found to be insignificant, Clark and van Wincoop (2001) do not predict business cycle convergence for the euro area after the adoption of a single currency. De Haan et al. (2002) fail to arrive at a clear answer as to whether the further integration of euro area countries would lead to business cycle convergence. Using pre-war data going back to 1929, they find that business cycles in the US have become less synchronised over time. Significant evidence for convergence is also not provided when the analysis is restricted to post-war data or uses a different number of subperiods. These results, together with the findings for Western Germany (as a second benchmark) and the OECD, do not allow precise conclusions about the potential impacts of the common European currency to be drawn. Wynne and Koo (2000) compare standard deviations and correlation coefficients of business cycle variables across, on the one hand, US Federal Reserve districts, and, on the other, EU countries. Although no clear statement can be made on whether high standard deviations result primarily from synchronous business cycles with different magnitudes or rather from a low degree of synchronisation, lower standard deviations in the cyclical components of employment and GDP can generally be observed in the US.

Imbs (2004) focuses on the determinants of synchronisation, also using US state level data. Estimating a system of simultaneous equations by applying a three-stage least squares (3SLS) approach, he tries to isolate the direct effects of inter-sectoral and intra-sectoral trade, financial integration and sectoral specialisation on the degree of business cycle synchronisation between 24 selected countries as well as between US states. Although the results for the latter are only discussed briefly and are part of a sensitivity analysis that is not reported in the published version of the paper, Imbs (2004) provides evidence that all of the posited determinants of business cycle synchronisation exert a significant effect.

Beine and Coulombe (2003) and Wakerly et al. (2006) focus on features of the business cycles in Canadian regions. In order to find out whether the adoption of the US dollar is preferable for Canadian regions, Beine and Coulombe (2003) investigate the evolution of business cycles in Canadian provinces relative to the US cycle. They find that correlations between the US cycle and that of the central provinces Ontario and Quebec tended to increase over time, whereas the correlations of the other provinces with the US decreased. Due to this strong heterogeneity between provinces, Canada does not seem to be an optimal currency area. Wakerly et al. (2006) obtain similar results and also report large asymmetries in regional output fluctuations, mainly due to similar levels of technology, as measured by total factor productivity, as well as due to similarity in preferences, as identified using the permanent income hypothesis.

The experience of the US in particular, as reported by Partridge and Rickman (2005), raises concerns about the usual practice of assessing OCAs in terms of cyclical correlation. In the US, close synchronisation can be observed for the period from 1971 to 1998. On the one hand, the analysis suggests that the US best fulfilled OCA criteria in the 1970s, a period in which US monetary policy is viewed as being particularly ineffectual. On the other hand, successful monetary policy during the 1990s was accompanied by a decline in synchronisation, and this business cycle de-coupling did not seem to affect the efficiency of monetary policy. Thus, standard OCA theory does not help to explain US monetary policy. A further lesson can be drawn from the US experience. Behavioural factors such as the political support for US monetary policy or structural factors which are linked to the effectiveness of monetary policy may play an important role for the success of a common monetary policy. The overall implication of this study for the euro area is "*that monetary unions can succeed in a wider range of settings than imagined, such as an inclusive euro area that expands to the UK and elsewhere*".

2.1.6 Literature on Identifying Business Cycle Shocks

2.1.6.1 Structural and Global VAR Models

The analysis of correlation between shocks in different countries could potentially provide information on the symmetry of these shocks. Fidrmuc and Korhonen (2003), who estimate bivariate structural VAR models using an approach suggested by Bayoumi and Eichengreen (1992) for the euro area and the individual countries, compare the estimated supply and demand shocks of every country with those of the euro area model. Their aim is to provide empirical evidence on the degree of structural shock symmetry between the New Member States (NMS) and the euro area. The correlation of demand shocks with the euro area appears to be lower than the correlation of supply shocks for most of the NMS. Moreover, most NMS exhibit lower scores than the current euro area countries when tested for macroeconomic shock correlation in relation to the euro area aggregate.

The Global VAR (GVAR) approach, introduced by Pesaran et al. (2004) for modelling interdependencies among many countries, provides a solution to the degrees-of-freedom problem by estimating country-specific VARs with exogenous variables (VARX). Foreign variables are modelled as exogenous. Those exogenous variables are specific to individual countries and every country's foreign variables are a weighted sum of all other countries' corresponding variables in the world. The weighting is typically determined based on trade shares or GDP shares. Pesaran et al. (2004) show that country-specific VARX models can be combined in a convenient way for computing the coefficients of a global VAR; that is, a VAR that comprises the variables of *all* countries covered in the model. Ultimately, all countries' variables are endogenous in the global VAR, although foreign variables are exogenous in country-specific VARs.

Dees et al. (2007) consider the euro area as a single country and investigate the linkages between it and the rest of the world in the GVAR framework. Their sample covers the period from 1979 to 2003. The global model includes 26 economies. Each country-specific VAR comprises 6 domestic variables (real output, inflation rate, real exchange rate, real equity prices, a short-term and a long-term rate of interest), 5 foreign variables (the domestic variables minus the real exchange rate) and 1 further global exogenous variable (oil prices). However, structural shocks and their dynamic effects on the variables are not identified in this framework. Instead, the authors concentrate on the dynamic responses of the variables to a shock based on a certain equation for a specific country. Since no initial structural identification is carried out, they employ generalised impulse response functions as described in Pesaran and Shin (1998) for their analysis. They are interested, among other things, in the dynamic effects of a shock to the US short-term interest rate on US and euro area variables. Such a shock leads to different impulse response patterns in the US than in the euro area. Surprisingly, the impact response of US output is positive, but it becomes insignificant after two quarters; whereas the response in euro area output is insignificant from the outset. Similarly, the US inflation rate rises in the first two periods after the shock, while the euro area inflation rate does not.

In addition to the dynamic analysis with respect to country-specific shocks, the GVAR framework allows for the modelling of global shocks, too. Dees et al. (2007) compute global shocks to a certain variable as a weighted-average of country-specific shocks.

The only structural shock identification carried out to date is US monetary policy shocks by Dees et al. (2007). The US model is included in the GVAR as the first country-specific model. Furthermore, it does not contain foreign variables. The authors follow the strategy discussed by Sims and Zha (1998) for the identification of monetary policy shocks. The dynamic responses to a monetary policy shock by the US and the euro area variables are not much different than their generalised responses to a shock to the US short-term interest rate mentioned above.

2.1.6.2 Factor Models

Factor models which, in contrast to classical VAR models, can contain many variables, provide another possibility for distinguishing between world and country-specific shocks as well as spillovers between countries. Stock and Watson (2005) estimate 2 common factors and 7 country-specific shocks with a Factor-Structural VAR for the G7 economies. The VAR comprises the GDP growth rate of the G7 countries. Global shocks are the 2 common components of the seven-variable VAR. Moreover, the spillover effects are modelled such that the country-specific shock of one country cannot have an impact on the GDP growth of another country before the quarter in which the shock took place has elapsed. Global shocks, on the other hand, are allowed to have an impact effect. The first relevant finding for our study is that international synchronisation has not increased recently. Instead, two coherent cyclical groups have emerged among the G7 countries: The English-speaking group and the euro area group. Secondly, the decrease in international synchronisation is due to a decrease in the volatility of global shocks.

Eickmeier (2006) estimates a large model with 296 variables for investigating business cycle transmission from the US to Germany. Her sample covers the period from 1975 to 2002. The variables used are real and nominal variables for the US and German economies. The movements of these variables are related to a small number of factors (8 according to tests) which follow a VAR process. The empirical framework allows a distinction to be made between common and idiosyncratic components (shocks). Eickmeier (2006) also imposes some restrictions on the VAR process of the factors in order to estimate US supply and real demand shocks. Her approach has two advantages. First, one can compute the dynamic effects of structural shocks of one country on the variables of another country. Second, conclusions can be drawn on the importance of various channels for business cycle synchronisation. Eickmeier (2006) finds that US supply and demand shocks *"affect the US economy and the German economy largely symmetrically"*. Our study also finds that common shocks to Germany and the US would lead to a high correlation between these two countries; see section 5.2. Moreover, trade and relative price movements are found to be the most important channels of business cycle transmission. The role of financial markets, on the other hand, is not clear. Given that Germany is the largest economy in the euro area, these conclusions can also be expected to apply to the relationship between the US and the euro area.

Kose et al. (2005) investigate the evolution of the G7 business cycles with a so-called dynamic factor model. Unobserved dynamic factors determine, together with country-specific shocks, the evolution of output, consumption and investment in the modelled G7 countries. The so-called G7 factor is common to all countries. The evolution of the variables is additionally driven by a country-specific factor that is common for the variables of that country, and an idiosyncratic shock. The authors analyse the relative influence of these three factors in three different sub-periods: the Bretton Woods period (1960-72), the period of common shocks (1972-86) and the globalisation period (1986-2003). Although the share of common shocks increases in the latter two periods, it cannot be clearly concluded that the global shocks are most important in business cycle fluctuations in the globalisation period. In particular, the share of global shocks decreases in the globalisation period relative to the previous one. The share of global shocks increases steadily, however, in the output fluctuations of France and Italy. Thus, the overall impact of global shocks in the euro area is ambiguous. This assessment is also corroborated by our own empirical work (see section 5.2).

2.1.7 Literature on Risk Sharing and Fiscal Federalism

The synchronisation of business cycles and other macroeconomic variables in a monetary union such as the euro area becomes less crucial if mechanisms of risk sharing are in place. Such mechanisms can partly substitute for the loss of national monetary policy when it comes to stabilising asymmetric shocks and asymmetric business cycle fluctuations in a monetary union. According to an argument by Mundell (1963) that has been further developed by McKinnon (2001), a monetary union is conducive to risk sharing through portfolio diversification. Furthermore, greater business cycle synchronisation in a monetary union such as the euro area may not be necessary or useful since this would reduce the scope and function of risk-bearing mechanisms, as such mechanisms are based on divergence rather than convergence in business cycles.

In OCA theory there are two forms of international risk sharing that potentially alleviate the impact and adjustment burden from asymmetric shocks in a monetary union: (i) federal tax-transfer systems provide automatic stabilisation by transferring resources from countries in a boom to economies in a recession, e.g. such as that caused by an asymmetric shock that has hit the monetary union; (ii) cross-country holdings of financial assets contribute to risk sharing and diversification between countries since part of the burden of asymmetric shocks will be transferred to foreign holders of domestic assets, particularly stocks,[1] and vice versa. This form of risk sharing has been mostly investigated by estimating the degree of consumption smoothing across borders. The possibility of cross-border holdings of financial assets not only applies to regional risk sharing in a monetary union like the euro area but also has a global equivalent in the form of global risk sharing and consumption smoothing. The ongoing process of globalisation and financial market integration has dramatically increased the potential for risk sharing at a global level.

Empirical evidence on the euro area case finds that both forms of cross-country risk sharing are fairly weak – and are more than likely to remain so – certainly when compared with mature monetary unions/federations like the US and Canada. This is not surprising given a number of crucial dimensions in which the euro area currently differs from mature monetary unions like the US. Firstly, the euro area (and European Union) are not designed to be fiscal federations in accordance with the principals of fiscal federalism. Instead, the federal fiscal tax and spending powers are very small (the EU budget does not exceed 1% of EU GDP) when compared to the federal budget in the US. This implies, for example, that the

---

[1] Foreign direct investment (FDI) represents another type of cross-country financial asset holding that could be relevant in this respect. Using a panel of 25 OECD countries for the period 1981-2001, Schiavo (2007) estimates the effect of currency unions on bilateral FDI flows. The approach is in a similar vein to the larger literature that has tried to estimate the trade effects of currency unions; see Rose (2000). A seperate EMU effect is considered for the euro area countries. It is found that currency unions, including the euro area, have a significant positive effect on bilateral FDI flows.

amount of allocation, redistribution and stabilisation that occurs through the federal budget in the US is completely absent in the euro area. Part of the fiscal stabilisation remains at the national level in that automatic stabilisers are let free to do their stabilising (subject to the constraints of the Stability and Growth Pact). Proposals to develop alternative insurance and transfer schemes that could compensate for the virtual absence of a federal fiscal system in the euro area have received some academic interest but their introduction appears unlikely in light of current political and economic circumstances.

Furthermore, the effects of risk sharing trough the financial system are generally found to be lower in the euro area then in the US. Kalemli-Ozcan et al. (2004) find that, although financial integration in the euro area has increased over time, the frequency with which idiosyncratic shocks are smoothed through risk sharing in the euro area financial system remains fairly low: smoothing by the financial sector is in the range of 10% of income over the period from 1993 to 2000, whereas it reaches 55% in the US case.[2] Kalemli-Ozcan et al. also investigate whether risk sharing is conducive to higher specialisation, higher asymmetry in output and lower asymmetry in income as a result of increases in opportunities to share risk across member countries in monetary unions. While this hypothesis is supported for the US case, it is not confirmed for the EU case. The authors find that incomes are actually more asymmetric than production despite an increase in risk sharing. The low initial degree of risk sharing is suggested to be responsible for these differences.

Possible explanations for the limited role of risk sharing in the euro area financial system could be the still substantial home bias in investment behaviour and the fragmentation of the European banking system, as compared to the US case. These factors are likely to adjust over time such that risk sharing through financial markets in the euro area is likely to strengthen, but this is a very gradual process. Nevertheless, according to the methodology developed by van Wincoop (1994), this means that there are potential benefits from increased risk sharing in the euro area on the order of a 2 to 3% increase in permanent consumption. Also, the European Commission (2008) strongly emphasises the potential gains from financial integration by virtue of greater risk sharing. Yet in order to achieve this, further efforts are required to enhance the efficiency and liquidity of euro area financial markets, to promote the cross-border provision of retail financial services, to improve the efficiency of corporate and government bond financing and to ease regu-

2 Asdrubali et al. (1996) find an even higher degree of risk sharing in the case of the US for the sample 1963-90. In their examination of smoothing by capital markets, federal government spending and taxation and credit markets, they calculate that the first channel absorbs 39 per cent, the second 13 per cent and the third 23 per cent of shocks to gross state products. Using the same approach, Marinheiro (2003) estimates for the EU15 are 9 per cent, 5 per cent and 19 per cent for the period 1981-90, respectively, i.e. a smoothing of 32 per cent (vs. 81 per cent for US states during the same period).

latory and supervisory costs for financial intermediaries operating in a multi-jurisdictional environment.

Indirect tests of risk sharing that test consumption smoothing across countries using consumption, GDP and GNP correlations also fail to find strong support for consumption smoothing across the euro area; see Marinheiro (2003), among others. If consumption correlations across countries exceed the output or GDP correlations, this could form indirect evidence of partial international risk sharing. Similarly, a lower correlation between output (GDP) and income (GNP) may suggest the presence of international risk sharing via cross-country holdings of financial assets and the presence of consumption smoothing between countries. In a similar vein, regressions of consumption differentials on output differentials in a monetary union and of output differentials on income differentials can be used to test for risk sharing. In the first case a lower association between consumption differentials and output differentials could reflect increasing risk sharing. In the second case a lower association between output and income differentials could be due to increased risk sharing. Again, basically all studies find lower risk sharing for the euro area as compared to other, more mature monetary unions.

Lastly, it is important to note that causality may also run the other way around: risk sharing through the financial system may foster convergence in a monetary union but (convergence inside) the monetary union itself may foster financial integration and increased risk sharing through the financial system as investors will find it easier to diversify their investments across the member countries of a stable and integrated monetary union.

In conclusion, the role of risk sharing in the EMU is currently limited. Over the long term, risk sharing through the development of a federal fiscal system and in particular through the euro area financial system is likely to increase.

2.2 Determinants of Business Cycle Synchronisation

2.2.1 Trade Integration

Trade is regarded as the major transmission channel for business cycles and a prime variable behind cyclical synchronisation. In empirical studies, trade intensity between countries is often found to play a significant role in business cycle correlations and to be the only robust determinant of synchronisation. Although an "empirical consensus" has emerged concerning the importance of trade, there have been contradictory findings concerning its effects. According to the Heckscher-Ohlin theorem, for instance, greater openness to trade is likely to foster specialisation due to comparative advantage and economies of scale. This is posited to lead to lower economic synchronisation if a high share of industry-specific shocks within countries exists. Thus, an idiosyncratic shock in a certain sector may not spread that easily across borders due to the absence of that industry in other countries. However, if trade between countries is dominated by intra-industry trade, the removal of trade barriers leads to a diffusion of demand shocks across countries. In addition, if trade induces technological and knowledge spill-overs, higher output correlations should be the result.

According to Frankel and Rose (1998), bilateral trade results mainly from increasing intra-industry trade. They consider the net effect of total trade and provide empirical evidence that inter-industry trade does not play an important role for synchronisation compared to intra-industry trade. These findings are supported by subsequent studies by Gruben et al. (2002), Calderón et al. (2002) and Imbs (2004). Compared to the results obtained by Frankel and Rose (1998), however, their conclusions point to somewhat weaker trade effects, but they nevertheless support the view that trade intensity has a positive impact on business cycle synchronisation. In particular, Imbs (2004) shows that the main effect of business cycle co-movement results from intra-industry trade. In addition, Akin (2007) shows that the volume of this kind of trade has risen significantly from 1970 to the globalisation period, particularly in developed countries. Baxter and Kouparitsas (2005) and Böwer and Guillemineau (2006) apply extreme bounds analyses to check for robustness in many determinants of business cycle correlation. Both studies find that trade is robustly connected with business cycle synchronisation and thus support the view of Frankel and Rose (1998), but Böwer and Guillemineau (2006) also emphasise that, compared to other determinants of synchronisation, trade has lost relative importance since the introduction of the euro in 1999.

A challenge for econometric analyses is that trade intensities between countries and business cycle correlations are endogenous, a property that renders OLS estimates inconsistent. Most researchers handle this problem by applying instrumental variable techniques (IV) and typically use a set of gravity variables such as geographic distance measures and border dummies as instruments to identify the trade effect. However, as de Haan et al. (2005) point out, such an approach *"is not appropriate as the gravity variables not only affect trade intensity but are also related to some other variables that affect business cycle synchronisation"*. As a consequence, unless one is able to include all variables that influence trade and business cycle correlation, estimates will be biased. An alternative approach is to conduct a time-series analysis that allows the use of *predetermined* variables and to check for lead and lag relationships in order to alleviate the similarity problem that plagues static econometric approaches.

In addition to the type of trade (inter- vs. intra-industry), the type of shock (demand or supply) and their similarities (common or idiosyncratic shocks) are also crucial for identifying the effect of trade on business cycle synchronisation. Increased trade will lead to increased co-movement of business cycles if the main sources of shocks are demand shocks that are common across countries.

2.2.2 Currency Unions and Monetary Integration

The role of currency unions and monetary integration in promoting business cycle synchronisation is ambiguous. A coordinated monetary policy may promote synchronisation if it leads to more similarity of output fluctuations and also if there are indirect effects from an increase in bilateral trade intensity through exchange rate stability. Monetary policy in a currency union implies a better coordination of reactions to common shocks, but may be less efficient when member countries are frequently hit by idiosyncratic shocks. A currency union removes a means of buffering asymmetric external shocks through exchange rate adjustments, leaving adjustments to fiscal and structural policies. Decreasing synchronicity of member countries' business cycles may be a consequence of giving up exchange rate control.

Artis and Zhang (1999) find that ERM membership promoted a shift to business cycle similarity. Frankel and Rose (2002) find evidence for the trade channel of monetary integration, showing that a currency union has a strong and very significant effect on increasing bilateral trade between member states. However, other studies have come to different conclusions. De Haan et al. (2002) analyse correlation across US States, German states and 18 OECD countries and do not find significant evidence for increasing homogeneity over time. Whereas trade seems to foster convergence, stable exchange rates act as a countervailing force. Clark and van Wincoop (2001) as well as Baxter and Kouparitsas (2005) do not find similar monetary policy to be an important determinant of business cycle correlation, again supporting the conception that monetary integration can be both a stabilising and a decoupling factor for synchronisation. By analysing an OECD country sample over the period from 1960 to 2001, Otto et al. (2001) conclude that similarity between monetary policies does not make much of a contribution to international growth correlations. Their results instead suggest that it is the similarity of economic characteristics and institutions that explains much of the observed correlations.

A study by Dubois et al. (2007) uses a hypothetical, counterfactual analysis by investigating questions such as: What if the euro had never been introduced? How would national output and inflation rates have developed over time? The authors use Global VARS and compare outcomes of "true" GVARs and several "counterfactual" GVARs that are based on the absence of a common currency. According to this scenario analysis, small countries in particular benefit in terms of output gains from joining the ERM, whereas a clear effect for the larger countries cannot be identified.

2.2.3 Fiscal Policy

Constraints on fiscal policy induced by the Stability and Growth Pact (SGP) may reduce the risk of asymmetric policy shocks, but adhering to the criteria of the SGP also reduces a nation's ability to counteract country-specific shocks through the use of expansive fiscal policies. Both of these implications of the SGP have very different effects on business cycle synchronisation. In empirical studies, the fiscal policy positions of various countries are generally compared in terms of government spending to GDP and budget deficit/surplus. According to theory, a higher discrepancy between these measures should be linked to less correlated business cycles.

Darvas et al. (2005) provide evidence for a positive impact of complementary fiscal policies on synchronisation in a panel of OECD countries. Another important result of their study is that output correlation is higher in phases with lower budget deficits, a finding that implies a positive effect of the SGP on synchronisation. Thus, closer coordination of fiscal policies and the limitation of budget deficits may sustain the emergence of more symmetric business cycles. A study by Fatás and Mihov (2003) further corroborates the positive output effects of institutional restrictions on fiscal policy by showing that the intensive usage of discretionary fiscal policies leads to increased output volatility. Furthermore, Akin (2007) finds in a cross-section of 47 countries that similarity in bilateral fiscal policies fosters output synchronisation.

Böwer and Guillemineau (2006) observe that a lower bilateral discrepancy in output is correlated with lower differentials in budget deficits. A robustness test, however, indicates that this effect is more significant between 1980 to 1996 than between 1997 and 2006.

Clark and van Wincoop (2001) examine the standard deviation of budget deficit differentials and correlations in budget deficits and show that fiscal policies are more similar in countries with comparable sizes of government and that budget deficits are more correlated with a larger public sector. Based on OLS and IV techniques applied to a sample of 14 EU countries, the authors find no evidence of more coordinated policies leading to either higher or lower business cycle synchronisation. They further conclude that this does not mean that monetary and fiscal policies have no effect on business cycles. The net effect on correlations can be small when country-specific policy is both a source and a stabiliser of business cycles.

Overall, the recent literature suggests that similarity in fiscal policies (with respect to expenditures and budget deficits) has a positive effect on bilateral business cycle synchronisation. Whether the implementation of the Maastricht Treaty and the SGP has had a significant impact on correlations is not clear-cut. Böwer and Guillemineau (2006) report that the importance of fiscal policies has decreased since the introduction of the SGP.

2.2.4 Sectoral Structure

Convergence of business cycles is more likely to arise between countries that have similar production structures. If two economies have similar sectoral structures then these should respond in a similar way to *common* shocks. In such a case, the similarities of the business cycles will depend on the fraction of variation that is explained by common shocks in relation to overall shocks. If countries are more specialised in terms of very few common industries across countries, business cycles should be less synchronised due to little shock spill-over across borders. To shed light on this question, one has to look at the prevalent type of shocks affecting a country. A higher share of idiosyncratic shocks rather than common or global ones would indicate that a diversified sectoral structure has a negative impact on the symmetry of business cycles and vice versa.

It is important to note that if trade integration has a negative effect on synchronisation, then the mechanism of action might be sectoral structure. As predicted by classical models of international trade (Heckscher-Ohlin) as well as the New Economic Geography literature inspired by Krugman (1979, 1980), increasing international trade might induce the increasing specialisation of sectoral structures. This in turn might negatively affect the degree of synchronisation, thus generating a negative indirect effect of trade integration that potentially counters or even offsets its positive direct effect. This view has been famously expressed by Krugman (1991), who predicted that the trade-induced regional concentration of industries in Europe could render the euro area a less suitable currency area.

By analysing measures of distance and sectoral shares, Otto et al. (2001) find that similar industry structures are positively correlated with output co-movement. However, the results are not statistically significant. Testing for robustness confirms the fragility of the determinant as an important factor. In almost the same manner, Baxter and Kouparitsas (2005) and Böwer and Guillemineau (2006) conclude that structural similarity goes hand in hand with convergence, although the outcome is weak and generally not robust.

In contrast, Imbs (2004) as well as García Herrero and Ruiz (2007) find clear evidence that similar production structures tend to reduce bilateral output fluctuations. An interesting finding of Imbs (2004) is that the sectoral structure is generally more important for countries joining the euro area than for countries, like the UK, that did not enter. These countries tend to be more affected by idiosyncratic shocks.

Akin (2007) finds that the differences in economic structure across countries have not shifted over time. Furthermore, developed countries are more diversified than less advanced economies, which in turn leads to the conclusion that the synchronisation of business cycles is higher between industrialised countries.

2.2.5 Financial Market Integration

Despite the prominent role financial market integration has played in economic globalisation in past decades, in the context of international business cycle synchronisation, it can be regarded as one of the determinants least researched in the existing literature. This can mainly be attributed not to a lack of interest in the matter itself, but to several methodological problems arising in empirical studies. These will be reviewed in detail in section 4.1.1. Nevertheless, some important venues for empirical research and also to a certain extent relevant results have emerged in the literature.

From a theoretical point of view, the assessment of the effects of financial integration on business cycle synchronisation suffers from the fact that there are numerous possible direct and indirect effects that can also potentially contradict themselves. Furthermore, there are several interdependencies with other factors such as trade integration and the sectoral specialisation of production. These complex interactions are well-documented by Imbs (2004), among others. Theoretical predictions about the direct effect of financial integration on the synchronisation of output movements are equivocal. First of all, a high degree of financial linkage between two countries can result in, say, a decline in aggregate demand in these countries due to a falling stock market in one country. Furthermore, financial disturbances and crises can be propagated internationally by contagion effects in integrated financial markets, with negative effects both on demand (by affecting income streams generated through investment positions) and on supply (by affecting supply of capital to potential investors) in all affected countries. Even though this latter effect seems to be more important in developing countries, the recent crisis in the US mortgage debt market and its international aftermath highlight the possibility for such internationally correlated effects in developed countries, including those of the EU.

Aside from such direct effects, there are several indirect ways by which financial integration can potentially influence business cycle synchronisation. As illustrated in section 2.1.7, an increase in financial integration allows better international risk sharing. Thus, it enables economies to have better insurance against sector-specific output shocks and provides incentives for sectoral specialisation in an economy's production structure. This specialisation should in turn decrease the degree of international output synchronisation because the economies are exposed to different idiosyncratic shocks. On the other hand, by enhancing sectoral specialisation, economies can exploit their respective comparative advantages better and engage in international trade. This in turn could result in a higher degree of business cycle synchronisation, should the involved economies specialise in the same sectors and engage in intra-industry trade, or in a lesser degree of synchronisation, if mostly inter-industry trade takes place due to different specialisation patterns. In summary, from a theoretical point of view it is not clear whether these different direct and indirect effects offset each other and which effect dominates.

Turning to the results of the empirical studies, one is presented with a rather mixed picture. Imbs (2004) concludes that while financial integration tends to increase sectoral specialisation, its total effect on business cycle synchronisation is significantly positive. This direct positive effect is supported by Imbs (2006), who uses bilateral portfolio investment data, among other variables. The results of this study only partially support the positive indirect effects of financial integration on trade integration and specialisation. In addition, Imbs (2006) rejects the hypothesis that trade linkages lead to greater financial integration. Akin (2007) reports that a country's general financial openness has a strong positive effect on its trade integration. Furthermore, the global financial integration measure that is used is found to have a weak positive but sometimes insignificant effect on business cycle synchronisation, yet this effect is higher for countries with high financial openness. Otto et al. (2001) find several financial integration measures only have a significant positive effect on the synchronisation of output movements in single equation estimates, but the results potentially suffer from an omitted variable bias. Partially

similar results are obtained in Otto et al. (2003). In this study, equity market integration is also found to have a statistically significant positive effect in a multivariate framework. Bordo and Helbling (2003) attribute their inconclusive results regarding financial integration to data problems and do not reject the general idea that financial integration plays a role in determining synchronisation. Böwer and Guillemineau (2006) use a different approach; extreme bounds analysis. They find limited empirical support for the notion that bilateral capital flows (as proxied by bank flows) as well as differences of stock market indices play a role in determining business cycle synchronisation.
The results of Kalemli-Ozcan et al. (2010) challenge the results of Imbs (2004, 2006) and Akin (2007). In a novel panel-econometric approach using financial harmonisation in the EU as an instrumental variable for financial integration, the authors document a negative effect of banking market integration on synchronisation. They argue that Imbs and others do not correctly identify the causal effect of financial integration, and that, as a result, the finding of a positive effect is biased. This notion of a negative overall effect is corroborated by the results of García Herrero and Ruiz (2007). In a study of Spain, they provide evidence that financial integration, as measured by bilateral flows, can actually tend to reduce business cycle synchronisation. The authors attribute this to the fact that international financial integration might allow economies to decouple their production patterns. As mentioned, this study is only undertaken for Spain and not for a cross-section of many countries. Alongside such studies that estimate the direct and indirect effects of financial integration, there are other studies, such as Kalemli-Ozcan et al. (2004), that specifically concentrate on the interdependence of financial integration and sectoral specialisation. In their study, Kalemli-Ozcan et al. also find a negative indirect effect of financial integration on business cycle synchronisation due to an enhancement of sectoral specialisation.

In summary, the results of several previous studies seem to be supportive of the idea that in many cases financial integration promotes business cycle synchronisation, but sometimes this effect can be offset by indirect negative effects. Other studies such as Kalemli-Ozcan et al. (2010), however, come to opposing conclusions. Due to these conflicting results, empirical research on this topic is far from arriving at a definitive consensus. In any case it should be noted that low degrees of business cycle synchronisation can be regarded as less harmful in the presence of functioning and highly integrated financial markets. By shifting resources internationally and inter-temporally, integrated financial markets enable risk sharing and the smoothing of consumption and therefore ultimately increase economic welfare. On the whole, one can conclude that further research, especially research that takes more appropriate data into account, is needed to shed light on the question of the effects of financial integration. The investigation in section 4.1 pursues this line of inquiry.

2.2.6 Gravity Variables and Other Indicators

Empirical studies on the determinants of business cycle correlations usually also include a set of gravity variables that serve as instruments in IV-based estimations in order to identify trade effects. In addition, gravity variables are used as control variables that influence synchronisation. Typical gravity variables that characterise "natural" similarities between countries are border and language dummies, geographical distance and relative country size in terms of population or the economy, etc. A broad set of explanatory variables is used by Otto et al. (2001), who consider factors such as: the origin of legal system; accounting standards quality, using an index created by La Porta et al. (1998); structural economic reforms, using an index developed by Lehman Brothers; and openness to new technologies. Estimation results show that a higher quality of accounting standards, higher speed of technology adoption and a shared language are particularly important in establishing bilateral output correlations. In addition, a common border to have a substantial impact on business cycle synchronisation.

Akin (2007) emphasises membership in a Free Trade Area (FTA) and primary commodity exportation as important determinants of cyclical similarity. Baxter and Kouparitsas (2005) focus on the similarity of export and import baskets, and factor endowments. These studies yield the following results: FTA membership and commodity export similarity turn out to be insignificant variables. The similarity of trade baskets is negative and significant, but not robustly correlated to the convergence tendencies of business cycles. Other factor endowments with regard to (i) years of education, (ii) physical capital per worker and (iii) arable land per worker do not play an important role.

Böwer and Guillemineau (2006) check the robustness of a broad set of explanatory variables for business cycle correlation across euro area countries. The study finds a significant negative relationship between differences in cross-country competitiveness and business cycle synchronisation. Labour market flexibility correlation is also negative (i.e. high differences in flexibility are associated with less symmetry), but not significant or robust. The gravity variable of distance turns out to be significant and has the expected sign (i.e. lower distance is correlated with higher convergence of cycles). On the other hand, the gravity variable of relative population size shows no clear sign of any significant correlation.

Table 1. Literature summary on the determinants of synchronisation

Authors	Period	Main determinants analysed	Main conclusions
Afonso and Furceri (2007)	1980-2005		In an enlarged EMU the ability to smooth country specific shocks does not increase (only short and medium term considered). Business cycle synchronisation and international risk sharing are likely to increase with new EMU members.
Akin (2007)	1970-2003	Trade, financial openness, partner similarity, free trade area membership, exchange rate volatility, oil-import dependency	Trade integration is the most important determinant of synchronisation, financial integration has a weak positive effect, trade partner similarity has no effect.
Angeloni and Dedola (1999)	1970-97		In the last period synchronisation of output, stock market indices, aggregate and price increased.
Artis and Zhang (1997, 1999)	1961-93		Synchronicity has grown under ERM regime, results suggest existence of a European cycle.
Baxter and Kouparitsas (2005)	1970 and 1995	Bilateral trade, total trade, sectoral structure, export/import similarities, factor endowment, gravity variables	Bilateral trade is robust, industrial structure and currency union is not robust, distance is robust.
Bergman (2004)	1961:1-2001:4	Trade, monetary policy, fiscal policy, gravity variables (border, size, distance, EU membership)	EU country pairs more synchronised than non-EU-country pairs. Correlation higher with flexible exchange rates. Positive effect through economic and monetary integration (last 10 years). Trade (+)
Bordo and Helbling (2003)	1880-2001	Global and idiosyncratic shocks, supply and demand shocks, trade integration, asset market integration, exchange rate policy	Secular trend of increasing synchronisation. Global shocks dominant factor, cycle volatility declined, modest role of bilateral trade, financial integration delivers inconclusive result. No evidence for positive effect of membership in fixed exchange rate regime.
Böwer and Guillemineau (2006)	1980-2004	Bilateral trade, economic specialisation, flow of bank assets, interest rate differ-	Trade has a robust positive effect, monetary unions that foster intra-industry trade thus can become endogenously optimal. Stock mar-

		ence, exchange rate volatility, fiscal deficit, price competitiveness, stock market difference, geographical distance, labour market flexibility	ket integration has robust positive impact on co-movement.
Calderón et al. (2002)	1960-99	Bilateral trade specialisation / sectoral structure using several gravity variables	Trade has a positive impact on synchronisation (higher between industrialised countries). Asymmetric production structure lowers correlation.
Clark and van Wincoop (2001)	1963-97 (US-EU dataset), 1970-92 for employment and 1982-96 for GDP (EU regions)	Border, monetary and fiscal policy, geographical variables, production structure, trade	First: cycle correlation within the US is much higher than cross-country correlation in the EU. Second: these differences mostly related to borders between EU countries. Third: no significant drop recognisable in regard to the border factor. Finally: trade is the main factor that explains the border phenomena.
Darvas and Szapáry (2005)	1983-2002		Hungary, Poland and Slovenia achieved high synchronisation of GDP, industry and exports, not for consumption and services; other CEECs countries less or no synchronisation; GDP synchronisation within EMU.
Darvas et al. (2005)	1964-2003	Fiscal divergence	Fiscal convergence induces greater business cycle synchronisation.
De Haan et al. (2002)	1929-93, 1950-96	Trade, monetary integration	US states: higher cycle synchronisation not observed. German states: slightly higher synchronisation. OECD: Trade intensity and exchange rate volatility are factors for higher co-movement.
Doyle and Faust (2002)	1970-2002		No sign of a significant change in business cycle synchronisation. Higher correlation during recessions than during recoveries.
Frankel and Rose (1998)	1959-93	Bilateral trade intensity	Greater integration historically has resulted in more highly synchronised business cycles.
	1990-2003	Trade, financial linkages, similar productive structures, distance, language, access to sea costs,	Similar productive structures (+), financial integration (-), trade integration (+), sectoral shocks (+), common policies (+).

		member of euro area and EU, inflation differentials, exchange rate volatility, land area, population, oil dependency	
Gayer (2007)	1975:3-2007:1, 1980:1-2007:1		Since 1990s the growth in the euro area has narrowed considerably (except in 2002), maybe due to general decrease in volatility of business cycles.
Gruben et al. (2002)	1965-98	Intra- and inter-industrial trade, specialisation	No support for negative impact of specialisation on business cycles. High share of intra-trade may contribute to more synchronisation since industry-specific shocks not dominate common demand shocks.
Inklaar et al. (2005)	1970-2003	Trade, specialisation, monetary policy, fiscal policy, financial integration	Positive impact of trade integration as well as similar fiscal and monetary policies on business cycle synchronisation.
Imbs (2004)	1980-2000 1960-2000 1977-2001	Trade integration, financial integration, specialisation. Exogenous factors: geographical distance, linguistic similarity, common border	Strong positive effect of intra-industry trade, negative effect of specialisation, positive effect of financial integration.
Imbs (2006)	1960-2000	Trade integration, financial integration, specialisation	Financially integrated economies tend to have more synchronised cycles, while the effect of financial integration on sectoral specialisation remains unclear.
Kalemli-Ozcan et al. (2001)	1963-93	Specialisation	Specialisation results in less correlated output shocks, thus offsetting the impact of trade integration; output shocks do not necessarily cause asymmetric income shocks due to risk sharing.
Kalemli-Ozcan et al. (2010)	1978-2007	Financial integration	Positive effect of financial integration found in cross-sectional estimations; negative effect found in panel estimations
Massmann and Mitchell (2004)	1960-2001		A long-run trend for rising correlation between euro area business cycles; emergence of a common euro area business cycle not smooth and stable.

Otto et al. (2001)	1960-2001	Trade intensity, equity return spreads, exchange rate volatility, FDI intensity, interest rate spreads, industry structure, legal system, accounting standards, structural reform, openness to new technology, adjacency, language	Trade (+) and exchange rate volatility (-) important. Significant variables: good accounting standards, similar legal system, common language, openness to technology. Insignificant variables: similar MP, bond market integration, industry structure and structural reform
Otto et al. (2003)	1960-2000	Trade intensity, financial linkages (FDI, equity flows, bond market), monetary and exchange rate policy	Trade, integration of equity markets, exchange rate stability, similar economic structure and speed of technological adoptation have positive effect on synchronisation. Bond market integration and FDI intensity increasingly important.
Wynne and Koo (2000)	1963-92 1960-96 1950-95		Significant positive correlation between EU-6. Employment less volatile than output. Higher correlation between US districts compared to EU-15

Table 2. Literature summary on the determinants of synchronisation in US and Canada

Author	Period	Considered/significant determinants	Main conclusion
Beine and Coulombe (2003)	1961-2000	Similarity in production structure (+, but no test for significance), international and interprovincial trade (+, but no test for significance), persistence of shocks (+, but no test for significance).	Heterogeneity among Canadian regions concerning the synchronisation of the business cycle relative to the US, floating exchange rate between US and Canadian dollar not beneficial to Ontario and Québec
Clark and van Wincoop (2001)	1963-97	Similarity in production structure, bilateral and inter-regional trade (+), monetary and fiscal policy coordination	Business cycle correlations among US regions are significantly higher than among EU countries, differences are mostly related to European borders, no drop in the border effect over time, trade can account for most of the observed border effect
de Haan, Inklaar and Sleijpen (2002)	1929-97 (different subperiods for different variables)	Bilateral trade intensity (+), exchange rate volatility (-)	Business cycles in the US states have become less synchronised, business cycles in the Western German states have become more synchronised
Imbs (2004)	1960-2001 (different subperiods are)	Inter-industry trade (+), intra-industry trade (+), financial integration (+), similarity in sectoral specialisation (+)	Business cycle synchronisation can be explained by all considered determinants
Partridge and Rickman (2005)	1971-98	Volatility of the national cycle ()	Decline in synchronisation of US state business cycles over time, decline in overall US volatility as primary reason
Wakerly, Scott and Nason (2006)	1965-2002	Equalisation entitlement payments, regional immigration flows, having hosted the Olympic games, similarity in preferences and technology (+), similarity in industrial structure, similarity in labour market structure, common fiscal policy, money supply and demand shocks	Asymmetry of Canadian regional output fluctuations, no findings of convergence for Canadian regions

Wynne and Koo (2000)	1950-96 (different subperiods are considered for different variables)	-	Generally lower standard deviations between cyclical components in the US than in the EU

3 Descriptive Analysis

By Bas van Aarle, Marcus Kappler, Atilim Seymen, and Klaus Weyerstrass (The research paper: Weyerstrass, K., van Aarle, B., Kappler, M., and Seymen, A. (2011): Business Cycle Synchronisation with(in) the Euro Area: in Search of a 'Euro Effect', Open Economies Review, Vol.22, is partly based on this chapter).

In this chapter, we investigate whether the symmetry of output fluctuations in the euro area economies has increased over time and whether this synchronicity has grown since the inception of the common currency, reflecting the possible occurrence of a "euro effect". Evidence from countries outside the euro area is also considered. In particular, EU members outside the monetary union – the New Member States (NMS), Denmark, Sweden and the UK – and the non-EU, OECD countries will be included in the study. We discuss measurement issues with regard to business cycle synchronisation and convergence and we present a set of up-to-date stylised facts concerning business cycle characteristics in the euro area and beyond. A frequency domain analysis is also conducted which allows us to estimate dynamic business cycle correlations and leading and lagging relationships between the cycles of different countries. The main focus is on convergence with respect to the cyclical component of output. However, both real and nominal convergence is needed in order for a common monetary policy to be efficient for all participants. We therefore look beyond output gaps by also analysing convergence of budget balances, inflation rates and real long-term interest rates. A section is devoted to identifying clusters of countries that share similar business cycle patterns and another section compares regional business cycle conformity and convergence in US states with the findings for the euro area. The final section offers summaries and conclusions to this chapter.

3.1 Methods for Estimating the Cycle

In order to decompose the trend and the cycle components from observed real output, we examine several parametric and non-parametric approaches that have been proposed by Massmann and Mitchell (2004). In addition, a full structural production function approach as employed by the OECD is considered. After providing a brief outline of each method, we illustrate the differences and similarities of the outcomes by giving a synopsis of the estimated cycles for the aggregate real GDP of the 12 countries forming the euro area until the end of 2006 (euro area 12). The object of interest is whether the different methods produce similar assessments of fluctuations of real changes in GDP from the estimated long-term trend or whether the different methods imply fundamentally different views on the development of the business cycle over time.

- From the class of non-parametric methods, the most commonly used are the "band-pass filters" of **Baxter-King (BK)** and **Christiano-Fitzgerald (CF)**, which eliminate the trend and irregular components of a time series while preserving business cycle components. Both procedures are based on variations of two-sided moving averages to the time series and differ only in terms of the estimation of the weights given to the lead and lag components. Both filter variants require the specification of a typical cycle length, which we set at 1.5 to 8 years. The band-pass filter of BK requires the specification of a finite-order moving average for extracting the high-frequency component. For quarterly data we employ a symmetric moving average of 12 quarters and for monthly data, a moving average of 36 months. The symmetry of the filter implies that observations will be lost from both the beginning and the end of the original sample, which can be regarded as a serious constraint. Thus, we use the CF filter, as the asymmetric version does not have this requirement and can be computed to the end of the original sample.[3] Both filters are approximations of ideal filters and isolate the frequency, which can be set exactly prior to filtering.
- The **Hodrick-Prescott (HP)** filter obtains the trend components of a time series after selecting the degree of smoothness for the trend. The central variable in this method is the smoothing parameter λ, which is used to input indirect assumptions about the typical duration of the reference cycle in the computing procedure. If λ is close to zero, the smoothed component is equal to the original time series. This corresponds to the assumptions of standard real business cycle theory, according to which all output movements are equal to fluctuations in the potential value. In contrast, very large values for λ produce a smoothed component that corresponds to a linear time trend and all actual output developments around this time trend are assigned to the cyclical component. In practice, λ values of 1600 for quarterly data and of 100 for annual data have become established. In our calculations we use these standard parameters.
- Also considered is a symmetric **moving average (MA)** for estimating a smooth trend component of the underlying series. The estimate of the cycle is the difference between the observations and the MA, which in our study is also set to 12 quarters and 36 months, for quarterly and monthly data, respectively. The MA has the distinct advantage of being simple to compute and highly transparent.
- A similar property holds for the **first order difference (D1)** of seasonally adjusted series and for the **year-on-year difference (DIF4)** of time series. Although these transformations do not rely on a sophisticated statistical framework to decompose trend and cycle, they offer quite intuitive interpretations. Conse-

---

[3] Cf. Christiano and Fitzgerald (2003) for computational details.

quently, they are the transformations commonly referred to when new economic data are officially released and communicated by EUROSTAT. The basic assumption of these differencing methods is that the secular component of the series is a random walk without drift, that the cyclical component is stationary and that that the two components are uncorrelated (cf. Canova, 1998). However, the evident trend in the *level* of real GDP and industrial production questions the suitability of a random walk model with no drift for characterising the data generating process.

- The **linear regression model (TIM)** assumes that output fluctuates around a deterministic trend and that deviations from the trend are stationary and may be interpreted as cycle. However, such an assumption is in contrast with the usual outcomes of unit root tests, which imply that GDP is integrated or difference stationary. Technically, the cycle measure of the TIM is the residual of a time trend regression and intercept on the target variable. Note that detrending an integrated economic time series neglects the changes in the growth component of the series and leads to an overestimation of the variance and persistence of the cyclical component.
- An **unobserved components model (UC)** is also considered. The model assumes that output can be decomposed in a trend, a cycle and an irregular component. We use the same specification as Massmann and Mitchell (2004), who employ a smooth local linear trend model which goes back to Harvey (1993). In this model, the trend component is a second order random walk, while the cycle is specified as a trigonometric function. The cycle measure is the difference between the estimated trend and the actual output series. Model parameters are estimated via the Kalman filter recursion and numerical optimisation of the likelihood function. The unobservable trend component is obtained with the aid of the fixed interval Kalman smoother.
- The **production function approach (PFA)** of the OECD belongs to the class of multivariate methods for estimating the trend component of output and the output gap. It is a procedure which is only suited for decomposing real GDP. The concept of potential output is central to this method. It assumes that there is a macroeconomic production function that combines various input factors at any current level of available technology, and that potential output may be conceived of as the output of an economy subject to a given quantity of non-variable input factors and sustainable quantities of variable input factors. The PFA combines data on the potential labour input, the trend of total factor productivity and the capital stock with a production technology, typically of the Cobb-Douglas type.[4] The PFA offers a broad view on the cyclical movements of GDP in the sense that it combines information from a broad set of macroeconomic key variables. For the project, we use the quarterly output gap series of the Economic Outlook regularly published by the OECD.

---

4 Beffy et al. (2006) explain the PFA procedure used by the OECD in detail.

3.2 Methods for Measuring Synchronicity

Contemporaneous unconditional Pearson correlations computed either between the business cycles of individual countries and a reference country or computed as unconditional bilateral correlations are the most commonly employed measures for synchronicity (cf. table 1 in section 2). The first alternative allows one to examine whether a single country converges to a reference series – the euro area aggregate, in our case – while the second alternative allow one to examine the dispersion of business cycle similarities over a group of countries. To check for convergence, correlations are typically computed over different time periods using a fixed or rolling sample window. In particular, the first and the second moments help assess whether convergence takes place: *a rise in the mean of the correlations computed over consecutive periods coupled with a simultaneous decrease in the variance of the correlations is considered as evidence of increased synchronisation.* In the case of rolling samples, outcomes can be sensitive to the considered window length over which correlations are computed (Gayer, 2007). The window length should be wide enough to leave sufficient observations to compute precise correlation coefficients but short enough to study the time-varying pattern of business cycle correlations. In general, the optimal window size cannot be determined analytically but has to be determined from the outset.[5]

Mink et al. (2007) propose measures which do not rely on the computation of averages over a time interval but instead allow the computation of synchronicity measures per observation. The two measures proposed by Mink et al. (2007) take differences in cycle amplitudes *and* synchronicity into account. The synchronicity measure directly builds on the estimated output gaps and is given by

$$\rho_t = \frac{1}{N}\sum_{i=1}^{N}\frac{g_{it}g_{rt}}{|g_{it}g_{rt}|} \tag{1}$$

in which g_{it} is the gap of country i in period t and g_{rt} is the gap of the reference variable (euro area GDP, for instance). N is the number of countries in the group. The synchronicity measure lies between -1 and 1 but is transformed to a uniform [0,1] scale in order to facilitate interpretation: the scaled measure $\tilde{\rho}_t$ indicates the fraction of countries that have the same sign of the output gap of the reference cycle in period t. We denote this measure **MJH-SYNC** below. If this measure is computed on a per-country basis (by omitting the summations in equation (1) and adding i-index to ρ_t), the result is an index that takes the value -1 if the gap of country i has the opposite sign as the reference cycle in period t and 1 if it has the same sign.

---

5 Gayer (2007) remarks that "*if the window length is shorter than the mean length of the cycle, small phase shifts between otherwise identical cycles can lead to systematic, but artificial, drops in the association measure at the turning points of the cycles*".

The second synchronisation measure also takes the similarity of cycle amplitudes into account. It is computed as

$$\gamma_t = -\frac{\sum_{i=1}^{N} \left| g_{it} - g_{\tau t} \right|}{\sum_{i=1}^{N} \left| g_{it} \right|} \qquad (2)$$

By construction, an increase in γ_t signals an increase in business cycle co-movement. This measure is based on a scaled distance between output gaps of the country group and the reference cycle and may also be computed on a per-country basis in order to express the scaled distance between individual countries and a reference series. The co-movement measure γ_t will be denoted **MJH-COM** in what follows.

Most studies on business cycle synchronisation use correlation coefficients to characterise co-movement between output gaps, since correlation analysis provides an appropriate assessment of cyclical synchronisation. De Haan et al. (2005), for instance, review other procedures which involve coherence measures, phase-adjusted correlations or concordance indices as in Harding and Pagan (2002), and diffusion indices that measure the share of countries in recessions if a certain area is in a recession.

However, a drawback of analysing time-varying correlations in a descriptive manner is that such an approach cannot assess whether an observed increase in correlations may be regarded as convergence from a statistical point of view. Massmann and Mitchell (2004) propose a test for convergence which is suited for assessing the significance of an observed trend in time-varying synchronisation measures for a group of countries. The test runs a regression of a time trend and an intercept on a vector of correlation coefficients in a dynamic panel data model. If convergence is taking place, a significant time trend will be observed. A similar regression approach can be undertaken with the standard deviations of correlation coefficients to test if homogeneity in terms of business cycle synchronisation has increased (or decreased) over time and particularly since 1999. We will leave this, however, to future work. A regression technique to test for convergence may also be applied to the co-movement (1) and synchronisation (2) measures. In section 3.4 we will use this approach to test whether cyclical convergence or divergence in the euro area can be verified.

3.3 Cycle Measures for Euro Area GDP

We start the descriptive analysis with a synopsis of the different measures for the cycle of aggregate GDP for the euro area. The considered procedures are outlined in section 3.1.

Figure 1 shows the time series graphs of the euro area business cycle over the period from 1970Q1 to 2007Q3, according to the different approaches outlined above.[6] The shaded areas highlight the periods of recession that have been identified by the CEPR Business Cycle Dating Committee and which have been updated for the periods after 2003Q3 with the aid of the Harding and Pagan (2002) dating rule. Table 3 contains a set of summary statistics which characterise these measures that have been computed over the common sample from 1991Q1 to 2007Q3. Visual inspection clearly demonstrates the sensitivity of the cycle to measurement.

Fig. 1. Cycle estimates for euro area GDP

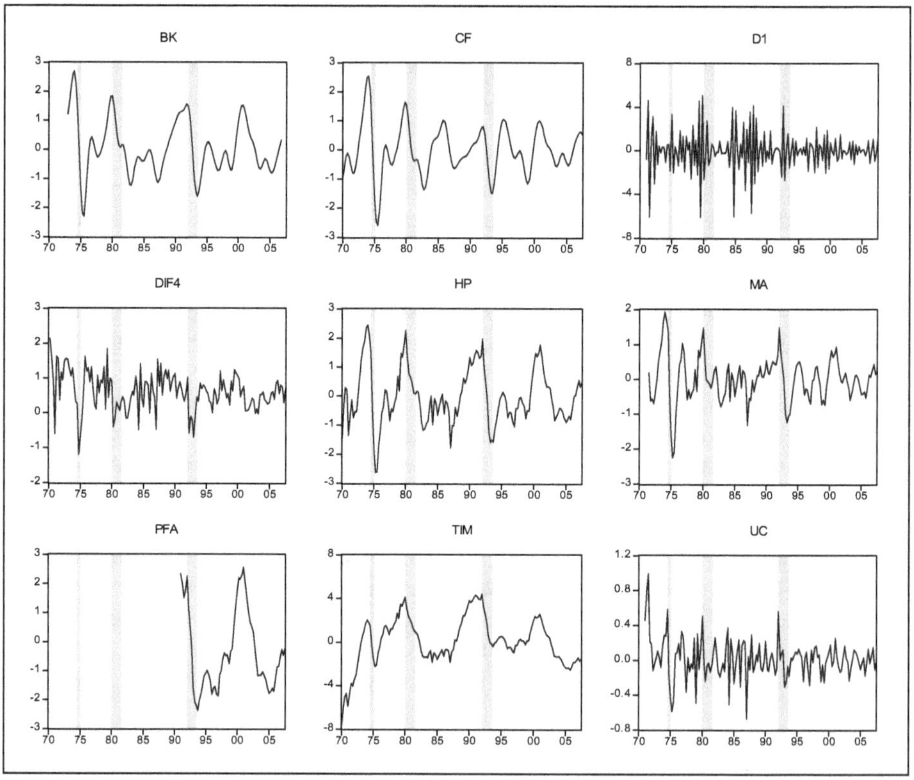

Notes: BK=Baxter-King, CF=Christiano-Fitzgerald, D1=first differences, DIF4=year-on-year differences, HP=Hodrick-Prescott, MA=moving average, PFA=production function approach, TIM=linear regression model, UC=unobserved components model.

6 For computation of the symmetric Baxter-King (BK) filter and the symmetric moving average (MA), the sample has been extended to 2009Q4 by inclusion of GDP projection from the OECD Economic Outlook. Note that the BK filter loses 12 quarters of observations at either side of the sample, while the MA filter reduces the sample by 6 quarters.

Table 3. Summary statistics of euro area cycle measures

	BK	CF	D1	DIF4	HP	MAC	PFA	TIM	UC
Mean	-0.00	-0.00	0.01	0.49	-0.04	0.00	-0.36	0.33	0.00
Median	-0.21	-0.05	-0.00	0.53	-0.22	0.02	-0.84	0.15	0.02
Maximum	1.57	1.07	4.14	1.26	1.98	1.49	2.57	4.42	0.56
Minimum	-1.59	-1.47	-2.65	-0.69	-1.58	-1.22	-2.36	-2.48	-0.30
Std. Dev.	0.81	0.65	1.14	0.39	0.88	0.52	1.41	1.77	0.14
Skewness	0.48	-0.26	0.38	-0.52	0.57	0.01	0.70	0.60	0.43
Kurtosis	2.48	2.45	4.71	3.69	2.51	3.08	2.19	2.83	5.41
Jarque-Bera	3.22	1.55	9.29	4.11	4.09	0.02	6.96	3.91	17.44
Probability	0.20	0.46	0.01	0.13	0.13	0.99	0.03	0.14	0.00

Notes: Sample period is from 1991Q1 to 2006Q4. See also notes to figure 1.

Table 4. Correlations of cycle measures

Correlation	BK	CF	D1	DIF4	HP	MAC	PFA	TIM	UC
BK	1.00								
CF	0.80	1.00							
D1	0.01	0.02	1.00						
DIF4	0.12	0.15	0.12	1.00					
HP	0.98	0.74	0.00	0.19	1.00				
MAC	0.89	0.84	-0.00	0.28	0.89	1.00			
PFA	0.92	0.54	-0.00	0.12	0.95	0.74	1.00		
TIM	0.78	0.44	-0.01	-0.01	0.79	0.63	0.82	1.00	
UC	0.39	0.45	-0.02	0.46	0.48	0.73	0.34	0.27	1.00
Probability	BK	CF	D1	DIF4	HP	MAC	PFA	TIM	UC
BK	-----								
CF	0.00	-----							
D1	0.92	0.89	-----						
DIF4	0.33	0.23	0.34	-----					
HP	0.00	0.00	0.97	0.13	-----				
MAC	0.00	0.00	0.99	0.03	0.00	-----			
PFA	0.00	0.00	1.00	0.33	0.00	0.00	-----		
TIM	0.00	0.00	0.96	0.93	0.00	0.00	0.00	-----	
UC	0.00	0.00	0.85	0.00	0.00	0.00	0.01	0.03	-----

Notes: The p-values reported are for testing the hypothesis that a single correlation coefficient is equal to zero. Sample period is from 1991Q1 to 2006Q4. See also notes to figure 1.

The cycles from the band pass filters (BK and CF), the HP, the PFA, the MA and the TIM show similar patterns that are formally confirmed by the correlation coefficients (see table 4). The first and fourth order differences (D1 and DIF4) of real euro area GDP and the unobserved components model (UC) produce cycle patterns that are generally more volatile than the outcomes of the other methods. The mean of the DIF4 and the TIM is positive implying that these procedures generate more positive than negative output gaps, while the PFA cycle is even negative on average over the common sample period (see table 3). However, the other procedures generate output gaps that (on average) cancel out. The maximum and minimum values of the gap measures illustrate the differences in amplitudes. The highest positive gap is estimated by the linear regression model (TIM) and this procedure also generates the lowest gap. Consequently, the TIM yields the cycle with the largest standard deviation. Overall, this exercise confirms the well-documented fact that our picture of the cycle mainly depends on how the cycle is measured (Massmann and Mitchell, 2004, Canova, 1998). This clearly advises us not to focus our attention on just one measure of the business cycle when looking for convergence. Therefore, whenever sensible, we look at several approaches for estimating the cycle to assess and test for synchronisation and convergence.

3.4 Stylised Facts on Synchronisation in the Euro Area

In this section we provide an up-to-date perspective on synchronisation and convergence in the euro area. While the broadest view of the business cycle is certainly provided by real GDP, many studies focus on industrial production indices as a proxy due to monthly data availability. Some even argue that one should look at stationary business and consumer survey data to circumvent the problem associated with the identification of the cyclical component from trending statistical data (Gayer and Weiss, 2006). The variable we use in the first step is real GDP for the 12 Member States of the euro area.[7] In order to check the robustness of the results to alternative measurements of the cycle, the different approaches for separating cycles from trend as outlined in section 3.1 are considered.

A window length of 6 years has been chosen for computation of the correlations over a fixed rolling window. This length is approximately in line with the average duration of completed business cycles for the euro area since 1970 (cf. figure 1). The averages of the correlations over the fixed rolling window (solid line) are shown in figure 2 together with the average correlations for a fixed observation period with the same length (dotted line). The rolling correlations refer to the *end points* of the windows, i.e. they compute the average correlation over the past window length. We focus on unweighted correlations and do not consider a weighting of correlation coefficients by country size as this would bias outcomes

---

[7] Lack of data availability prevents us from considering the new euro area members Slovenia, Malta and Cyprus in this more long-term oriented exercise.

mostly to the three large euro area economies. Gayer (2007) reports that the weighting of countries does not qualitatively alter findings.

Figure 2 shows that all cycle measures suggest a decrease in synchronisation for the recent past according to the rolling correlation measures. The dotted lines which represent average correlations for three non-overlapping periods of equal length – 1989Q1 to 1994Q4, 1995Q1 to 2000Q4 and 2001Q1 to 2006Q4 – show for most cycle estimates that business cycle synchronisation is at a high level and is steady over subsamples. The CF cycles imply a jump of synchronisation in the mid-1990s which is not observed for the other cycle measures. The drop in correlation that took place in 1997 coincides with the Asian emerging market crisis which had fairly diverse effects on the individual euro area countries (Gayer, 2007). This drop is captured by nearly all cycle estimates except for the one based on the fourth difference transformation. The final stage of the EMU – with the introduction of the euro in January 1999 – is accompanied by an increase in synchronisation. This well-known finding also emerges clearly in figure 2. Since 2003 a decrease in correlations can be observed, which seems not to have stopped yet. None of the cycle measures considered points upwards at the end of the sample.

Fig. 2. Mean of euro area correlations over a 6 year rolling window

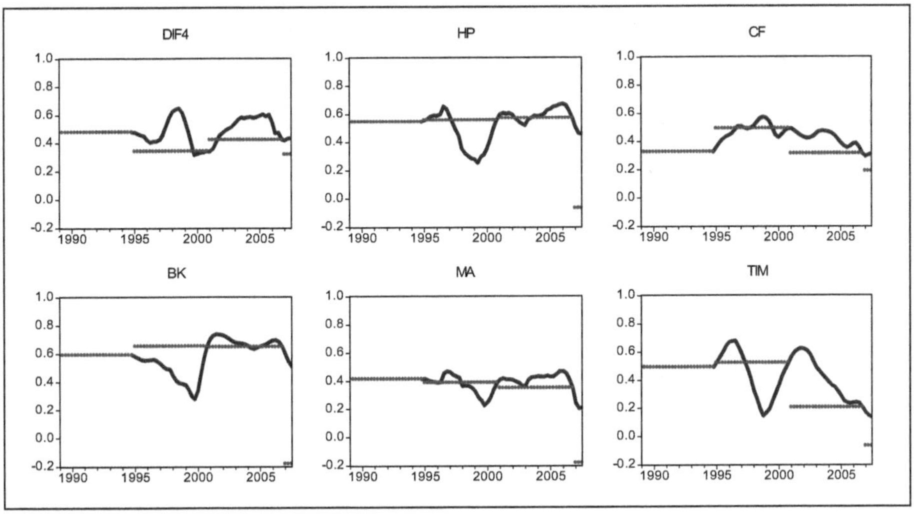

Notes: 6 year rolling window (solid line) and a fixed period of 6 years (dotted line). See also notes to figure 1.

The variance measures depicted in figure 3 support the previous findings. If an increase in mean correlation is found, it is typically accompanied by a decrease in dispersion and vice versa. In order to check the sensitivity of correlations outcomes to the window length, we repeated the exercise for a rolling window and a fixed sample of 4 years. The implication that synchronisation has declined since

2003 remains unchanged. Again, this conclusion is to a certain degree robust to the methodological choice of cycle measurement.

Fig. 3. Variance in euro area correlations over a 6 year rolling window

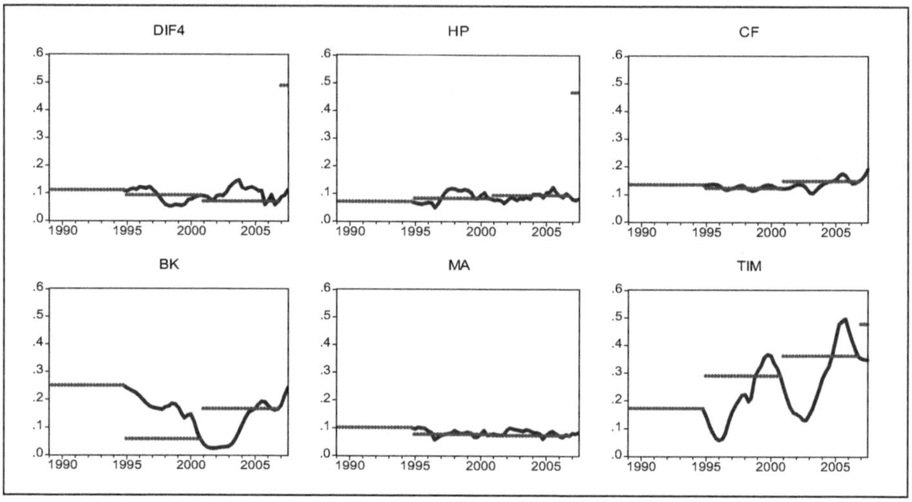

Notes: 6 year rolling window (solid line) and a fixed period of 6 years (dotted line). See also notes to figure 1.

Fig. 4. Mean of euro area correlations over a 4 year rolling window

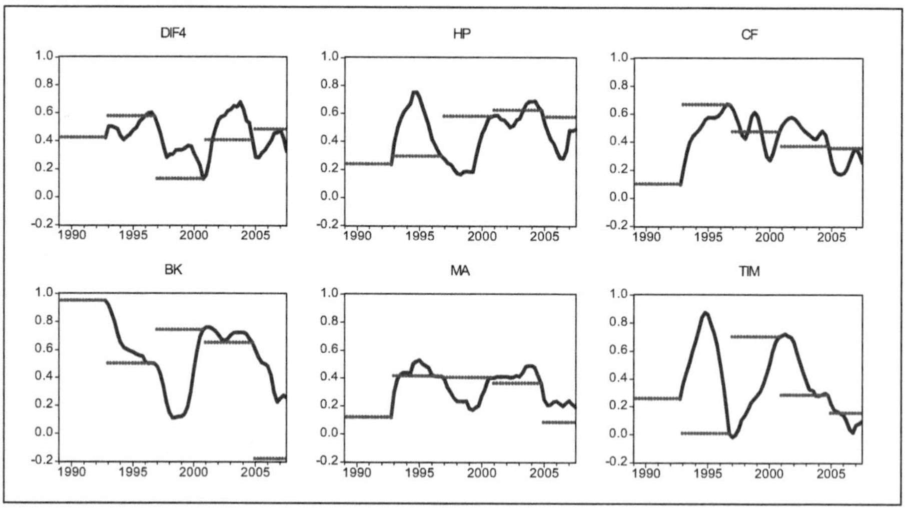

Notes: 4 year rolling window (solid line) and a fixed period of 4 years (dotted line). See also notes to figure 1.

Fig. 5. Variance of euro area correlations over a 4 year rolling window

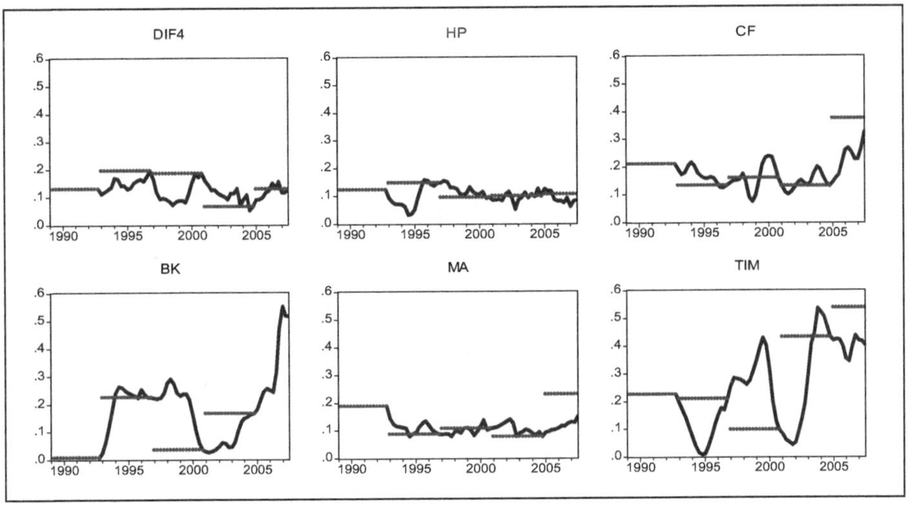

Notes: 4 year rolling window (solid line) and a fixed period of 4 years (dotted line). See also notes to figure 1.

Fig. 6. Correlations of Member States vis-à-vis the euro aggregate

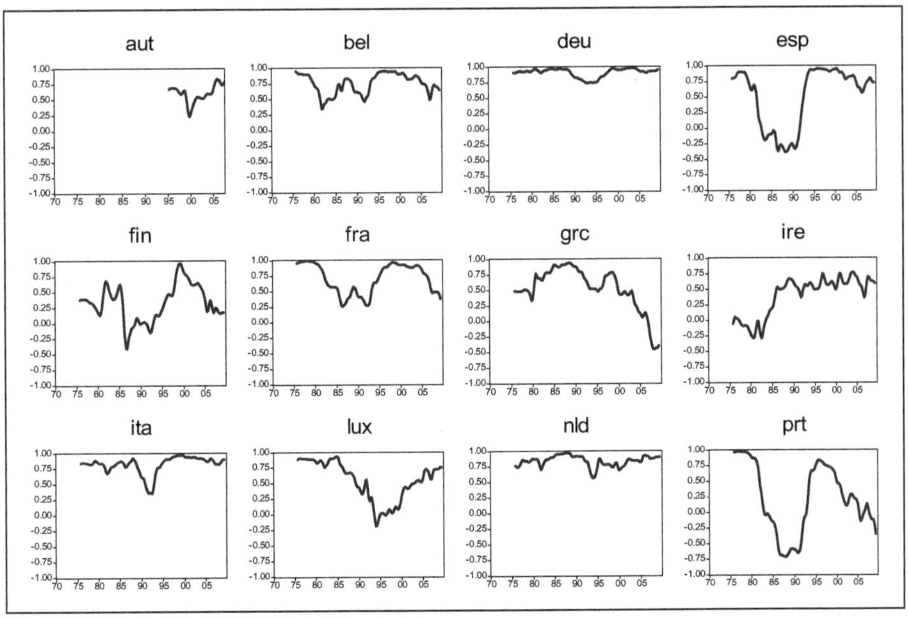

Notes: 6 years rolling window. CF filter based business cycles.

However, this broad picture of the development of mean correlations masks trends on the individual country level. Figure 6 shows the evolution of the correlations of the individual euro area countries vis-à-vis the euro area aggregate. The correlations are based on cycles which have been computed with the CF filter. These correlations basically confirm the results of previous studies, which show that particularly Greece and Portugal have had business cycles that have been uncoupled from the cycles shared by the larger European countries in recent years. Figure 7 and figure 8 show the synchronisation and co-movement measures proposed by Mink et al. (2007). These measures represent an alternative approach for assessing the degree of similarity in business cycles between countries that build on the signs of the output gaps (MJH-SYNC) and the distances between output gaps (MJH-COM). We use the output gap of the euro area 12 aggregate as the reference cycle. In order to reveal underlying trends in these measures, which are computed on a per-observation basis, a 6-year backward moving average of the MJH-SYNC and MJH-COM measure is included in the figures. The dashed lines in the graph show the five per cent critical values obtained from the simulation study by Mink et al. (2007).[8] Both measures fluctuate considerably over time and again illustrate that business cycle synchronicity is a dynamic rather than a static feature.

Fig. 7. MJH-SYNC together with a 6 year backward moving average

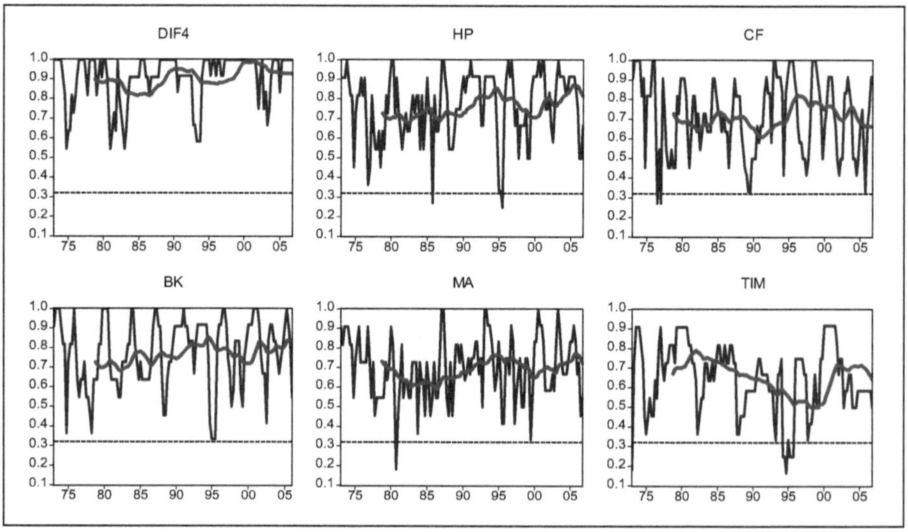

Notes: Five per cent critical values (---). See also notes to figure 1.

8 Values above these lines indicate that the estimated synchronisation and comovement measures are significantly different from a situation in which the business cycles fluctuate independently from one another.

In the case of synchronicity, figure 7 shows that all considered cycle measures lead to a fairly high level of synchronicity. The minimum and maximum values for the moving averages are 0.50 and 0.85, implying that most of the time the majority of the euro area countries have an output gap with the same sign as the euro area reference cycle.

Figure 8 displays the co-movement measure. Note that, by construction, this measure is bounded by zero from above. The results mirror the outcomes for the synchronisation measure. The measure is insignificant for many periods, particularly for the CF, MA and TIM detrending methods, yet is significant for the DIF4, HP and BK methods most of the time. For both similarity indices, it is difficult to detect a clear trend in the data that would imply convergence or divergence. In order to address this problem, we run a regression to check for the presence of a linear trend in these business cycle synchronicity measures.

Fig. 8. MJH-COM together with a 6 year backward moving average

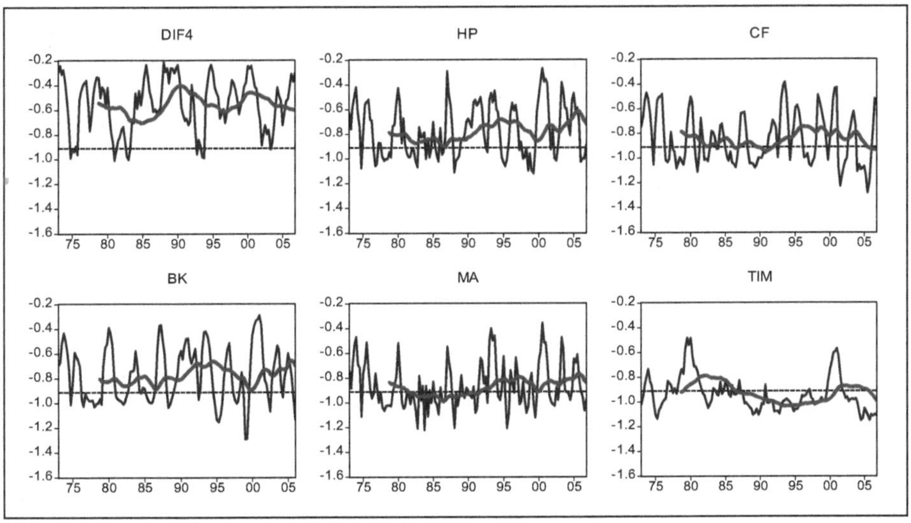

Notes: Five per cent critical values (---). See also notes to figure 1.

3.4.1 A Statistical Test of Convergence

The test is based on the sign and significance of the coefficient θ_p in the regression $\rho_t = c_p + \theta_p t + \varepsilon_t^p$, in which t is a linear time trend. A positive and significant coefficient indicates that synchronicity has risen over time and that convergence has taken place. In the exact same manner, the test is run by replacing ρ_t with the co-movement measures γ_t in order to test if convergence with respect to decreasing output gap distances can be detected.

Table 5 and table 6 present results of the convergence tests for three sample periods: (i) the complete observation period from 1973Q1 to 2006Q1, (ii) the period from 1980Q1 to 1998Q4 prior to the introduction of the euro which covers important developments towards European integration (completion of the Single Market Program, Treaty of Maastricht), (iii) the period from 1999Q1 to 2006Q1, which marks the introduction of the euro. Again, to check for the robustness of results several cycle measures are considered. Over the complete sample period, the regressions, which are based on the synchronisation index, yields for four out of six cycle measures a positive time trend (cf. column 2 of table 5). However, only the estimate of the convergence parameter θy for the year-on-year differences of GDP (DIF4) is significant; the other estimates imply that neither convergence nor divergence of synchronicity is statistically supported. For the period from 1980Q1 to 1998Q4, the DIF4-based synchronisation measure is again positive and significant while the TIM-based measure is negative and significant. For the last period, the latter measure again points to divergence.

Table 5. Test for convergence based on MJH-SYNC

Cycle measure	1973Q1 - 2006Q4	1980Q1 - 1998Q4	1999Q1 - 2006Q4
BK	0.00046 (0.44)	0.00015 (0.92)	0.00060 (0.90)
CF	-0.00042 (0.53)	0.00105 (0.46)	-0.00351 (0.42)
DIF4	0.00078 (0.08)	0.00218 (0.04)	-0.00049 (0.79)
HP	0.00083 (0.14)	0.00015 (0.91)	-0.00170 (0.76)
MA	0.00035 (0.50)	0.00127 (0.21)	-0.00028 (0.95)
TIM	-0.00079 (0.26)	-0.00375 (0.01)	-0.00949 (0.04)

Notes: Entries display $\hat{\theta}_p$ estimates. P-values are in parenthesis. The p-values are based on heteroskedasticity and autocorrelation consistent standard errors. See also notes to figure 1.

Turning to the co-movement based regressions, for the last two subsamples only the TIM cycle results in a significant coefficient estimate, but the sign is negative both for the 1980Q1 to 1998Q4 and for the 1999Q1 to 2006Q4 samples. The overall conclusion from this analysis is that business cycle convergence in terms of an increase in coinciding output gap signs as well as with respect to output gap distances is hardly supported by the data.

Table 6. Test for convergence based on MJH-COM

Cycle measure	1973Q1 - 2006Q4	1980Q1 - 1998Q4	1999Q1 - 2006Q4
BK	0.00026 (0.76)	-6.3E-05 (0.97)	-0.00337 (0.76)
CF	-0.00089 (0.27)	0.00154 (0.31)	-0.00558 (0.43)
DIF4	0.00045 (0.61)	0.00274 (0.11)	-0.00205 (0.73)
HP	0.00088 (0.28)	0.00080 (0.62)	-0.00337 (0.69)
MA	0.00053 (0.42)	0.00148 (0.19)	-0.00348 (0.53)
TIM	-0.00096 (0.15)	-0.00268 (0.01)	-0.01361 (0.00)

Notes: Entries display $\hat{\theta}_p$ estimates. P-values are in parenthesis. The p-values are based on heteroskedasticity and autocorrelation consistent standard errors. See also notes to figure 1.

3.5 Stylised Facts on Synchronisation in Non-Euro Area Countries

As discussed in the previous sections, business cycle synchronisation and macroeconomic convergence in general are – amongst many other factors – key requirements for the good function of a monetary union like the euro area. The functioning of the euro and the euro area is not only crucial for its member countries, but also for countries outside the euro area due to their economic linkages with the euro area. In fact, important questions could well be posed, such as: Has the introduction of the euro affected business cycle synchronisation within the euro area and between the euro and non-euro countries, both inside and outside the EU? What role do global convergence and synchronisation play? In this vein, we analyse business cycle synchronisation of other countries in relation to the euro area. In line with the findings of the analysis in the previous section, there could be many reasons why the degree of business cycle synchronisation of these other countries with the euro area has changed over time, including, among other things, the actual introduction of the euro area on January 1, 1999. Within the group of the non-euro countries we distinguish two subgroups: (i) the group of EU countries that are currently not members of the euro area (NMS, Denmark, Sweden and the UK)[9] and (ii) the group of non-EU OECD countries.

It is of interest to see how both groups may be synchronised with the euro area and how their synchronisation may have been affected by the creation of the euro area. For the first group, an additional and important aspect is that entering the euro area at some point in time is a real option/obligation. The analysis of this group could be undertaken from the perspective of the OCA, where a sufficient degree of business cycle synchronisation is one of the criteria. For the second group, adopting the euro is not an option. Nevertheless, it is also important to assess the degree of business cycle synchronisation of these countries with the euro area and to know if the introduction of the euro has had an effect. In the literature on business cycle synchronisation, the role of economic integration on business cycle convergence has been analysed first and foremost, and evidence of a positive relationship has been found; see in particular Frankel and Rose (1998), Imbs (2004) and Baxter and Kouparitsas (2005).

In this section we will build on the results of the previous section, asking similar questions concerning business cycle synchronisation and applying similar methodologies. In particular we analyse if there has been any change in business cycle synchronisation related to the introduction of the euro. To do so, we compare business cycle synchronisation before and after the introduction of the EMU, analyse the cross-regime behaviour of business cycles and consider global busi-

[9] Slovenia entered the euro area on 1 January 2007, Cyprus and Malta on 1 January 2008, but for consistency and comparability we treat these three countries here as if they have not yet entered the euro area, such that euro area in this section always refers to euro area 12.

ness cycle convergence and its link to synchronisation in the euro area. We also take a brief look at business cycle volatility since volatility could also be related to business cycle synchronisation. Concretely, we analyse whether business cycles have become less volatile and more synchronised in the world. It is possible that there are links between regional and global business cycle volatility and synchronisation: growing trade and financial integration of economies synchronises the effects of global shocks via cross-country output spillovers. Asymmetric shocks are partly absorbed by trade spillovers and more strongly shared globally in the case of higher integration. Thus, global integration is likely to contribute to lower volatility and higher synchronisation of business cycles on average. The IMF (2007) finds that trade integration has contributed positively to the observed decline of business cycle volatility for a sample of 78 countries during the period from 1970 to 2005.

In our study, the trend-cycle decomposition is achieved by taking (a) the HP filter and (b) year-to- year growth rates (DIF4). Note that in the case of the NMS the calculation of output gaps and other detrended variables is even more problematic than in the case of euro area countries: sample sizes are generally shorter, data less accurate, structural breaks omni-present and a long-run steady state of the economy not well defined. Despite such limitations, it is assumed that our data do approximate to a certain extent the true economic conditions. To obtain some degree of robustness in our results we include both growth rates and de-trended variables based on the HP filter in the analysis. Figure 9 shows for all countries the output gap and GDP growth rate. In most cases both measures of the business cycle seem comparatively similar, such that we can expect our results to be somewhat robust.

One important aspect that we analyse first is whether business cycle volatility has changed. In recent studies, several authors have found that business cycle volatility has tended to decline since the mid-1990s. Evidence has been found in particular for lower volatility in the US (where it has been dubbed the "Great Moderation" by Blanchard and Simon, 2001), but this decline in business cycle volatility seems also to have had more global dimensions. Various explanations have been proposed to explain this observed decline in volatility, including higher trade and financial integration, lower exchange rate and terms-of-trade volatility, increasing consumption smoothing, better monetary and fiscal management, a "good-luck" factor in the sense of smaller and less frequent macroeconomic shocks, as well as technical and institutional aspects such as more efficient inventory management and deregulation. Taken all together, these developments can be expected to explain the observed increased stability of business cycles in many countries and of the global economy as a whole. Overall, there is no clear consensus on the relative importance of each of these factors for the drop in business cycle volatility (neither with regard to the US or the euro area).

For the euro area an additional aspect may be taken into consideration, namely the possibility that the creation of the euro itself has contributed to a change in business cycle volatility. Obviously, that would be an important finding since it would mean that adopting the euro has led to a shift in business cycle volatility in the euro area countries, apart from other factors that may play a role, such as a global shift in business cycle volatility.

Fig. 9. Output gaps (GAP) and real GDP growth rates (PCRGDP)

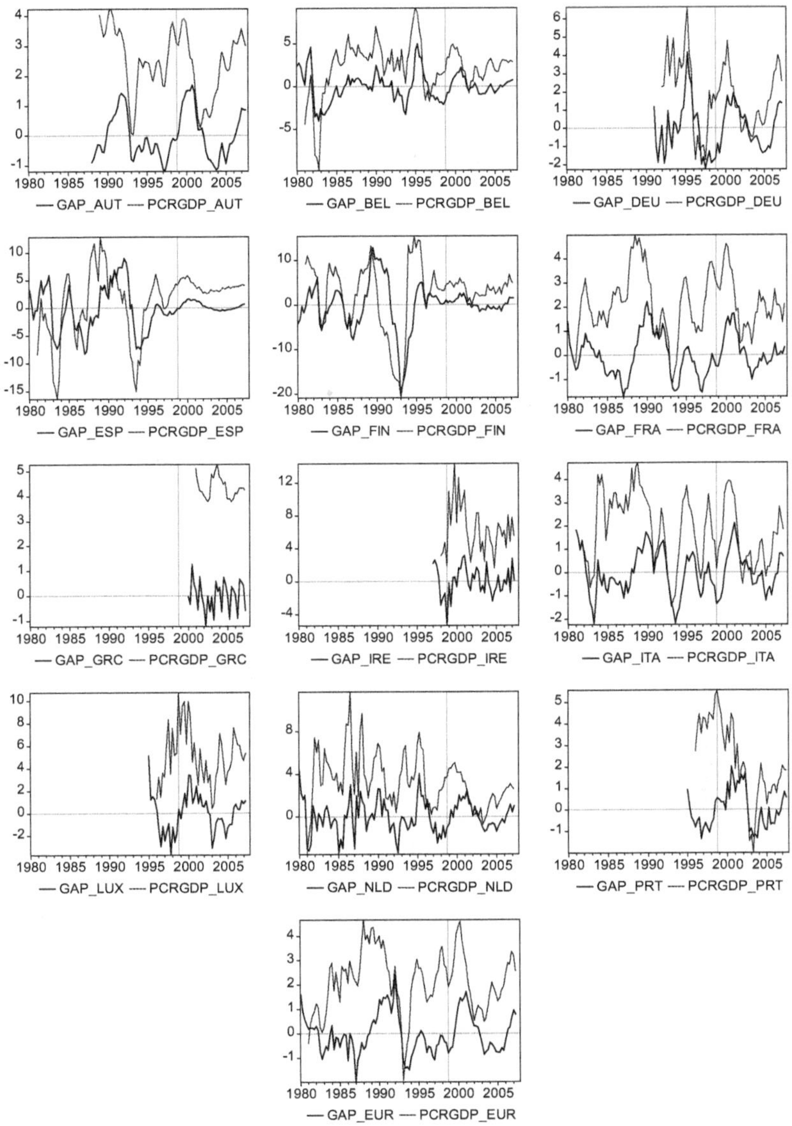

(a) Euro-12 countries

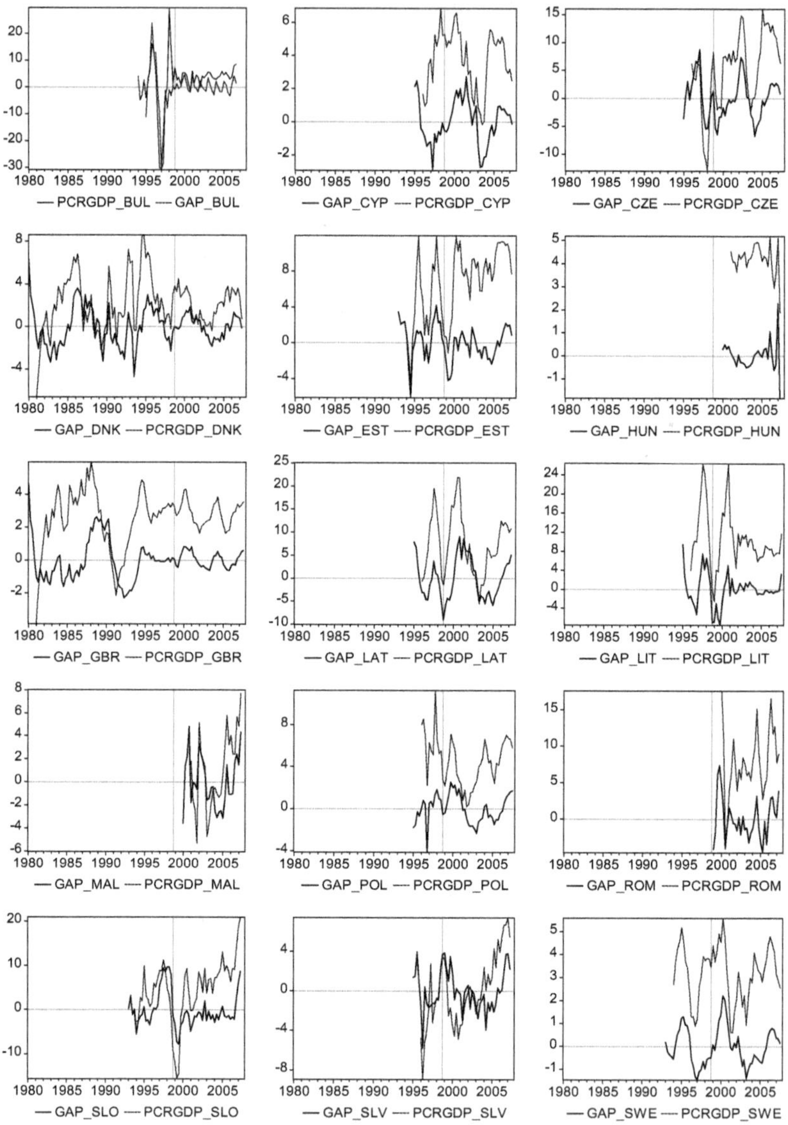

(b) non euro-12 EU-27 countries

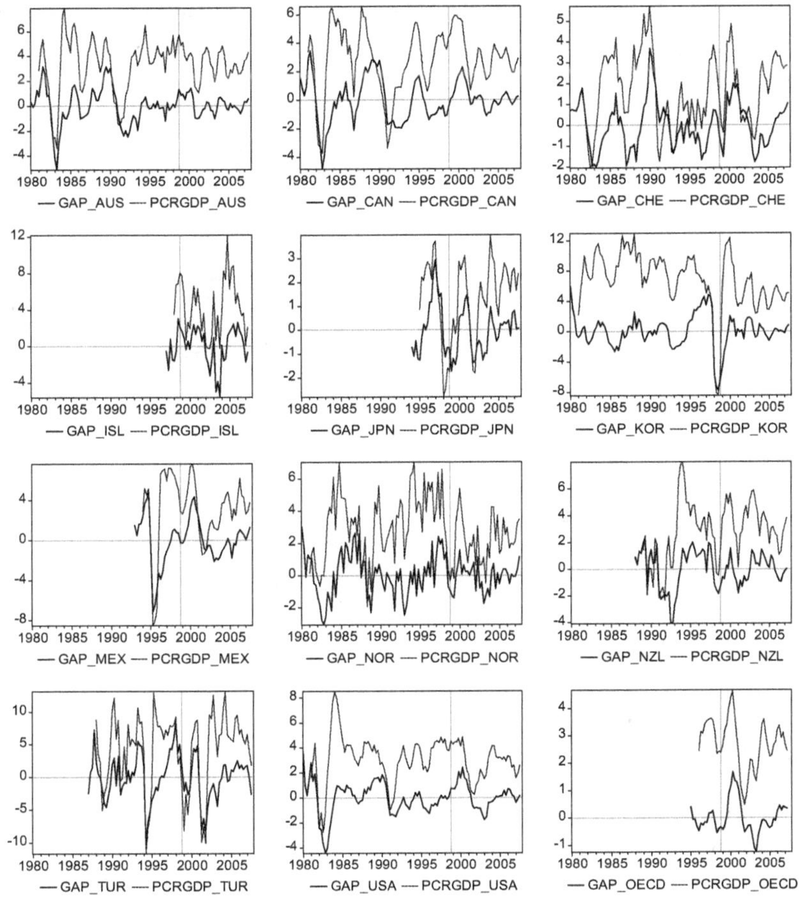

(c) non-EU countries

Whether the introduction of the euro has had a negative, no, or positive effect on business cycle volatility is again an empirical question similar to that concerning the euro's effect on business cycle synchronisation. From a theoretical perspective there could be reasons for both positive effects (i.e. on macroeconomic policy management; effects stemming from integration) and negative effects (i.e. less national coordination of monetary and fiscal policy; loss of exchange rate as shock absorber in the case of asymmetric shocks; the "increased specialisation" argument). Similar to our analysis of the role of the creation of the euro area on business cycle synchronisation, we are interested here is knowing if there is a "euro effect" on business cycle volatility. We can determine business cycle volatility in the euro area and the other countries in our sample in a straightforward manner: Figure 10 summarises the stylised facts about business cycle volatility. To proxy business cycle volatility we calculate both the standard deviation of the output gap (a) and real GDP growth rates (b).[10]

Fig. 10. Business cycle volatility

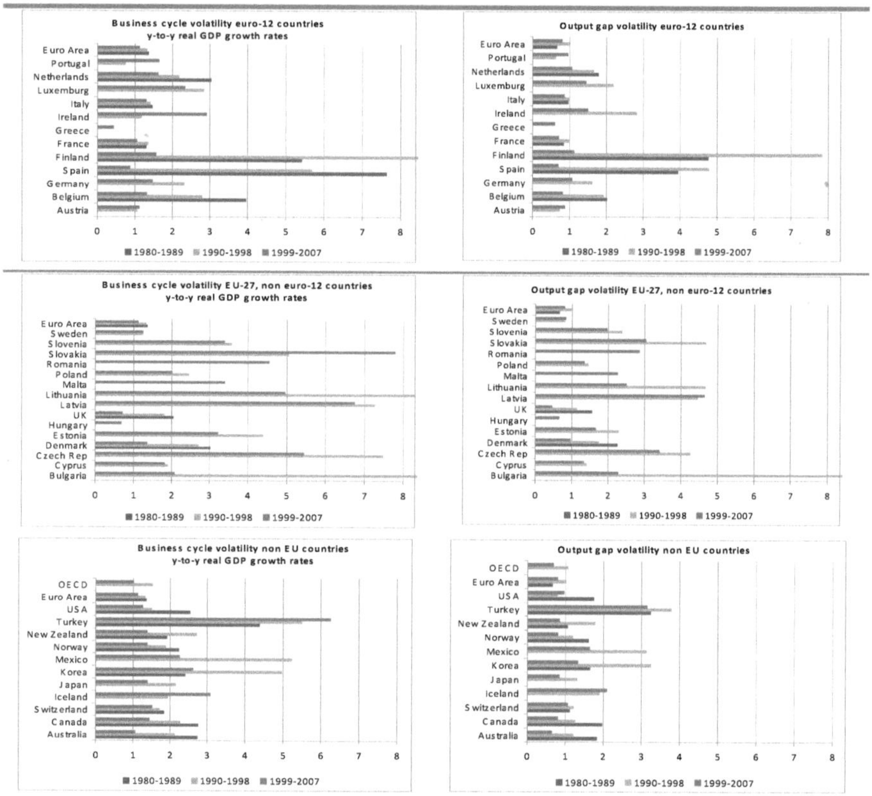

(a) (b)

Notes: real GDP growth rates (a) and output gaps (b), 1980-2007.

For most countries, business cycle volatility is somewhat lower in the period 1999-2007 compared to the period 1990-98 and to the period 1980-89, to the extent that data are available for this latter period. Thus there is indeed some tendency towards declining business cycle volatility which may in the euro area be attributable to some degree to the introduction of the euro. At the same time, the volatility of many non-euro countries and of the aggregate OECD business cycle has fallen since 1990, pointing to a global dimension in this process of declining volatility. Compared to the US, the reduction in business cycle volatility is actual-

10 In their analysis of business cycle volatility in Germany, Buch et al. (2004) also use these two measures. Evidence is found for a small decline in volatility of the German business cycle since the early 1990s.

ly smaller in the euro area. In most cases the observed changes are not so large, exceptions being in particular Finland, most NMS, Korea and Mexico. The observed heterogeneity between euro area countries in the size of the reduction in business cycle volatility has also been noted by the European Commission (2007) in its analysis of business cycle volatility in the euro area. Results also vary somewhat depending on whether output gaps or real GDP growth rates are used, e.g. in the case of Ireland, Latvia and Slovakia.

Table 7. Correlations of output gaps

	Austria	Belgium	Germany	Spain	Finland	France	Greece	Ireland	Italy	Luxemburg	Netherlands	Portugal	Euro Area	OECD
Austria	1.00													
Belgium	0.92	1.00												
Germany	0.81	0.71	1.00											
Spain	0.90	0.80	0.87	1.00										
Finland	0.89	0.85	0.84	0.81	1.00									
France	0.88	0.87	0.73	0.89	0.80	1.00								
Greece	0.19	0.22	0.07	0.13	0.21	0.16	1.00							
Ireland	0.46	0.50	0.57	0.47	0.53	0.49	-0.01	1.00						
Italy	0.80	0.77	0.90	0.86	0.84	0.79	0.16	0.54	1.00					
Luxemburg	0.81	0.74	0.78	0.80	0.72	0.79	0.05	0.44	0.65	1.00				
Netherlands	0.86	0.81	0.90	0.90	0.83	0.83	0.07	0.44	0.89	0.75	1.00			
Portugal	0.75	0.65	0.74	0.78	0.66	0.74	-0.02	0.35	0.75	0.68	0.81	1.00		
Euro Area	0.92	0.85	0.95	0.95	0.91	0.88	0.14	0.57	0.93	0.83	0.94	0.80	1.00	
OECD	0.87	0.91	0.62	0.73	0.83	0.86	0.26	0.46	0.61	0.78	0.69	0.55	0.77	1.00

	Bulgaria	Cyprus	Czech Rep	Denmarl	Estonia	Hungar	UK	Latvia	Lithuania	Malta	Poland	Romania	Slovakia	Slovenia	Sweden	Euro Area	OECD
Bulgaria	1.00																
Cyprus	-0.01	1.00															
Czech Rep	0.06	0.34	1.00														
Denmark	0.21	0.84	0.27	1.00													
Estonia	0.29	0.47	0.53	0.57	1.00												
Hungary	0.10	0.35	-0.22	0.38	0.00	1.00											
UK	0.20	0.28	-0.53	0.37	0.02	0.41	1.00										
Latvia	0.01	0.77	0.44	0.73	0.49	0.07	0.32	1.00									
Lithuania	-0.37	-0.04	0.04	0.08	0.03	-0.04	0.06	0.37	1.00								
Malta	-0.30	0.43	0.53	0.52	0.39	-0.01	-0.09	0.68	0.61	1.00							
Poland	0.26	0.43	-0.40	0.60	0.29	0.48	0.85	0.35	0.06	0.06	1.00						
Romania	0.42	0.29	0.02	0.28	0.48	0.13	0.34	0.19	-0.36	-0.14	0.41	1.00					
Slovakia	-0.41	-0.03	0.18	-0.14	-0.34	-0.11	-0.30	-0.09	0.09	0.22	-0.26	-0.32	1.00				
Slovenia	0.16	0.47	0.29	0.54	0.43	0.01	0.10	0.32	-0.26	0.27	0.30	0.25	-0.10	1.00			
Sweden	0.22	0.68	0.11	0.84	0.50	0.47	0.60	0.65	0.11	0.40	0.77	0.36	-0.14	0.49	1.00		
Euro Area	0.29	0.74	0.16	0.77	0.53	0.23	0.66	0.86	0.20	0.42	0.58	0.36	-0.30	0.37	0.79	1.00	
OECD	0.21	0.63	-0.15	0.75	0.43	0.62	0.76	0.51	0.11	0.25	0.80	0.36	-0.26	0.36	0.90	0.77	1.00

	Australia	Canada	Switzerland	Iceland	Japan	Korea	Mexico	Norway	New Zealand	Turkey	USA	Euro Area	OECD
Australia	1.00												
Canada	0.23	1.00											
Switzerland	0.05	0.77	1.00										
Iceland	-0.13	0.50	0.52	1.00									
Japan	0.19	0.45	0.52	0.34	1.00								
Korea	0.55	0.43	0.34	-0.21	0.06	1.00							
Mexico	0.22	0.88	0.82	0.49	0.61	0.29	1.00						
Norway	0.29	0.41	0.58	0.44	0.37	0.21	0.51	1.00					
New Zealand	0.49	-0.23	-0.59	-0.27	-0.12	0.08	-0.36	-0.10	1.00				
Turkey	0.48	0.34	0.10	0.18	0.56	0.12	0.39	0.17	0.27	1.00			
USA	0.36	0.73	0.60	0.52	0.69	0.12	0.86	0.48	-0.17	0.61	1.00		
Euro Area	0.03	0.71	0.92	0.32	0.45	0.34	0.79	0.43	-0.53	-0.03	0.48	1.00	
OECD	0.32	0.81	0.83	0.47	0.76	0.28	0.95	0.53	-0.32	0.50	0.91	0.77	1.00

Notes: Common sample 2000:I-2007:II. Own calculations from OECD and Eurostat data.

As previously discussed in section 3.1, the analysis of business cycle synchronisation relies on various measures to determine business cycle synchronisation between countries. Table 7 and 8 provide the contemporaneous correlations of output gaps and real GDP growth rates of the euro area-12 countries, the NMS and the group of non-EU countries. We display bilateral correlations and correlations with the euro area aggregate and the OECD aggregate (approximating here the "global economy").

Table 8. Correlations of real GDP growth rates (y-to-y)

	Austria	Belgium	Germany	Spain	Finland	France	Greece	Ireland	Italy	Luxemburg	Netherlands	Portugal	Euro Area	OECD
Austria	1.00													
Belgium	0.83	1.00												
Germany	0.73	0.53	1.00											
Spain	0.74	0.40	0.78	1.00										
Finland	0.79	0.74	0.78	0.60	1.00									
France	0.64	0.64	0.50	0.54	0.62	1.00								
Greece	-0.09	-0.08	-0.14	-0.02	0.10	0.15	1.00							
Ireland	0.15	0.32	0.33	0.15	0.34	0.27	-0.05	1.00						
Italy	0.54	0.52	0.77	0.68	0.74	0.62	0.20	0.43	1.00					
Luxemburg	0.55	0.43	0.57	0.41	0.37	0.46	-0.23	0.19	0.29	1.00				
Netherlands	0.72	0.58	0.86	0.83	0.74	0.70	-0.03	0.25	0.86	0.50	1.00			
Portugal	0.31	0.15	0.45	0.35	0.25	0.36	-0.10	0.09	0.43	0.45	0.61	1.00		
Euro Area	0.82	0.68	0.95	0.81	0.85	0.71	-0.02	0.35	0.87	0.57	0.94	0.49	1.00	
OECD	0.79	0.87	0.46	0.31	0.71	0.68	0.08	0.25	0.35	0.59	0.44	0.08	0.60	1.00

	Bulgaria	Cyprus	Czech Rep	Denmark	Estonia	Hungary	UK	Latvia	Lithuania	Malta	Poland	Romania	Slovak Rep	Slovenia	Sweden	Euro Area	OECD
Bulgaria	1.00																
Cyprus	0.13	1.00															
Czech Rep	0.10	0.50	1.00														
Denmark	0.33	0.73	0.49	1.00													
Estonia	0.43	0.37	0.49	0.64	1.00												
Hungary	-0.47	0.17	-0.22	0.08	-0.13	1.00											
UK	0.20	-0.10	-0.63	-0.01	0.00	0.30	1.00										
Latvia	0.09	0.70	0.51	0.60	0.39	-0.09	-0.03	1.00									
Lithuania	-0.38	-0.46	-0.14	-0.39	-0.20	0.10	-0.05	-0.02	1.00								
Malta	-0.07	0.35	0.68	0.64	0.48	0.11	-0.32	0.51	0.16	1.00							
Poland	0.49	0.17	-0.25	0.51	0.43	0.11	0.68	0.10	-0.30	0.12	1.00						
Romania	0.48	0.39	0.00	0.29	0.33	0.00	0.48	0.32	-0.41	-0.13	0.49	1.00					
Slovak Rep	0.27	0.31	0.36	0.49	0.20	0.01	-0.11	-0.03	-0.47	0.43	0.44	0.15	1.00				
Slovenia	0.44	0.41	0.44	0.78	0.69	-0.21	0.01	0.37	-0.53	0.54	0.61	0.35	0.65	1.00			
Sweden	0.40	0.40	0.36	0.74	0.64	0.07	0.31	0.41	-0.36	0.51	0.69	0.44	0.57	0.78	1.00		
Euro Area	0.43	0.61	0.25	0.61	0.60	-0.08	0.36	0.82	-0.10	0.30	0.47	0.50	-0.07	0.42	0.53	1.00	
OECD	0.33	0.35	0.02	0.62	0.58	0.34	0.60	0.28	-0.19	0.36	0.86	0.40	0.43	0.61	0.82	0.60	1.00

	Australia	Canada	Switzerland	Iceland	Japan	Korea	Mexico	Norway	New Zealand	Turkey	USA	Euro Area	OECD
Australia	1.00												
Canada	0.18	1.00											
Switzerland	0.14	0.61	1.00										
Iceland	-0.26	0.31	0.38	1.00									
Japan	0.07	0.46	0.63	0.26	1.00								
Korea	0.59	0.69	0.46	-0.23	0.23	1.00							
Mexico	0.12	0.78	0.81	0.36	0.72	0.47	1.00						
Norway	0.40	0.38	0.65	0.34	0.35	0.51	0.51	1.00					
New Zealand	0.50	0.12	-0.37	-0.27	-0.12	0.38	-0.16	0.10	1.00				
Turkey	0.42	0.42	0.27	0.11	0.61	0.30	0.53	0.21	0.21	1.00			
USA	0.32	0.58	0.63	0.38	0.72	0.36	0.80	0.51	-0.03	0.66	1.00		
Euro Area	-0.01	0.62	0.85	0.15	0.55	0.49	0.77	0.50	-0.28	0.08	0.42	1.00	
OECD	0.27	0.71	0.85	0.28	0.83	0.53	0.94	0.58	-0.12	0.59	0.88	0.60	1.00

Notes: Common sample 2001:I-2007:II. Own calculations from OECD and Eurostat data.

A number of stylised facts appear from these tables. Firstly, in most cases, while the results are relatively similar between both methods of business cycle measurement, the analysis of output gaps produces in general slightly higher correlations than growth rates. With the exception of Greece and Ireland (and Portugal in the case of real GDP growth rates), all euro area countries' output gaps and real GDP growth rates correlations with the euro area aggregate are above 0.6. Among the non-EU countries, Switzerland displays a high correlation with the euro area, whereas most others display much less co-movement of their business cycles with the euro area. Importantly, the euro area business cycle itself is strongly correlated (0.77 in the case of output gaps and 0.6 in the case of real GDP growth rates) with the aggregate OECD cycle, which we loosely interpret here as an adequate representation of the global business cycle.[11] Concerning business cycle

11 In a more detailed analysis one would need to take into account that the euro area share in the OECD is not negligible and correct accordingly. The weight of the euro area 12 in the total OECD amounts to 28 % (PPP-adjusted GDP share in the year

synchronisation with euro area countries, tables 7 and 8 thus suggest that Greece and Ireland do not score optimally at present, and that Cyprus, Denmark, the UK, Latvia, Sweden and Switzerland are highly synchronised and could probably do fairly well in the euro area. Finally, the tables suggest that the euro area is in turn highly synchronised with the global economy.

In most cases we are able to calculate pair-wise correlations for a considerably longer sample period and it is therefore of interest to explicitly distinguish between the period before the introduction of the euro and after the introduction and see if there are differences between both periods in terms of business cycle synchronisation. Figure 11 displays the business cycle correlations – measured again by correlations of output gaps and real GDP growth rates – measured for the three different country groups in three sequential periods: (i) the EMS period, 1980-89; (ii) the pre-EMU period, 1990-98; and the (iii) the euro area period 1999-2007. We also calculate the weighted and unweighted averages and the weighted and unweighted variances: an increase in synchronisation between groups of countries can be defined as an increase in the average business cycle correlation together with a decrease in the variance of business cycle correlations, such that business cycles on average are more similar and there is a reduction of heterogeneity between countries in their degree of business cycle synchronisation with the euro area economy. A number of stylised facts appear from these figures. We summarise them in the following sections.

3.5.1 Regional Integration: The Euro Area

As noted in other studies, the early 1990s was a period of business cycle divergence in the euro area.[12] However, business cycle convergence increased again in most countries during the second half of the decade and afterward. This is seen in the average and variance of correlations and in practically all cases in the individual country cases as well. This outcome is found both with regard to correlations in output gaps and real GDP growth rates. In the 1999 to 2007 period business cycle synchronisation again reached the normal level of around 0.7. The analysis in figure 11 is too crude to pick the observed phases of "re-coupling and decoupling" of euro area business cycles that was observed in section 3.4, where it was shown using a less crude analysis with moving correlations that business cycle synchronisation in the euro area typically remains at a relatively high level, while experiencing considerably fluctuations.

2000). Since this observation would apply to other OECD countries as well, this would imply a need for much more detailed analysis, which is not pursued here.

12 The first half of the 1990s was marked by a set of idiosyncratic shocks and developments, including the German reunification shock and its aftermath, the crises in the EMS and the fall of communism in Eastern Europe, to name a few. In addition, lack of monetary and fiscal policy convergence and coordination is likely to have played a role in business cycle divergence during the first half of the 1990s.

Fig. 11. Synchronisation with euro area

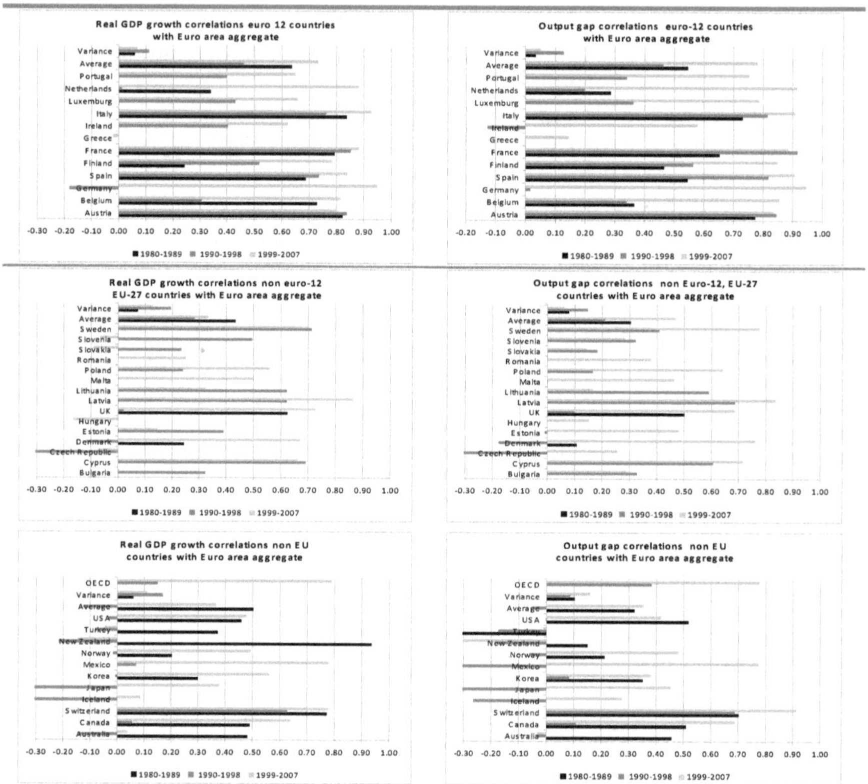

(a) (b)

Notes: real GDP growth (a) and output gap (b) correlations, 1980-2007.

3.5.2 Other EU Countries: Synchronisation but at a Lower Level

The business cycles of the EU countries not in the euro-12 are clearly less synchronised on average (0.40 in the case of output gaps and 0.3 in the case of real GDP growth rates) than most euro-12 countries with the euro area aggregate. Their synchronisation is currently comparable to that of the Members States in the period before adopting the euro. However, most countries display the similar dynamics in that synchronisation was low and/or declining in the 1990s, but increased again after 1999. Exceptions are Slovenia, Slovakia, Lithuania and Bulgaria, which actually witnessed a small decline in business cycle synchronisation with the euro area. Business cycle synchronicity of the New Member States the euro increased further in the years prior to euro adoption, as was the case in countries like Portugal, Italy and Spain in the period after the Maastricht Treaty was signed and a strong convergence path was pursued. In many cases, the level of trade and investment integration between the NMS and the euro area is similar to that of current Member States, implying potential benefits from decreasing transaction costs and decreasing risk of asymmetric shocks. In addition, if the endogeneity hypothesis of Frankel and Rose (1998) applies, acceding to the euro area should contribute to additional trade, investment and business cycle synchronisation. Denmark, Sweden and the UK also deserve attention: their business cycle synchronisation with the euro area is at a high level, implying that – at least as far as this criteria is concerned – the decision to enter the euro area should not be viewed as a dramatic one.

3.5.3 The Euro Area and Global Convergence

In the third panel of figure 11 we display non-EU country business cycle synchronisation with the euro area as well as the synchronisation of the euro area and the global economy.

Fig. 12. Non euro-12 EU-27 countries vis-à-vis the euro aggregate

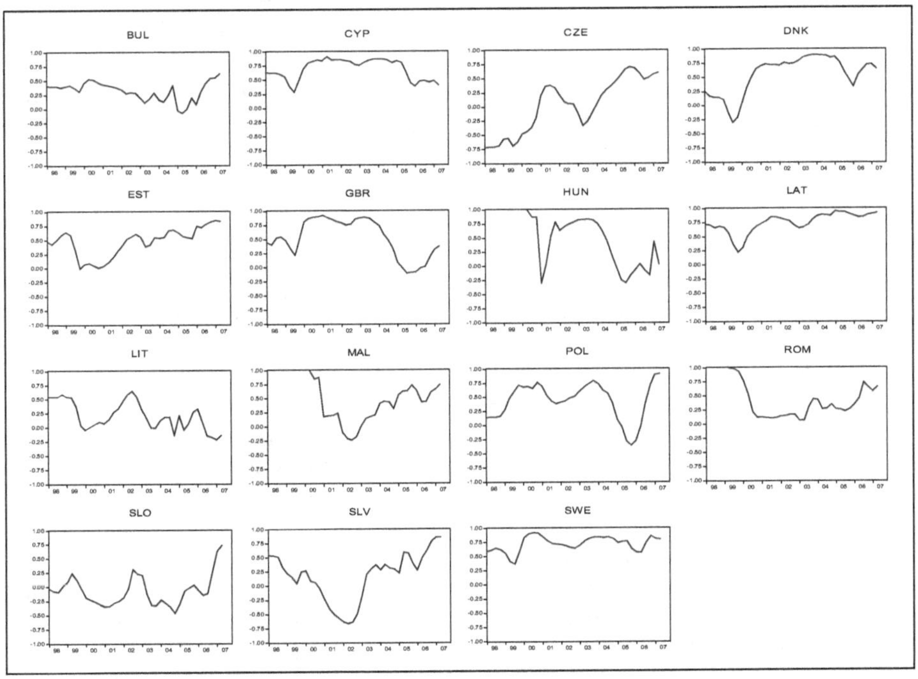

Output gap correlations of non euro-12 EU-27 countries vis-à-vis the euro aggregate over a 4 year rolling window.

Fig. 13. Non EU countries vis-à-vis the euro aggregate

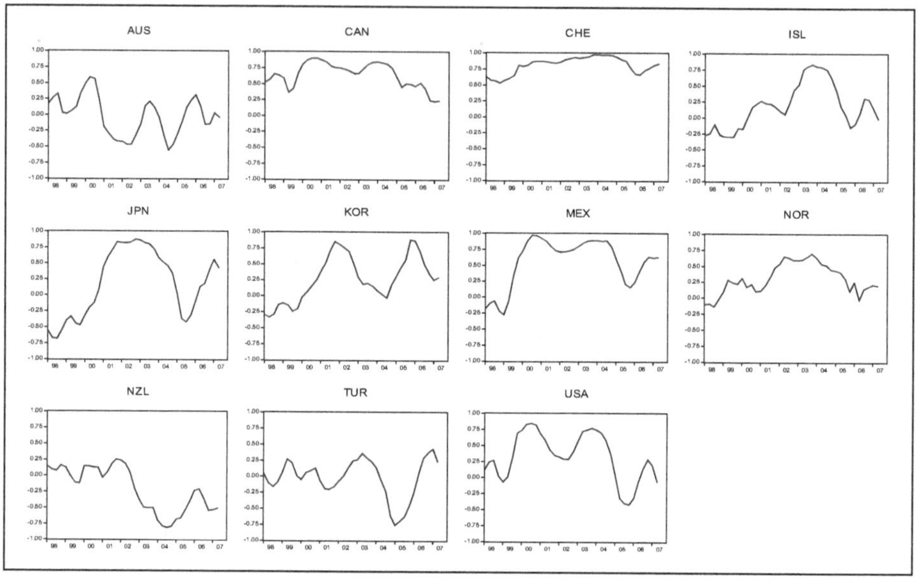

Output gap correlations of non EU countries vis-à-vis the euro aggregate over a 4 year rolling window.

We find that there is some increase of synchronisation with the euro area in this group, although this group also clearly contains a cluster that is – not surprisingly – hardly synchronised with the euro area (Turkey, New Zealand, Iceland and Australia). Synchronisation between the euro area and the global cycle has increased considerably so that we can certainly speak of a "global convergence effect" that affects the euro area in the recent period in the sense that global spillovers on the euro area economy increase in importance.

However, the values in figure 11 are averages for three distinct periods and allow only in a very crude manner the identification of whether the pattern of business cycle synchronisation is changing. We can, however, tease out the presence (or absence) of a "euro effect" on business cycle synchronisation by computing the correlations over successive intervals of four years (i.e. a four-year "rolling window"). We thus calculated four-year rolling window output gap correlations to gain a better insight into the dynamics of business cycle synchronisation with the euro area. Figure 12 shows results for the group of EU-27 countries that are currently not a member of the euro area and figure 13 displays outcomes for the non-EU countries. Here we concentrate on output gaps but results turn out to be similar when using growth rates. Again, the rolling correlations refer to the end points of the windows, i.e. they compute the average correlation over the past window length. From figure 12 we see that several countries such as Cyprus, Latvia and Sweden maintained a high and steady degree of cyclical synchronisation with the euro area during the period from 1994Q1 to 2007Q3. Others such as Lithuania, Hungary and the United Kingdom have de-coupled from the euro area movement in recent years. Since 1999, a steady increase in synchronisation with the euro area reference cycle is clear for the Czech Republic, Slovenia and Slovakia but also for Malta and Estonia.

Figure 13 shows the cyclical correlations of the non EU countries vis-à-vis the euro aggregate in a time-varying manner. A high degree of co-movement with the euro area can be observed for Switzerland, whereas New Zealand, Turkey and Australia clearly have had cycles that were generally not much related to the cyclical movements observed in the euro area. Interestingly, the output gaps of the US and the euro area aggregate have also become more dissimilar recently.

3.6 Coherence, Phase Effects and Dynamic Correlations

The previous sections analysed the euro area business cycle properties in the time domain and looked for changes in static correlations computed over different subsamples to study the change in co-movement over time. In this section, we apply concepts that are defined in the frequency domain in which time series are described as being constituted of an infinite number of components with different periods and amplitudes. The aim of such a decomposition is to determine the importance of different cycle frequencies in accounting for the behaviour of a variable. Components that are not repeated over time have zero frequencies (or infinite periods) and noisy components correspond to very high frequencies (or short periods). In between lie the business cycle frequencies that account for all other movements in the series. In contrast to the analysis in the time domain, we are able to conduct a frequency-by-frequency analysis once the series has been transformed in its spectral representation. In particular, this allows us to concentrate on the most dominant frequencies of our cycle measures and leave aside components with frequencies that account only for a minor fraction of business cycle movements. Static cross-correlations are defined over the complete frequency range and thus do not allow us to focus on the most important cyclical components. For instance, when two series are correlated at low frequencies (the long run swings in the series) but to a lesser extent at higher frequencies (the short run swings) then the estimated static correlation will be a mixture of these correlations, hiding interesting dynamic relationships. A further advantage of analyses in the frequency domain is that it offers simple and intuitive statistics that reveal lead and lag relations between two cycle series for which time domain counterparts are not that easily defined.

We use the concepts of *coherence* and *dynamic correlation* to determine the correlation between components of individual countries' cycles and a reference cycle over the range of the most dominant frequencies. Coherence is the frequency domain analogue of the cross-correlation function in the time domain and ranges from 0 to 1. However, this measure disregards the phase effect between different cycle series, i.e. this measure is completely independent of the position in time of two series. It determines only whether two series have the same pattern or not, independent of the position in time. Dynamic correlation, introduced by Croux et al.

(2001), is a measure of the correlation between the components that takes the phase shift between those components into account. It is also computed frequency-by-frequency or over a frequency band and ranges between -1 and 1. Dynamic correlation reduces to static correlation if the complete frequency range is considered. A third measure that is of interest is the *phase effect*, which represents the shift in time between the components of two series for each frequency (or over a frequency band). The phase effect tells us the relative cyclical position of a countries' cycle when compared to a reference cycle. Thus, it allows us to assess the lead and lag relationship between cycles. The concepts of coherence, dynamic correlation and phase effect are closely related: If the phase effect is small in a range of frequencies, the absolute value of dynamic correlation and the value of coherence will be almost identical. In contrast, if the phase effect is pronounced, important differences between coherence and dynamic correlation will result. Taken together, these measures can provide us with important information regarding in-phase correlation, overall dynamic correlation and lead/lag relationships between the cycles of the euro area countries.

We present results for individual countries' cycles vis-à-vis the euro area cycle. We also include the UK, the US and Japan which represent relevant economies outside the euro area. In addition, we compute coherence, dynamic correlation and phase effects between individual countries' cycles and major economies such as Germany, France, the UK, Japan and the United States as the respective reference cycle. Frequency domain analyses require large enough observation periods in order to obtain precise estimates of the population spectrum. Therefore, our analysis relies on the fixed sample period from 1970Q1 to 2006Q4 and excludes Austria, as quarterly GDP observations are not available prior to 1989Q1. Since we are not interested in the values of coherence, dynamic correlation and phase effects at every frequency, following Azevedo (2002), we compute the means of these measures over frequency bands that encompass the most dominant ones, i.e. those that represent the major fluctuations in the cycles. Again, cycles are extracted with the aid of the Christiano-Fitzgerald (CF) band-pass filter. The computational details can be found in the appendix.

Figure 14 reports the mean coherence and mean phase effect between each country and the euro area reference cycle. The horizontal axis shows the phase effect, which gives the position of each country relative to the euro area cycle. A positive value X means that the countries' cycle is X quarters ahead of the euro area cycle. The vertical axis shows the coherence measure. It should be noted that to interpret the phase effect consistently, the dominant cycles (frequencies at which the spectrum of the cycles has a peak) of the two series should not be very different and the estimate of the phase effect is less accurate when the true coherence is low. A higher coherence results in higher precision of the phase estimate. The dominant cycles are estimated in the range between 4.6 years (Portugal) and 6.4 years (Greece). Thus, our estimates of the mean phase effects should not be affected by the small discrepancies in dominant cycles.

Turning to the results in figure 14, mean coherence is high except for Finland and phase effects are in the range of -2.5 and 2 quarters implying that although the patterns of the business cycles between the considered countries and the euro area cycle are fairly similar, the timings of the cyclical positions are different. Countries that lead the euro area cycle by almost two quarters are the Netherlands, Greece and the US. Germany, Finland, France and the UK are also ahead of the reference cycle, but to a lesser extent. In addition, while countries like Italy, Spain, Belgium, Portugal and Japan show a lagging tendency, countries such as Ireland and Luxembourg are almost in-phase with the euro area. High correlation is indicated by the estimated mean dynamic correlation (Table 9). Dynamic correlation between the euro area business cycle and the cycle of the individual country is lowest for Finland, Portugal and the UK.

Fig. 14. Countries vis-à-vis the euro area: mean coherence and phase effect

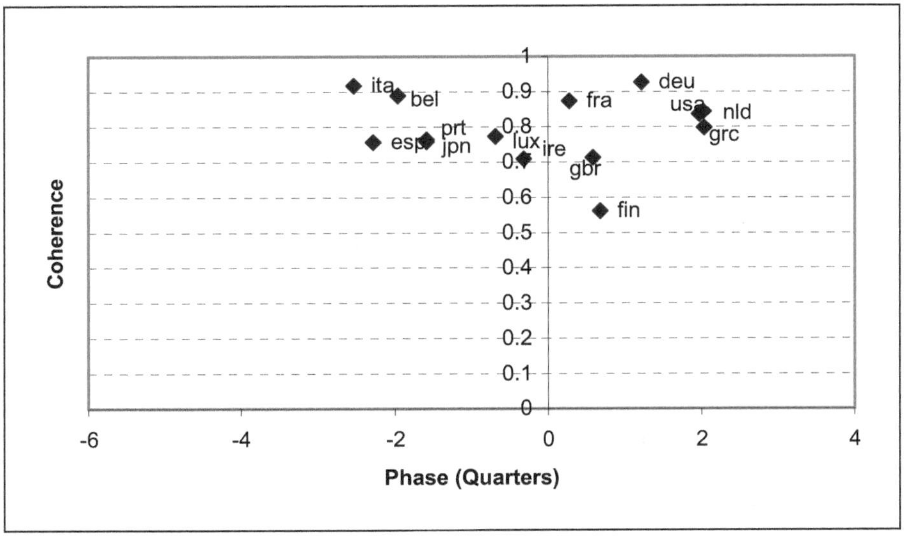

Table 9. Countries vis-à-vis the euro area: mean dynamic correlation

bel	deu	esp	fin	fra	grc	ire	ita	lux	nld	prt	usa	gbr	jpn
0.81	0.88	0.66	0.33	0.82	0.74	0.68	0.78	0.76	0.75	0.63	0.73	0.63	0.79

The next figures compare the cyclical positions of individual countries against selected large economies. The mean coherence, mean phase effect and mean dynamic correlation estimates presented in figures 15 to 19 and tables 10 to 14 provide a more diverse picture of the individual countries' cyclical relations.

Firstly, we compare individual countries cycle position versus the US cycle. The outcomes are shown in figure 15 and table 10. Conspicuous results are the pronounced phase effects: The phase of most countries' cycles lag, on average, behind the phase of the US cycle and the estimated mean phase effect is high for several countries. Italy and Belgium seem to lag behind the US cycle by more than four quarters. Leading countries are Spain, Greece and Finland. Using the example of Italy, the relation between coherence, phase and dynamic correlation can be seen clearly: For Italy, the mean phase effect is estimated very high (ca. -5 quarters) and the estimated mean coherence value is also high (0.88). At the same time, dynamic correlation only amounts to 0.38. While the coherence measure only assesses the correlation of the cyclical patterns, independent of the phase shift between the cycle components, the dynamic correlation takes this shift in time into account and therefore both concepts yield very different correlation estimates.

Fig. 15. Countries vis-à-vis US: mean coherence and phase effect

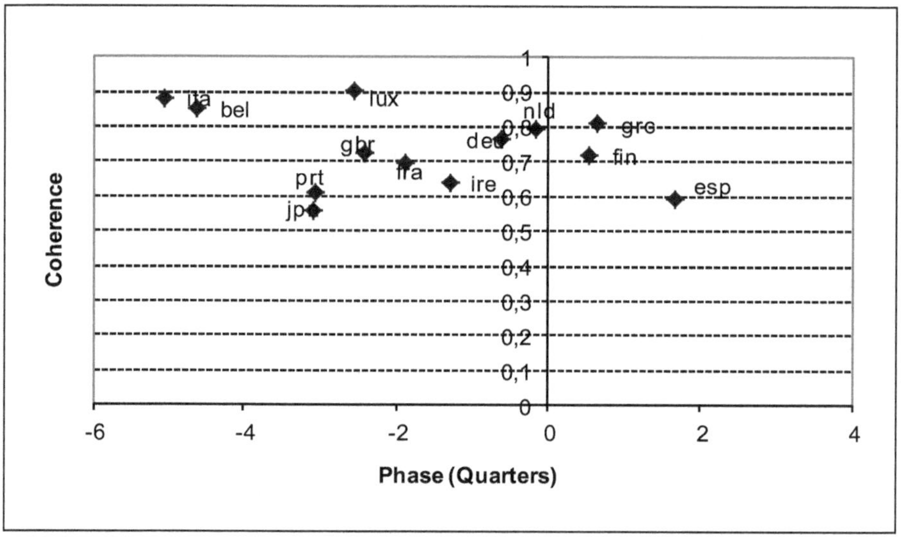

Table 10. Countries vis-à-vis US: mean dynamic correlation

bel	deu	esp	fin	fra	grc	ire	ita	lux	nld	prt	gbr	jpn
0.53	0.67	0.43	0.11	0.70	0.79	0.40	0.38	0.84	0.64	0.41	0.68	0.50

When we use Germany as the reference cycle (figure 16 and table 11), mean phase effects and mean coherence are slightly more pronounced than in the euro area reference case. We find five countries (Spain, Japan, Belgium, Portugal and the Netherlands) that lead the German cycle by more than one quarter. Finland's lead is estimated at almost three quarters but it has to be noted that the measured phase for Finland might have lower precision due to a low coherence estimate. The other countries are more in-phase with the German cycle, except for Italy for which we find a mean phase effect of minus three quarters. Dynamic correlation ranges between -0.07 (Finland) and 0.88 (The Netherlands). Other countries besides Finland that exhibit, on average, a low dynamic correlation with the German cycle are Spain (0.34), Portugal (0.41) and the UK (0.35).

Fig. 16. Countries vis-à-vis Germany: mean coherence and phase effect

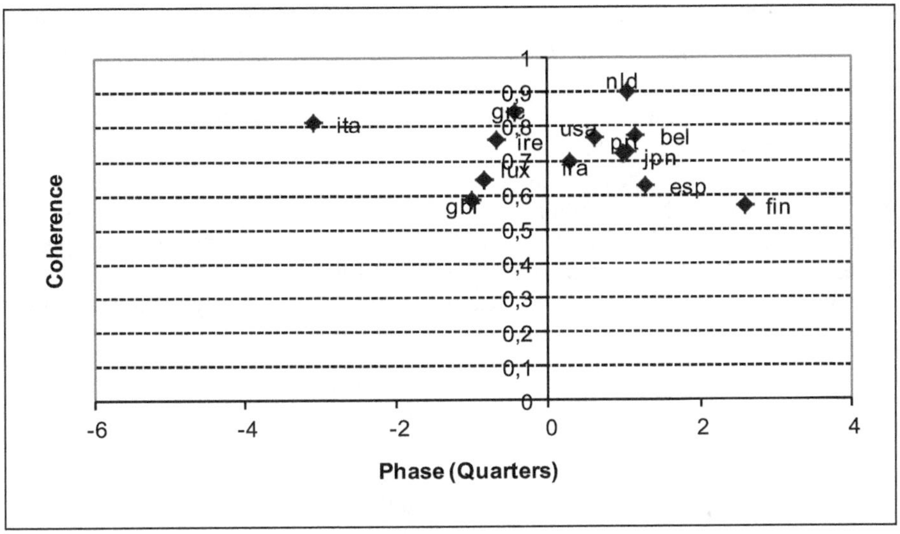

Table 11. Countries vis-à-vis Germany: mean dynamic correlation

bel	esp	fin	fra	grc	ire	ita	lux	nld	prt	usa	gbr	jpn
0.52	0.34	-0.07	0.52	0.81	0.56	0.52	0.62	0.88	0.41	0.67	0.35	0.65

Fig. 17. Countries vis-à-vis France: mean coherence and phase effect

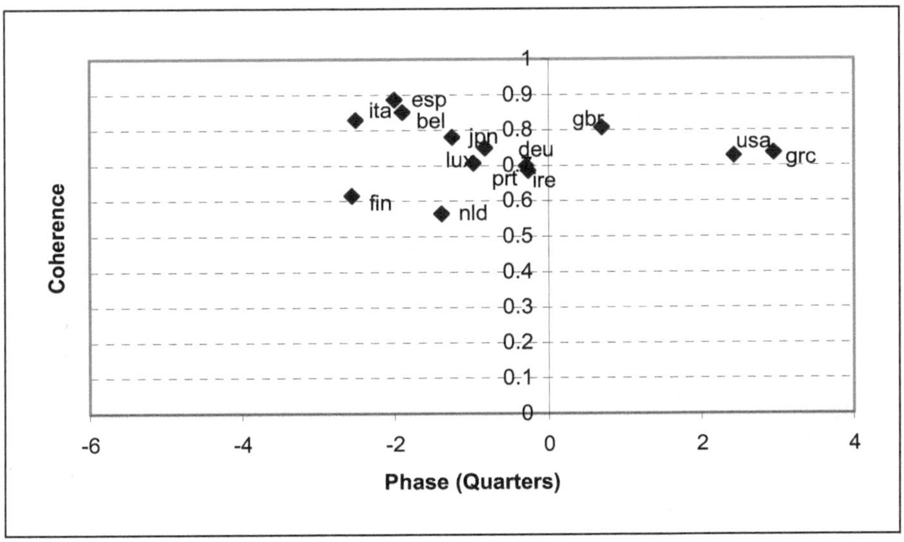

Table 12. Countries vis-à-vis France: mean dynamic correlation

bel	deu	esp	fin	grc	ire	ita	lux	nld	prt	usa	gbr	jpn
0.73	0.53	0.83	0.55	0.61	0.69	0.58	0.69	0.44	0.60	0.74	0.88	0.68

The individual countries' cycles in comparison with the British business cycle are shown in figure 18 and table 13.

The individual countries' results vis-à-vis the French cycle are presented in figure 17 and table 12. More countries lag behind the French cycle than lead it. The leading countries (the UK, the US and Greece) have phase shifts between approximately one and three quarters, while Greece and the US seem to lead the French cycle with the highest phase shift. Mean coherence and mean dynamic correlation is on average higher than it is in the German reference case.

Fig. 18. Countries vis-à-vis the UK: mean coherence and phase effect

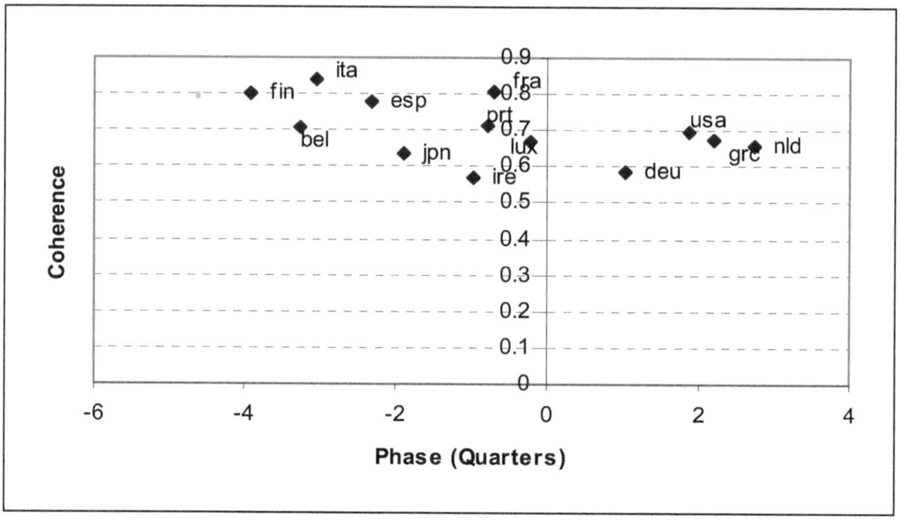

Table 13. Countries vis-à-vis the UK: mean dynamic correlation

bel	deu	esp	fin	fra	grc	ire	ita	lux	nld	prt	usa	jpn
0.48	0.35	0.66	0.49	0.85	0.49	0.34	0.50	0.68	0.17	0.53	0.68	0.47

Lastly, we compare individual countries' cyclical positions versus the Japanese cycle (figure 19 and table 14). It stands out that mean coherence varies substantially between countries, which implies that the pattern of the Japanese business cycle is more "idiosyncratic" than the other countries' cycles. A looser connection between Japan and the rest of the world is also reflected in the dynamic correlation estimates. The estimated phase effects range from -2.5 to 3.5 quarters, with Greece, the US, the UK and France as leading countries.

Fig. 19. Countries vis-à-vis Japan: mean coherence and phase effect

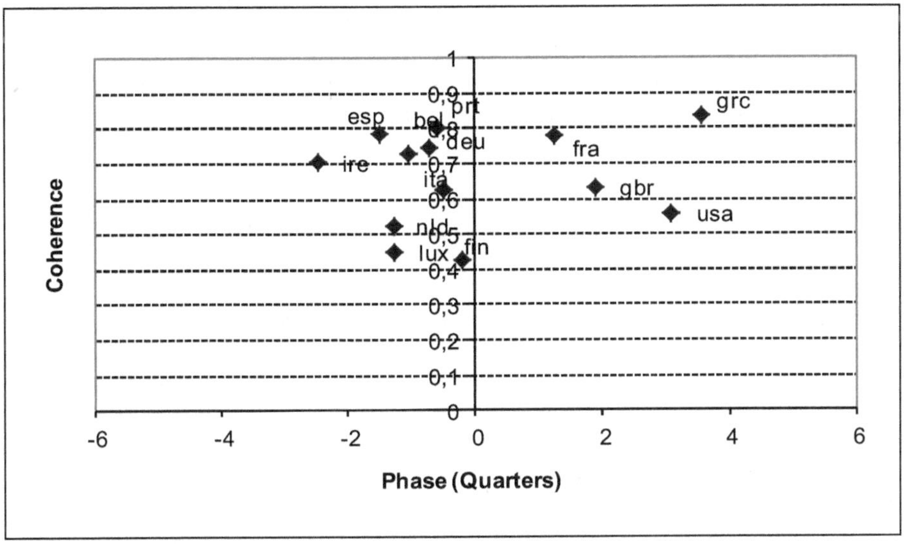

Table 14. Countries vis-à-vis Japan: mean dynamic correlation

bel	deu	esp	fin	fra	grc	ire	ita	lux	nld	prt	usa	gbr
0.69	0.65	0.73	0.29	0.67	0.72	0.67	0.59	0.46	0.39	0.75	0.50	0.47

To summarise the outcomes of the frequency domain analysis, we generally find that coherence and dynamic correlation among the considered countries are fairly high, falling below 0.5 only in few cases. Although a comparison with the static correlation exercises should be made with caution, this outcome is broadly in line with the findings in the preceding sections. The distinctive advantage of a frequency domain analysis is that it allows one to look at phase shifts between the countries' cyclical positions. We indeed find such phase shifts to be present and of relevant magnitude in many cases. Our results revealed that the US leads the euro area business cycle and the cycles of the other considered economies. In the case of the euro area, the US business cycle leads by approximately two quarters, which is not a crucial phase shift. With regard to the US cycle, the positive phase shift is highest vis-à-vis the Japanese cycle. Greece is also ahead of the other countries in most cases. Italy, Spain and Belgium are among the countries that lagged behind the phases of the respective reference cycles in most cases. From the non-euro area countries, the UK emerges as having the lowest dynamic correlation against the euro area cycle although the phase shift is not of relevant magnitude. Thus, the British cycle has a pattern which is less related to the euro area cycle than most other countries' cycles. From the euro area Member States, Finland is an outlier. Finland's dynamic correlation with the euro area cycle is measured around 0.33, a comparably low value. This result, which appears less pronounced in the static correlation measures shown in figure 6 of section 3.4, makes clear that it is a worthwhile exercise to look at narrower business cycle frequency bands to assess the complete picture of synchronisation. Portugal and Spain are also among the Member States that show relatively low values of dynamic correlation with the aggregate cycle. Taken together, it is the European "periphery" that shows a looser connection with the cyclical movements in the euro area aggregate than the euro area "core", a stylised fact reported previously in preceding sections.

3.7 Macroeconomic Convergence beyond GDP Cycles

According to the OCA arguments, a monetary union requires a sufficient degree of macroeconomic convergence to remain viable. Macroeconomic divergences are the result of asymmetries in macroeconomic shocks or policies in addition to the differences in transmission mechanisms that absorb macroeconomic shocks; differences in transmission mechanisms reflect in particular the differences between countries in their institutional configurations. In particular, recurring and persistent divergences may ultimately provoke the breaking-up of a monetary union, with nations deciding to re-establish national currencies, as history has shown. Both real and nominal convergence are needed in order for a common monetary policy to be efficient for all participants. In case of real and/or nominal divergence, a common monetary policy will be less and less fitting to the needs of most of the participating countries and may therefore contribute to macroeconomic divergence.

In this section we will have a closer look at real and nominal convergence in the euro area and also at the question of whether convergence patterns have changed since the introduction of the euro. We narrow the analysis of real convergence to output gaps and budget balances and of nominal convergence to inflation rates. Real long-term interest rate convergence is also considered as it contains an element of nominal convergence (nominal interest rates and inflation rates), thus yielding information on real convergence. Of considerable interest in the case of real interest rates is that real interest rate differentials have narrowed since the introduction of the euro, as the prime interest rate is determined by the ECB. Nevertheless, significant inflation differentials continue to persist in the euro area. In principal, therefore, inflation rates could serve as an indicator for analysing the effects of introducing a common currency.[13]

Figure 20 displays the GDP-weighted dispersion of output gaps, inflation rates, budget balances and real interest rates in the euro area. All variables are collected for the period 1990Q1 to 2007Q4.

---

13 A similar remark applies to real exchange rate variability.

Fig. 20. GDP-weighted dispersion in the euro area

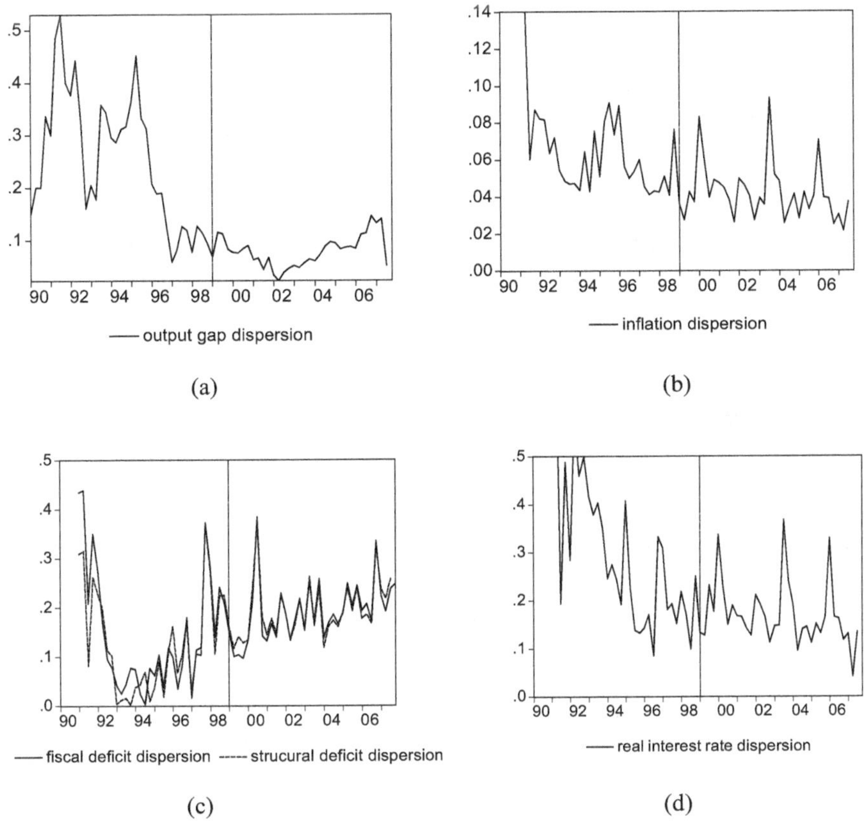

Notes: Source: own calculations from Eurostat and OECD data.

Output convergence is measured in panel (a) by the standard deviation in the GDP-weighted output gap[14] differentials between the individual Member States and the euro area aggregate in each period. According to this measure, output gap convergence increased especially during the 1990s and has been relatively low and constant since then. *Inflation convergence* in the euro area according to panel (b) has been relatively stable since 1990 with an occasional temporary upward shock to dispersion. Inflation is measured by the quarterly growth rate of the seasonally adjusted GDP deflator. In 2007, inflation dispersion appears to start rising somewhat in the euro area group, possibly because of a different pass-through of energy and global food price rises, e.g. due to different weights of energy and food in national HICPs.

---

14 Output gaps are based on the HP filtered real GDP series (using a smoothing coefficient λ of 1600).

Fiscal convergence is an important precondition for the efficient functioning of a monetary union. Even if the members of a monetary union fulfill (most of) the dimensions of the OCA, diverging fiscal policies can lead to diverging economic adjustments in a monetary union.[15] In fact, in many cases in history the main causes of the breaking-up of monetary unions can be traced back to fiscal divergences and imbalances. The potential building-up of fiscal imbalances with subsequent consequences on the stability of the common currency was indeed a major concern for the architects of EMU: as a solution to control fiscal imbalances, the fiscal framework of the Stability and Growth Pact with its set of fiscal checks-and-balances was proposed in the Maastricht Treaty.

In a straightforward but relatively crude manner, fiscal dispersion is measured here by the standard deviation of the differences between national and euro area fiscal deficit to GDP ratios (weighting countries by their purchasing power adjusted GDP weights). This measure – used also by De Bandt and Mongelli (2000) in their analysis of fiscal convergence in the pre-EMU period – measures in a rough way the degree of fiscal convergence in the euro area. We find that fiscal convergence took place essentially during the years 1992-95, when countries were preparing themselves to meet the entrance criteria for the EMU, a conclusion also reached by De Bandt and Mongelli (2000). Since then fiscal convergence has been slightly on the decline again.

For comparison, we also display the cyclically adjusted fiscal deficits, since any output gap convergence will also lead to converge in fiscal deficits if automatic stabilisers are substantial – as they are in the euro area. It is therefore also of interest to isolate this effect and consider as well any convergence of structural deficits since this would reflect more purely the result of deliberate policy actions in a monetary union like the euro area. Structural deficits are calculated using the EU Commission's (2006) calculations of budgetary cyclical sensitivities, which range from 0.27 in the case of Lithuania to 0.65 in the case of Denmark and for most countries between 0.40 and 0.50 (EA12 average: 0.47, EU15 average: 0.49 and EU27 average: 0.44). A cyclical sensitivity of 0.5 implies that an increase in the output gap by one percentage point shifts the budget balance by 0.5% of GDP. Government revenues are more sensitive to business cycles than government spending (government consumption, government investment and government transfers). These automatic fiscal stabilisers play an important role in stabilising macroeconomic shocks.

As countries in the euro area do not differ very much in their budgetary sensitivities, a change in the focus of analysis from current to structural deficits is not likely to greatly alter the outcomes concerning deficit dispersion. Indeed, the cyclically adjusted deficits display similar divergence patterns as the current deficits and also display a slight increase since 1996. In other words, the automatic stabilisers contribute practically nothing to (additional) fiscal dispersion (because of

15 Darvas et al. (2005) find evidence that fiscal convergence is indeed associated with synchronisation of business cycles in their panel of OECD countries during the 1964-2003.

the similarity between countries in the size of the automatic stabilisers). In addition, the introduction of the euro has not contributed to a reduction in fiscal dispersion, notwithstanding the noticeable fiscal consolidation that has been achieved in many countries. The differences between fiscal convergence based on current or structural fiscal deficits are likely to be larger if one considers the entire EU27 below, since differences in budgetary elasticities will be larger than in the EA12 group.

In conclusion, the small upward trend in fiscal divergence since the introduction of the euro on January 1, 1999, stands in contrast to the dispersion of output gaps, inflation rates and real interest rates that all have remained constant since then (cf. figure 20). The introduction of the euro has been conducive to low and stable output and inflation dispersion but perhaps at the cost of some increase in fiscal dispersion.

Another interesting way to look at the effects of the introduction of the euro on macroeconomic convergence is to compare the group of euro area (EA12) countries with the group of the EU countries that has remained outside the euro area. Any systematic differences between both groups may be related to the workings of the common currency as in most other ways these two groups do not seem to differ systematically. Similarly, any systematic difference between both countries that is manifest since 1999 may be the result of the first group participating in the euro area and the other group's exclusion.

In figure 21 output gaps, inflation rates, fiscal deficits to GDP and real interest rate dispersion in relation to the euro area aggregate economy are displayed not only for current Member States but also for the other group of non euro, EU27 countries.

Countries are not weighted by GDP as in figure 1 since we want to analyse both countries inside and outside the euro area. As is more or less to be expected, we see that the group of EA12 have on average lower dispersion in relation to the euro area aggregate output gap, inflation rate, fiscal deficit and real interest rate than non euro area countries. The difference between the EA12 and the rest of the EU is however not overwhelmingly large and narrows for output and inflation during the period 2000-06. Taken together, these stylised facts additionally suggest that the second group is converging to the euro area average in terms of output gaps and inflation and that fiscal and real interest rate convergence is practically absent in both groups alike.

Fig. 21. Unweighted dispersion in the euro area and the rest of the EU

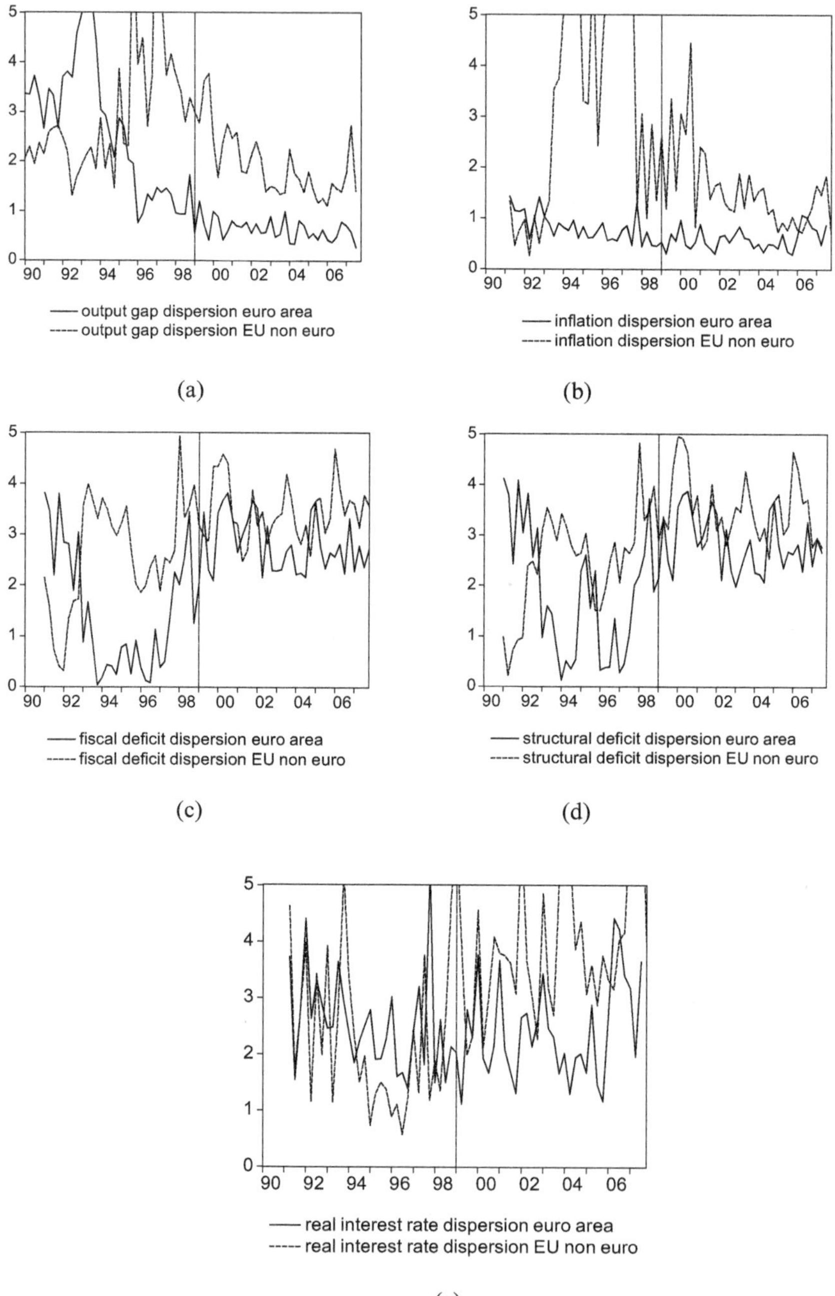

3.7.1 Business Cycle Persistence

One business cycle characteristic that plays an important role in the propagation of shocks is business cycle persistence. It is also a factor that can be helpful in analysing business cycle convergence in a monetary union like the euro area: if national cycles do not display the same persistence, the transmission of similar shocks will not be the same over time.[16] Some countries may display higher volatility but less persistence in the adjustments after the shock, as the persistence of business cycles is often linked to the underlying structural features and institutional settings of the countries, including size and openness. To the extent that countries differ in these dimensions, they will also differ in the persistence of business cycle fluctuations and their degree of business cycle synchronisation (even if only symmetric shocks take place).

In some studies, such as OECD (2002), the AR(1) coefficient is used as a rough but straightforward summary measure of persistence. It is of interest to take a closer look at differences in business cycle persistence in the euro area as well as to conduct a comparison of the set of countries that acceded to the EU in 2004 and 2007 and those that are preparing or recently acceded to the euro area. Table 15 displays the persistence and volatility of output gaps, inflation rates and budget balances (to GDP). Persistence is measured by the AR(1) coefficient and volatility by the standard deviation over the sample. The sample runs from 1990:Q1 to 2007:Q4, but in a considerable number of cases the actual sample is shorter due to data limitations (particularly with regard to fiscal deficit data) or other obvious reasons (e.g. in the case of Bulgaria only the period after the end of 1996 when an output collapse and hyperinflation hit the country is considered; for Finland the exceptional recession of 1992-93 [and the period before] is not included).

Smaller countries and the acceding countries are in many cases characterised by somewhat higher volatility and somewhat lower persistence than the euro area as a whole and than the larger Member States. As noted above, such differences in persistence and volatility are likely to reflect the underlying structural differences between countries (including size) that lead to different transmissions of macroeconomic shocks and policies (including the common monetary policy) and to different degrees of business cycle synchronisation in a heterogeneous monetary union like the euro area. As these structural differences are typically highly persistent as well, these stylised facts concerning differences in macroeconomic persistence and volatility are very likely to characterise the euro area in the long term as well.

---

16 Impact effects of shocks and persistence in the transmissions of those shocks are sometimes combined in the concept of "resilience" to shocks, a term frequently used in the context of "optimal currency areas":

Table 15. Persistence and volatility, EU countries

	output gap persistence	output gap volatility	inflation persistence	inflation volatility	deficit persistence	deficit volatility
Aut	0.94	0.81	0.89	0.29	0.48	1.79
Bel	0.83	1.48	0.24	0.34	0.72	3.27
Deu	0.80	1.36	0.37	0.42	0.76	1.75
Esp	0.93	3.44	0.45	0.46	0.27	1.66
Fin	0.75	1.55	0.29	0.75	0.65	1.82
Fra	0.88	0.87	0.34	0.21	0.74	1.54
Grc	0.80	0.30	0.75	1.52	-	-
Ire	0.33	1.79	-0.02	1.44	0.50	2.01
Ita	0.86	0.93	0.39	0.62	0.23	1.59
Lux	0.61	1.60	0.33	0.72	0.46	3.16
Nld	0.71	1.40	0.26	0.35	0.72	1.79
Prt	0.77	0.89	0.73	0.43	-	-
EU	0.96	1.65	0.40	0.36	0.86	0.99
Dnk	0.68	1.40	0.42	0.49	0.95	1.99
Swe	0.88	0.83	0.49	1.09	0.67	1.85
Gbr	0.89	0.88	0.26	0.54	0.89	2.30
Bul	0.57	7.19	0.35	5.55	0.34	2.94
Cyp	0.76	1.27	0.21	0.53	0.51	0.23
Cze	0.77	3.73	0.49	1.23	0.34	2.78
Est	0.64	1.95	0.27	3.58	0.56	2.23
Hun	0.52	0.60	0.33	2.03	0.36	3.13
Lat	0.84	4.47	0.50	1.57	0.46	1.73
Lit	0.60	3.11	0.53	1.91	0.29	1.87
Mal	0.48	2.20	0.20	0.72	0.32	3.68
Pol	0.65	1.35	0.44	1.95	0.75	1.49
Rom	0.49	2.81	0.30	3.86	0.17	2.70
Svk	0.82	4.09	0.32	1.10	0.87	3.63
Slv	0.58	2.10	0.32	0.81	0.78	1.43
EU27	0.91	0.64	0.65	0.41	0.87	1.30

Sample: 1990Q1-2007Q4.

3.7.2 Inflation, Output Growth and Shocks

One aspect that complicates macro-economic analysis and management in the euro area is the interaction between country-specific factors (such as asymmetric shocks and country-specific institutions), euro area factors (such as the common monetary policy and fluctuations of the euro) and global factors and developments. As discussed in more detail in the literature overview, several studies have recently been undertaken that analyse the role of the global business cycle and global convergence in an increasingly integrated world.

In this context, it is of interest to carry out a simple analysis on the effects of country-specific, euro-wide and global shocks on individual EU countries using a VAR approach. Instead of taking a panel data approach, we estimate a small VAR model for each country. This has the advantage of allowing for heterogeneity in shock propagation mechanisms. The estimated VAR models are very simple and include country *i*'s quarterly real GDP growth and country *i*'s quarterly inflation rate (measured by the quarterly growth rate of the GDP deflator), euro area quarterly real GDP growth and inflation rates and the OECD aggregate quarterly real GDP growth and inflation rates. All variables are seasonally adjusted. For most EA12 countries the sample runs from 1991Q1 to 2007Q3 and for the NMS from 1995Q3 to 2007Q3; in a few cases the samples are shorter. In the case of Germany, France and Italy we use euro area variables that exclude these countries on their turn, since these three countries constitute, respectively, 32 per cent, 24 per cent and 21 per cent of euro area GDP.

The model is estimated as an ordinary VAR using up to 4 lags and the shocks are not given a structural factorisation and interpretation, i.e. inflation shocks cannot be interpreted as supply shocks and output growth shocks as demand shocks, following Bayoumi and Eichengreen (1992) and subsequent SVAR based studies on the symmetry of aggregate demand and supply shocks. The advantage, on the other hand, of this simple approach is that we can use the reduced form innovations to determine directly the correlation of country *i*'s inflation and real GDP growth innovations with the euro area and OECD shocks and the impact of these shocks on country *i*, using the impulse response functions and variance decompositions of generalised impulses[17] to euro area and OECD inflation and growth. Table 16 provides correlations of inflation and real output growth shocks in the EU countries with the EA12 aggregate and OECD aggregate.

As expected, countries differ to some degree in the correlations of domestic inflation and growth shocks with the EA12 and the OECD aggregates, reflecting the heterogeneities between countries and the joint presence of both idiosyncratic and common shocks driving output growth and inflation. In many cases, the correlations of inflation innovations are somewhat smaller than real output growth innovations, both in the case of correlations with the EA12 and OECD aggregates, and both for the group of EA12 countries and the group of other EU countries. This suggests more idiosyncrasies in inflation shocks than in growth innovations. Correlations with the EA12 inflation and output growth shocks are on average higher for the EA12 countries than the other EU countries. There are also exceptions here, such as Denmark, Sweden, the UK and Poland, which display higher correlations. The observed differences in correlations point at some heterogeneities in inflation and growth shocks in individual countries, in comparison with the shocks observed in EA12 and OECD inflation and growth rates.

The variance decompositions determine how much of the observed variance in inflation and growth rates can be related to each type of shock. We find that both in the case of inflation and real output growth, domestic shocks explain a major fraction of the observed variance. In the case of real output growth the share of

---

17 Generalised impulses create an orthogonal set of innovations that does not depend on the VAR ordering like a Cholesky decomposition or the structural VAR of Bayoumi and Eichengreen (1992).

variance explained by euro area shocks and OECD shocks is most cases larger than in the case of inflation: euro area shocks and OECD shocks each typically contribute 10% to 15% of the variance in real output growth in most countries, which is somewhat higher than the 5% to 10% in the case of inflation explained by inflation shocks coming from the euro area and OECD.

Figure 22 plots the impulse response functions (+/- 2 s.e. bands) of real GDP growth in the Member States to a generalised one-standard-deviation shock to euro area growth. The impact and subsequent transmission of shocks to euro area output growth depend on the structural characteristics of the different countries. Growth in all countries (except Greece) reacts positively to a positive growth shock in the euro area and the impact effect is relatively similar in most cases. Some heterogeneity across countries is observed in the persistence of the adjustments to the euro area shock, but in practically all cases the shock is practically absorbed after a year.

The effect of shocks to real output growth in the OECD on growth in the euro area is additionally displayed in the last graph, which shows a similar, small but significantly positive effect during the first year after such a shock occurs. This also illustrates the relevance of global shocks to the euro area (and their transmission) and the desirability of taking them into account in order to obtain a full picture of the impact and transmission of macroeconomic shocks in the euro area.

Table 16. Correlations and variance decomposition of inflation and output growth shocks

Correlation	AUT	BEL	FIN	FRA	GER	GRE	IRE	ITA	LUX	NET	POR	SPA	EA12	DEN	SWE	GBR	BUL	CZR	CYP	EST	HUN	LAT	LIT	MAL	POL	ROM	SLO	SLV
Inflation shocks																												
OECD inflation shocks	0.16	0.18	0.18	0.35	0.44	-0.21	-0.11	0.21	0.20	0.03	-0.05	0.14	0.26	0.34	0.03	-0.08	0.28	-0.12	0.15	-0.06	0.18	-0.14	0.22	0.35	-0.04	0.11	0.05	0.14
EA12 inflation shocks	0.21	-0.02	0.06	0.30	0.58	-0.28	-0.15	0.58	0.01	0.10	0.12	0.34		0.21	-0.06	0.18	-0.17	-0.05	-0.05	-0.03	0.03	-0.13	0.37	0.26	0.00	0.03	0.17	-0.05
Real output growth shocks																												
OECD real output growth shocks	0.30	0.17	0.27	0.51	0.37	-0.16	0.29	0.42	0.33	0.04	0.08	0.16	0.65	0.33	0.31	0.42	-0.07	0.05	0.06	0.09	0.12	0.18	-0.01	0.47	0.18	0.28	-0.01	-0.02
EA12 real output growth shocks	0.34	0.37	0.30	0.51	0.40	0.12	0.45	0.39	0.18	0.25	0.24	0.45		0.36	0.38	0.30	0.06	-0.17	0.00	0.20	0.20	0.21	0.00	0.07	0.23	0.04	-0.09	-0.04

Variance Decomposition	AUT	BEL	FIN	FRA	GER	GRE	IRE	ITA	LUX	NET	POR	SPA	EA12	DEN	SWE	GBR	BUL	CZR	CYP	EST	HUN	LAT	LIT	MAL	POL	ROM	SLO	SLV
Inflation																												
Domestic inflation shocks	59.8	68.7	63.3	52.5	49.3	54.5	82.6	57.6	73.3	89.6	52.5	66.6	82.9	74.1	91.0	87.6	75.4	81.5	84.7	94.8	45.5	84.1	80.3	58.5	69.9	76.3	66.3	78.1
OECD inflation shocks	8.4	10.8	11.4	36.5	13.8	5.9	1.4	4.2	5.1	0.3	7.4	10.6	8.4	10.7	0.4	1.1	9.9	9.9	2.3	1.8	24.3	3.2	5.4	11.7	5.2	6.9	9.0	4.1
EA12 inflation shocks	9.1	0.7	4.7	6.0	9.0	7.6	5.4	28.3	6.9	1.1	8.1	11.4		1.9	3.0	4.6	7.5	1.2	2.1	1.5	5.1	4.3	9.7	7.3	2.0	3.4	4.3	3.9
Domestic real output growth shocks	5.2	5.6	2.1	0.5	8.4	1.6	5.4	2.4	5.0	0.1	5.7	2.5	2.5	1.3	3.8	0.3	0.5	1.1	1.0	0.6	14.4	0.9	1.3	0.5	2.3	1.0	0.8	2.1
OECD real output growth shocks	16.0	3.1	12.2	2.1	12.0	3.6	0.9	3.0	7.0	0.5	8.5	4.8	6.1	1.2	1.1	3.3	6.2	4.1	5.0	0.4	0.9	1.9	1.6	5.9	1.5	7.8	3.6	3.2
EA12 real output growth shocks	1.4	11.1	6.3	2.4	7.5	26.7	4.4	4.4	2.7	8.4	17.8	4.1		10.8	0.6	3.1	0.6	2.2	4.9	0.8	9.9	5.6	1.7	16.2	19.2	4.5	16.2	8.6
Real output growth																												
Domestic inflation shocks	10.7	1.7	3.4	0.8	25.9	24.4	11.0	2.6	5.1	3.8	25.7	13.0	1.2	0.9	1.2	7.2	1.2	13.4	0.8	3.6	25.8	1.4	3.5	5.4	7.5	14.4	12.8	14.3
OECD inflation shocks	1.0	1.4	4.5	8.1	6.1	6.8	3.8	2.3	6.1	1.2	7.3	3.4	3.5	3.9	0.5	7.2	16.1	20.2	3.6	4.8	33.8	4.7	0.1	2.0	1.1	1.1	9.7	1.7
EA12 inflation shocks	1.1	0.3	3.7	3.1	8.8	1.9	17.5	1.0	2.1	1.0	4.4	12.0		3.6	2.0	2.9	14.9	3.1	4.3	11.5	3.8	14.1	19.5	8.0	8.4	12.2	4.4	5.2
Domestic real output growth shocks	81.8	78.4	75.2	45.8	32.5	25.4	58.0	65.4	74.0	74.4	47.1	48.6	47.6	76.7	74.2	57.0	64.3	56.2	74.7	65.7	32.7	54.5	72.5	38.2	64.0	62.3	68.8	77.9
OECD real output growth shocks	4.5	5.9	6.3	33.2	11.2	21.8	4.6	26.3	10.0	5.2	5.0	4.2	47.7	11.2	17.3	21.5	0.8	3.5	11.4	8.7	0.5	24.0	3.0	20.0	7.4	7.3	2.3	0.8
EA12 real output growth shocks	0.9	12.3	6.8	9.0	15.5	19.7	5.1	2.3	2.7	14.4	10.6	18.9		3.6	4.8	4.3	2.6	3.7	5.2	5.6	3.4	1.2	1.5	26.4	11.7	2.7	2.0	0.1

Fig. 22. Impact and transmission of euro area and OECD growth shocks

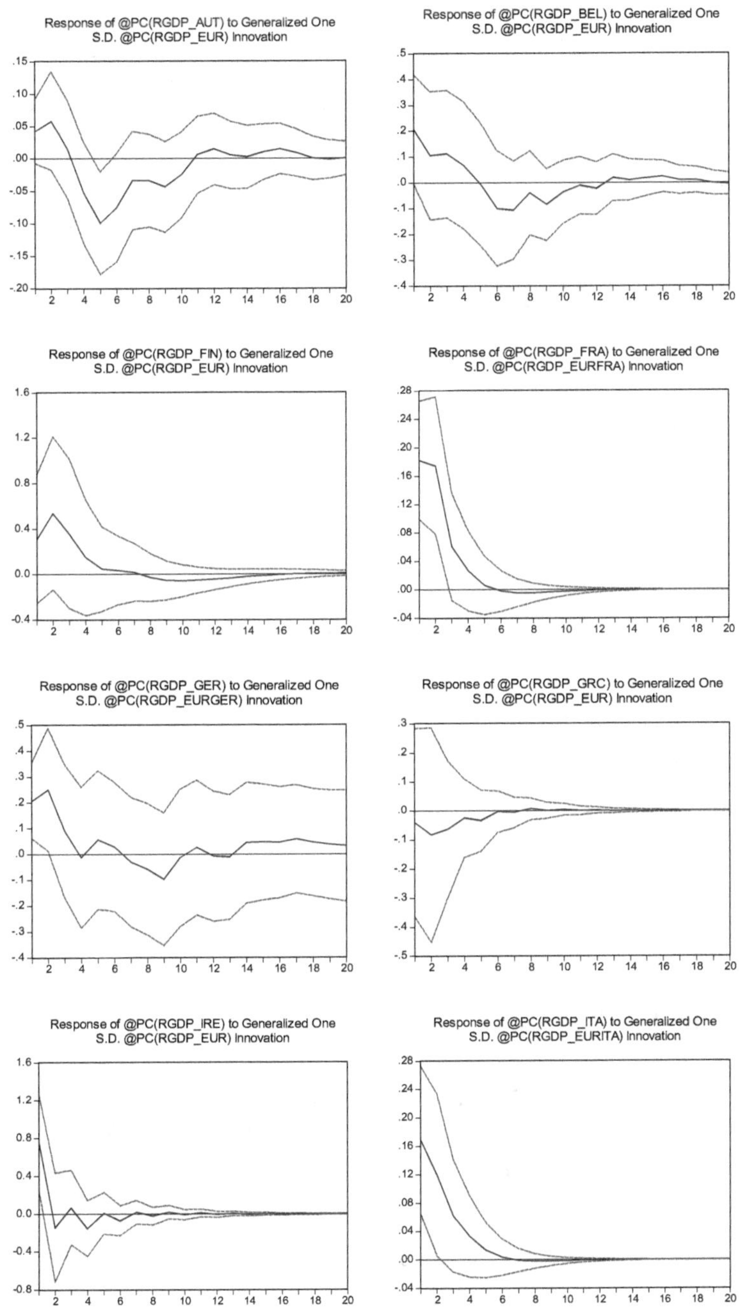

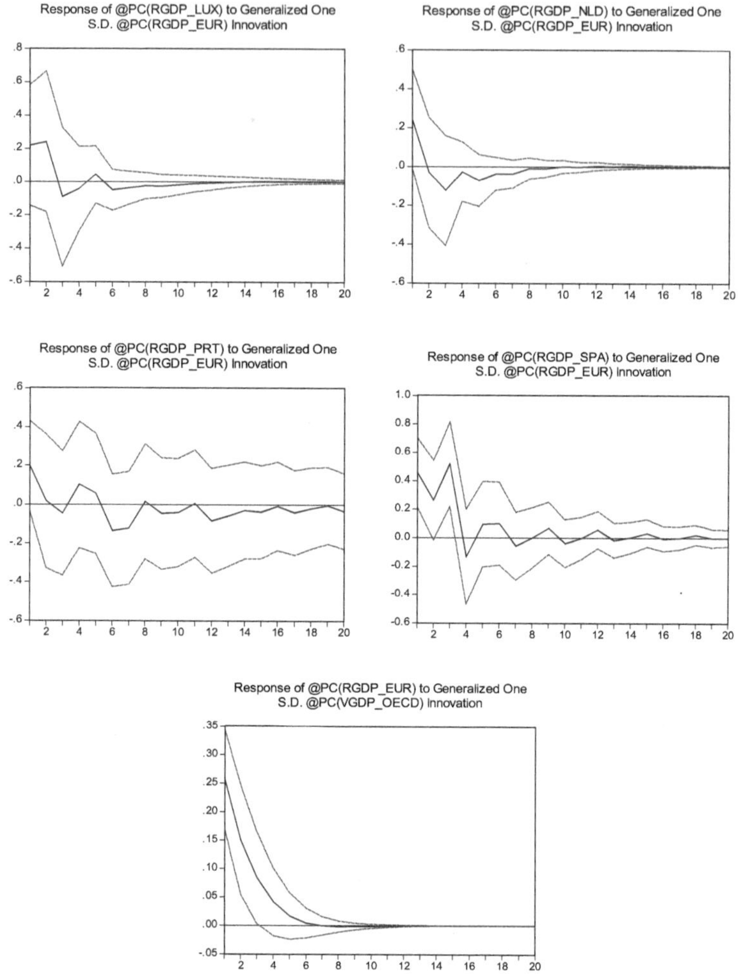

3.8 Cluster Analysis

This section analyses if there are clusters of countries within the euro area and the OECD that can be identified in terms of business cycle synchronisation, due to, say, geographical dimensions or institutional similarities.

3.8.1 Methodology

By means of a hierarchical cluster analysis, a set of variables is divided into groups (clusters) sharing similar characteristics. With regard to business cycle synchronisation, the variables of interest are output gaps which have been estimated with the asymmetric Christiano-Fitzgerald (CF) filter. For the cluster analysis, we opt to use the asymmetric Christiano-Fitzgerald band pass filter as the preferred method for separating the cycle from the trend. The decision for this method is mainly motivated by two reasons. Firstly, it belongs to the class of time series filters which are most commonly used in studies of business cycle convergence and synchronisation and therefore facilitates the comparison of our results with the outcomes of other studies. Secondly, this filter allows the extraction of a precise business cycle frequency band (1.5 to 8 years) which seems most appropriate for examining synchronisation and convergence. Furthermore, the asymmetric CF filter suffers less from the familiar end-point problem which plagues, among others, the Hodrick-Prescott (HP) filter. For the determination of the clusters, the Ward method is applied (see, e.g., Graff, 2006).

The Ward method is based on the Euclidean distance, where the distance between two items, *x* and *y*, is the square root of the sum of the squared differences between the values of the items:

$$\sqrt{\sum_i (x_i - y_i)^2} \tag{3}$$

with x_i and y_i defined as the output gaps of countries x and y in period i. The purpose of the Ward algorithm is to calculate for all possible clusters the means of the variables of interest and the Euclidean distances. The clusters are then determined on the basis of the minimum increase of the Euclidean distance. The linkage function specifying the distance between two clusters is computed as the increase in the "error sum of squares" (*ESS*) after fusing two clusters into a single cluster. The Ward method seeks to choose the successive clustering steps so as to minimise the increase in the *ESS* at each step.

The *ESS* of a set X of N_X values is the sum of squares of the deviations from the mean value. Hence, the *ESS* is given by the following expression:

$$ESS(X) = \sum_{i=1}^{N_X} \left| x_i - \frac{1}{N_X} \sum_{j=1}^{N_X} x_j \right|^2 \tag{4}$$

Mathematically, the linkage function, i.e. the distance between clusters X and Y, is described by the following expression:

$$D(X,Y) = ESS(XY) - [ESS(X) + ESS(Y)] \tag{5}$$

where XY is the combined cluster originating from fusion clusters X and Y. In contrast to other clustering methods which focus on the distance between the clusters, the Ward algorithm maximises the homogeneity within the groups. This method seems to be best suited in the context of business cycle synchronisation, as the idea behind the identification of clusters of similar business cycle characteristics is to find groups of countries sharing common business cycles rather than focus on the differences of the business cycle characteristics between countries in different clusters.

3.8.2 Empirical Results

In this section, the empirical results of the cluster analysis conducted for the book are presented. The analysis is performed for the 12 countries forming the euro area until the end of 2006 (euro 12). If the euro area countries are analysed in a larger context such as the OECD, the resulting cluster patterns may be different from the separate analysis for these countries, since in the larger sample some euro area countries may experience a higher synchronisation with some countries outside the euro area than with other euro area Member States. As an example, it might be possible that the business cycle of the euro area country Ireland is more similar to the business cycle of the UK, a non-member state, than to the business cycle of the euro area member Greece. Hence, in addition to the analysis for the euro area, a separate cluster analysis is performed for 30 OECD countries. The clustering is based on the quarterly output gaps estimated over the period 1970Q1 (where available) until 2007Q3. The result of the cluster analysis for the euro area is visualised in the form of a so-called dendogram which can be found in figure 23.

The analysis of the cluster structure is carried out by inspecting the dendogram from left to right, i.e. starting at the lowest level of aggregation. The length of the horizontal lines visualises the distance between the clusters. As an example, Finland exhibits a business cycle that is quite distinct from the other countries in the sample (see figure 23).

At the lowest level of aggregation, one cluster of two countries and one of three countries are formed, while the remaining countries do not pertain to any cluster. The first group of countries with similar business cycles is formed by the Netherlands and Austria. At the next stage, this group is joined by Germany. The second cluster is made up of Belgium, France and Spain, joined by Italy at the second stage. At the first stage, Greece and Portugal do not belong to any cluster. It is only at the second stage that these two countries merge into a separate cluster. Finally, three countries do not pertain to any cluster at this stage. These are Ireland, Luxembourg and Finland. At the next stage, the Netherlands, Austria and Germany remain in a separate cluster. A second group is made up of Belgium, France, Spain, Italy, Greece and Portugal. Only after these two clusters have merged to one cluster in the next step, Ireland joins this group, and Luxembourg and Finland join this single group successively at the last stages. Table 17 summarises the findings of the cluster analysis for the 12 euro area countries.

Fig. 23. Dendogram for the euro area countries

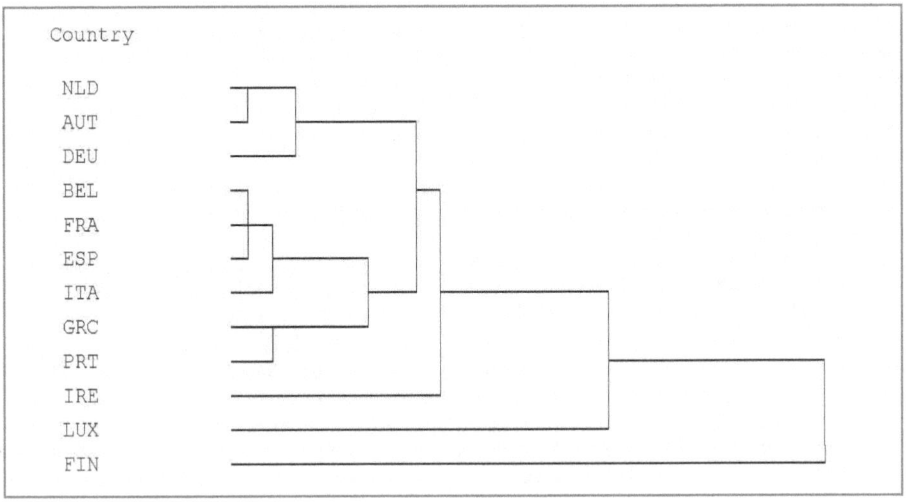

Table 17. Business cycle clusters of euro area (12 countries)

<table>
<tr><th>Stage 1</th><th>Stage 2</th><th>Stage 3</th><th>Stage 4</th><th>Stage 5</th><th>Stage 6</th></tr>
<tr><td>Netherlands, Austria</td><td rowspan="2">Netherlands, Austria, Germany</td><td rowspan="2">Netherlands, Austria, Germany</td><td rowspan="7">Netherlands, Austria, Germany, Belgium, France, Spain, Italy, Greece, Portugal, Ireland</td><td rowspan="8">Netherlands, Austria, Germany, Belgium, France, Spain, Italy, Greece, Portugal, Ireland, Luxembourg</td><td rowspan="9">Netherlands, Austria, Germany, Belgium, France, Spain, Italy, Greece, Portugal, Ireland, Luxembourg, Finland</td></tr>
<tr><td>Germany</td></tr>
<tr><td>Belgium, France, Spain</td><td rowspan="2">Belgium, France, Spain, Italy</td><td rowspan="4">Belgium, France, Spain, Italy, Greece, Portugal</td></tr>
<tr><td>Italy</td></tr>
<tr><td>Greece</td><td rowspan="2">Greece, Portugal</td></tr>
<tr><td>Portugal</td></tr>
<tr><td>Ireland</td><td>Ireland</td><td>Ireland</td></tr>
<tr><td>Luxembourg</td><td>Luxembourg</td><td>Luxembourg</td><td>Luxembourg</td></tr>
<tr><td>Finland</td><td>Finland</td><td>Finland</td><td>Finland</td><td>Finland</td></tr>
</table>

Based on these results, the business cycles of the twelve euro area countries in the sample are perhaps best represented as falling into three distinct clusters, with three individual countries that stand alone. The first cluster comprises the Netherlands, Austria and Germany. The second group consists of Belgium, France, Spain and Italy. Greece and Portugal form the third cluster, while Ireland, Luxembourg and Finland are quite different from the other countries.

Table 18 shows the bilateral cross correlations between the output gaps of the twelve euro area countries in the sample.

Table 18. Correlations between output gaps of EUR12 countries

	Aut	Deu	Nld	Bel	Fra	Ita	Esp	Grc	Prt	Ire	Fin	Lux
Aut	1.00											
Deu	0.68	1.00										
Nld	0.83	0.74	1.00									
Bel	0.45	0.55	0.61	1.00								
Fra	0.34	0.30	0.49	0.83	1.00							
Ita	0.20	0.52	0.44	0.79	0.79	1.00						
Esp	0.49	0.66	0.48	0.75	0.65	0.66	1.00					
Grc	0.25	0.40	0.21	0.24	0.19	0.41	0.42	1.00				
Prt	-0.03	0.29	0.02	0.38	0.41	0.56	0.53	0.51	1.00			
Ire	0.32	0.44	0.43	0.61	0.41	0.43	0.50	-0.14	0.16	1.00		
Fin	-0.30	-0.13	-0.03	0.47	0.60	0.54	0.32	-0.14	0.13	0.39	1.00	
Lux	0.51	0.25	0.49	0.29	0.24	0.07	0.14	0.17	-0.24	-0.14	-0.05	1.00

Notes: Output gaps have been calculated by applying the full-sample Christiano-Fitzgerald filter to quarterly GDP. Sample period is from 1970Q1 to 2007Q3.

The output gaps have been calculated by applying the full-sample Christiano-Fitzgerald filter to quarterly real GDP over the period 1970Q1 to 2007Q3. Hence, the table shows the input data for the above cluster analysis. The three clusters identified in the previous analysis are separated by horizontal lines. As expected, the business cycle synchronisation is highest within the clusters. The table also reveals the observation that, on average, the business cycles of Ireland, Luxembourg and Finland are only loosely correlated to the cyclical variations of the other euro area countries.

In the following, the clusters will be related to factors that may be important determinants of business cycle synchronisation, such as geographical proximity, trade linkages, fiscal policy and institutional similarities. Annual bilateral trade figures were taken from the IMF Direction of Trade database. Fiscal policy indicators (the overall and the cyclically adjusted primary budget balances in relation to GDP) were taken from the database of the OECD Economic Outlook. Institutional indicators may be found in the database of the Fraser Institute and in the dataset provided by Nickell (2006). The Fraser Institute publishes a Freedom of the World index for more than 120 countries (see Gwartney and Lawson, 2007). The overall index consists of several sub-indices such as a labour market regulation index, a business regulation indicator and an overall regulation index. Data are provided for the period from 1970 to 2005, but for the period from 1970 to 2000 data are only available in five-year intervals. Annual data are only published from 2000 onwards. For the present analysis, the missing data within the five-year periods have been constructed by linear interpolation. For some indicators and countries, the dataset starts at later points in time. As an example, the business regulation indicator is available only from 1995 onwards. Nickell (2006) provides a set of OECD indicators for labour market institutions in 20 OECD countries (from the euro area 12, Greece and Luxembourg are missing in this dataset). The dataset contains annual data for the period from 1960 to 2004, but for some indicators and countries the time period is shorter.

Regarding geographical proximity, in the first cluster Austria and Germany as well as Germany and the Netherlands share common borders, but this does not pertain to the pair Netherlands-Austria, which nevertheless exhibits a high degree of business cycle synchronisation. Moreover, some countries sharing a common border are found in different clusters. Examples are Belgium and the Netherlands as well as Spain and Portugal. In the second cluster, Belgium and France, France and Spain as well as France and Italy have common borders. The third cluster combines two countries (Portugal and Greece) which are in geographical terms quite distant from each other.

An important source of business cycle synchronisation is bilateral trade intensity. Following, e.g., Böwer and Guillemineau (2006), for each pair of countries the bilateral trade intensity is defined as the sum of bilateral exports and imports, divided by the sum of total exports and imports of both countries. Looking at the first cluster of countries, Austria and Germany as well as Germany and the Netherlands show high bilateral trade intensities, while Austria and the Netherlands do not trade as much with each other. These latter two countries are indirectly related to each other *via* their individual close trade linkages with Germany. In the second cluster, all countries exhibit high bilateral trade intensities; the only exception being the pair Belgium-Spain. In this case, the geographical distance is also relatively high. On the other hand, the trade linkages of Belgium are highest with Germany and the Netherlands, countries that are in a different cluster. The countries of the third cluster, Greece and Portugal, show a high bilateral trade intensity. However, due to geographical proximity, Spain is the most important trading partner for Portugal.

Differences in the cyclical position of the euro area countries may also be related to diverging fiscal policies. If fiscal policy divergence is a reaction to asymmetric shocks, then differences in fiscal policies may lead to more business cycle synchronisation. If, on the other hand, fiscal policy is itself a source of business cycle shocks, then diverging fiscal policies are associated with more heterogeneous business cycles (see, e.g., Darvas et al., 2005). The fear that diverging fiscal policies might reduce business cycle coherence in the euro area was one of the reasons for including the deficit criterion both in the Maastricht Treaty and in the Stability and Growth Pact (SGP). Different measures may be considered as indicators of the fiscal policy stance. One obvious candidate is the overall budget balance in relation to GDP. This indicator is used in the Maastricht Treaty and the SGP. However, the overall budget balance is to a considerable degree endogenous to the business cycle, since automatic stabilisers induce a rising deficit in a cyclical downturn and an improvement in an upturn. The cyclically adjusted budget balance is a measure of changes in the fiscal position of a country apart from business cycle influences. Furthermore, the overall budget balance contains interest payments on outstanding public debt. This expenditure item does not reflect the current fiscal policy stance. Hence, the primary budget balance, i.e. the budget balance adjusted for interest payments, is better suited as an indicator for discretionary fiscal policies. Based on these considerations, for the present study both the overall budget balance and the cyclically adjusted primary balance, each in relation to nominal GDP, are taken into account.

Over the period from 1980 to 1998, the countries of the first cluster, i.e. the Netherlands, Austria and Germany, had quite large overall budget deficits. In the period from 1999 to 2007, the average budget deficit ratio of Germany had only marginally improved, while the deficit ratios of the Netherlands and of Austria had improved considerably. Hence, since the introduction of the euro the fiscal positions of these three countries have exhibited some divergences. In terms of the cyclically adjusted primary budget balance (CAPB), as well, the fiscal policy stance of Austria and the Netherlands has been very similar since the introduction of the euro, while the CAPB of Germany was about one percentage point smaller. On the other hand, before 1999 the fiscal policies of Austria and Germany were more similar to each other and more distinct from that of the Netherlands. Based on the overall budget balance, in the second cluster Belgium and Spain on the one hand and Italy and France on the other hand show similarities, but there are substantial differences between these two sub-groups. While Belgium and Spain almost had balanced budgets from 1999 onward, France and Italy ran quite large deficits. However, over the period from 1980 to 1998, all four countries, and in particular Belgium and Italy, experienced high budget deficits, and the deficits of all four countries were considerably larger than those of the countries in the first cluster. Looking at the CAPB over the period since 1999, a somewhat different picture emerges. This indicator shows Spain and Italy having moderate surpluses, while Belgium has a larger surplus and France a smaller one. Before 1999, Spain, Italy and France exhibited similar fiscal policy stances with moderate deficits, while Belgium stands out with a surplus. The two countries of the third cluster, Portugal and Greece, ran high budget deficits both before and after the introduction of the common currency. However, based on the cyclically adjusted primary balance, the fiscal policy position of both countries has been almost balanced. Hence, while the overall budget balance differentiates this cluster significantly from the other countries, the differences in the CAPB are much smaller. Among the three remaining countries, Ireland and Luxembourg show more similar fiscal policies than Finland. Summarising these results, the overall budget balances are more similar within each cluster than between the clusters. However, when measuring the fiscal policy stance by the cyclically adjusted primary budget balance, the differentiation between the clusters is less clear-cut. During the financial and economic crisis in 2008-09, the fiscal position of all euro area countries deteriorated significantly, albeit to quite different extents. Both the working of automatic stabilisers (declining tax revenues, increasing expenditures, in particular for unemployment benefits) and discretionary policy actions were at play here. In a coordinated effort to combat the sharp decline in economic activity, almost all EU countries implemented substantial increases of public investment and consumption as well as tax reliefs. However, due to different starting positions in the budget balances at the outset of the recession and as the extent of the discretionary policies and the impact of the automatic stabilisers varied considerably between countries, the deterioration of the budget balances showed sizeable differences between the euro area countries, and these divergences were not closely related to differences in the cyclical position, since the economic downturn hit all industrialised countries nearly simultaneously.

Turning to the regulation indicators, the Freedom of the World indices for the three countries in the first cluster (Austria, Germany and the Netherlands) are very similar, particularly in the period since 1999. In the second cluster (Belgium, France, Spain and Italy), this indicator is also very similar, but on average it is somewhat lower than in the first cluster, indicating less labour and product market flexibility. In this respect, Belgian markets are more deregulated than those of the three other countries in the group. Greece and Portugal, which form the third cluster, are more different from each other than the countries of the other clusters. With regard to the Freedom of the World index, Portugal has more flexible markets than Greece. The three remaining countries not belonging to any cluster (Luxembourg, Finland and Ireland) exhibit considerably more flexible markets than the other euro area countries. Looking at two important sub-indices of the Freedom of the World index – labour market and business regulation – in each cluster the countries exhibit considerably more differences in their labour market regulations than in the business regulation index. Looking at the overall regulation indicator of Nickell (2006), the first cluster seems to be more homogeneous than the second cluster. In the second group, Italy and especially France have more regulated labour and product markets than Belgium and Spain. Due to missing data for Greece, the third cluster cannot be analysed. Summing these results up, the clustering of the labour and product market regulations is broadly in line with the clustering based on the output gaps. However, there are also some discrepancies. For example, over the period from 1999 to 2005 Belgium and Portugal had the same average Freedom of the World index, but they belong to different business cycle clusters.

The extent of business cycle synchronisation between the countries might also be influenced by industry structure. In particular, the share of manufacturing in total value added might be important, since industry is the sector that is most open to international competition and thus vulnerable to the international transmission of economic fluctuations and external shocks (see, e.g., Artis and Claeys, 2007). In the first cluster, the average share of manufacturing amounts to 18.7 per cent, slightly above the value of 16.6 per cent recorded for the second cluster. In the third cluster (Greece and Portugal), the importance of manufacturing is considerably lower (13.2 per cent). Finally, among the three countries not belonging to any cluster, the share of manufacturing varies between 7.9 per cent in Luxembourg and about 23 per cent in Finland and Ireland. However, within the first two clusters, there is also significant variation. This applies in particular to the first cluster, where the share of manufacturing ranges from 13.3 per cent in the Netherlands to 22.6 per cent in Germany. Hence, in some cases there is more variation within than between the clusters. Thus, the importance of manufacturing appears to explain only a small portion of business cycle synchronisation. However, during the 2008-09 recession the share of manufacturing in value added was of utmost importance for the degree to which countries were hit by the crisis. This pattern can be explained by the fact that during this period the downturn of economic activity led to plummeting exports. Hence, those countries with important manufacturing sectors and hence a large exposure to fluctuations in international demand experienced the sharpest fall in GDP. This shows clearly the importance of the source of a recession. If an economic downturn is caused by a drop in foreign demand, those countries with a relatively large industrial sector, particularly one specialised in the production of investment goods, will be especially hard hit. In such a case differences in the share of manufacturing in value added are thus crucial for the cross-country synchronisation of cyclical fluctuations.

The results of the cluster analysis in relation to possible factors driving business cycle synchronisation indicate that in general bilateral trade intensity and common borders are more important determinants of business cycle synchronisation than regulation, fiscal policies or the industry structure. However, as the recent recession has shown, the relative importance of the different factors may change over time. The exact contribution of the various determinants to the business cycle synchronisation has to be determined with regression techniques. This is the subject of chapter 4 of this book.

As mentioned above, extending the analysis to a larger sample of countries may affect the existing clusters, since some countries may show more business cycle similarities with countries outside the euro area than within. Hence, the cluster analysis was also performed for 30 OECD countries. The resulting dendogram can be found in figure 24.

At the first stage, six clusters of two or more countries are formed, while six countries do not belong to any cluster. These are Slovakia, the Czech Republic, Korea, Iceland, Mexico and Turkey. The first cluster of countries consists of the Netherlands, Austria, Belgium, France, Spain, Germany, Italy, Hungary, Switzerland and Norway. Another cluster is formed by Australia, New Zealand, the UK and Poland. Luxembourg, Denmark, the US and Canada comprise an additional cluster. Finally, there are three clusters consisting of two countries each: Greece and Portugal, Finland and Sweden as well as Ireland and Japan. At the second stage, a cluster emerges that contains all euro area countries except Ireland, together with Switzerland, Norway, Sweden, Poland, Australia, New Zealand and the UK. The second cluster is formed by Ireland, Japan and the Czech Republic, and the third group consists of Luxembourg, Denmark, the US, Canada and Iceland. At this clustering stage, Slovakia, Mexico and Turkey remain outside all country groups. When more clusters are merged, a large group emerges, consisting of the Netherlands, Austria, Belgium, France, Spain, Hungary, Germany, Italy, Switzerland, Norway, Greece, Portugal, Finland, Sweden, the UK, Poland, Australia, New Zealand, Slovakia, Ireland, the Czech Republic and Japan. The second cluster is made up of Luxembourg, the US, Canada, Denmark and Iceland. Korea, Mexico and Turkey remain separate. At the next stage, Mexico joins the US cluster, then Korea joins the larger cluster, and Turkey only joins the other countries at the final stage when there is just one cluster which consists of all countries. The various stages of clustering are summarised in table 19.

Fig. 24. Dendogram for the OECD countries

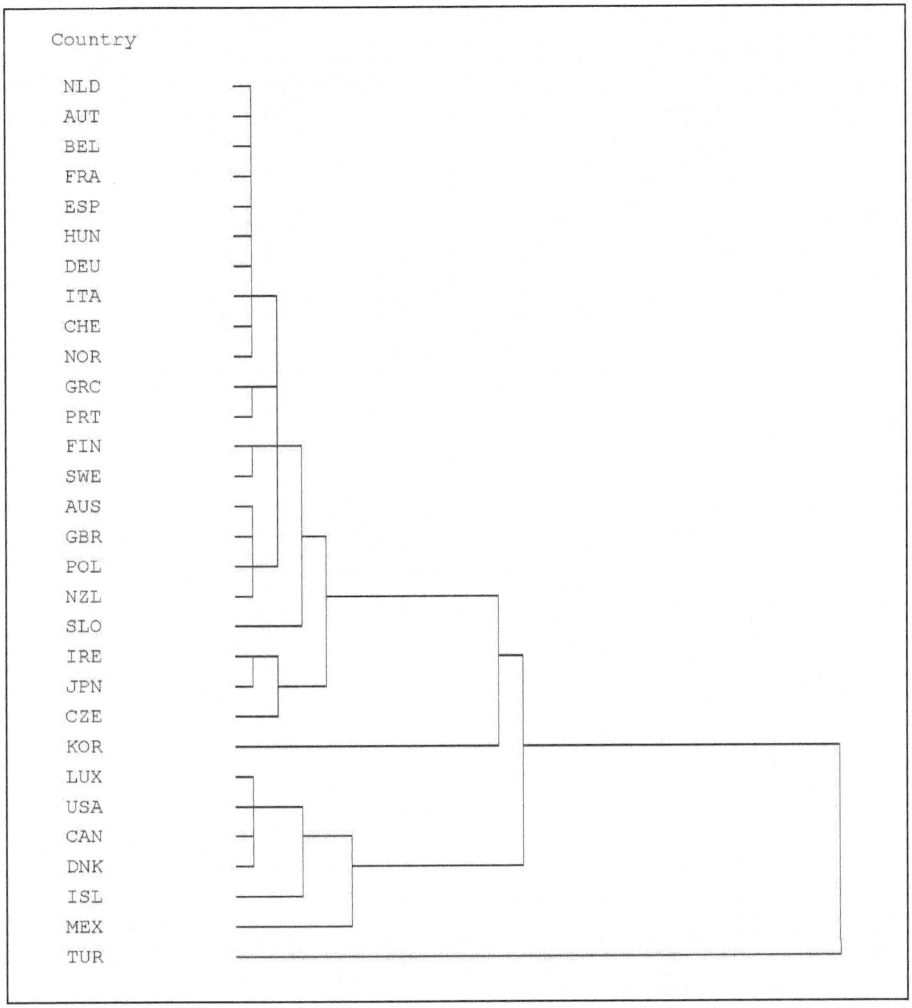

On a reasonable level of aggregation, three clusters emerge. The first one comprises all euro area countries in the sample (except Ireland and Luxembourg), plus the UK, Sweden, Hungary, Poland, Slovakia, Switzerland, Norway, Australia and New Zealand. In the second cluster, Ireland, Japan and the Czech Republic are grouped. The third cluster is formed by Luxembourg, Denmark, the US, Canada and Iceland. Korea, Mexico and Turkey are so different from the other countries that they do not belong to any cluster.

Table 19. Business cycle clusters of 30 OECD countries

<table>
<tr><th>Stage 1</th><th>Stage 2</th><th>Stage 3</th><th>Stage 4</th><th>Stage 5</th><th>Stage 6</th></tr>
<tr><td>Netherlands, Austria, Belgium, France, Spain, Hungary, Germany, Italy, Switzerland, Norway</td><td rowspan="4">Netherlands, Austria, Belgium, France, Spain, Hungary, Germany, Italy, Switzerland, Norway, Greece, Portugal, Finland, Sweden, Australia, New Zealand, Poland, GBR</td><td rowspan="5">Netherlands, Austria, Belgium, France, Spain, Hungary, Germany, Italy, Switzerland, Norway, Greece, Portugal, Finland, Sweden, Australia, New Zealand, Poland, GBR, Slovakia</td><td rowspan="7">Netherlands, Austria, Belgium, France, Spain, Hungary, Germany, Italy, Switzerland, Norway, Greece, Portugal, Finland, Sweden, Australia, New Zealand, Poland, GBR, Slovakia, Ireland, Japan, Czech Republic</td><td rowspan="11">Netherlands, Austria, Belgium, France, Spain, Hungary, Germany, Italy, Switzerland, Norway, Greece, Portugal, Finland, Sweden, Australia, New Zealand, Poland, GBR, Slovakia, Ireland, Japan, Czech Republic, Korea, Luxembourg, Denmark, US, Canada, Iceland, Mexico</td><td rowspan="12">Netherlands, Austria, Belgium, France, Spain, Hungary, Germany, Italy, Switzerland, Norway, Greece, Portugal, Finland, Sweden, Australia, New Zealand, Poland, GBR, Slovakia, Ireland, Japan, Czech Republic, Korea, Luxembourg, Denmark, US, Canada, Iceland, Mexico, Turkey</td></tr>
<tr><td>Greece, Portugal</td></tr>
<tr><td>Finland, Sweden</td></tr>
<tr><td>Australia, New Zealand, Poland, GBR</td></tr>
<tr><td>Slovakia</td><td>Slovakia</td></tr>
<tr><td>Ireland, Japan</td><td rowspan="2">Ireland, Japan, Czech Republic</td><td rowspan="2">Ireland, Japan, Czech Republic</td></tr>
<tr><td>Czech Republic</td></tr>
<tr><td>Korea</td><td>Korea</td><td>Korea</td><td>Korea</td></tr>
<tr><td>Luxembourg, Denmark, US, Canada</td><td>Luxembourg, Denmark, US, Canada</td><td rowspan="2">Luxembourg, Denmark, US, Canada, Iceland</td><td rowspan="3">Luxembourg, Denmark, US, Canada, Iceland, Mexico</td></tr>
<tr><td>Iceland</td><td>Iceland</td></tr>
<tr><td>Mexico</td><td>Mexico</td><td>Mexico</td></tr>
<tr><td>Turkey</td><td>Turkey</td><td>Turkey</td><td>Turkey</td><td>Turkey</td></tr>
</table>

Table 20 depicts the bilateral output gap correlations for the 30 OECD countries. Again, the identified clusters are separated by horizontal lines. For the countries in the second and third clusters, the business cycle synchronisation with the other economies in the respective cluster is clearly larger than the co-movement with the countries in the other clusters. For the large first cluster, the picture is less clear-cut. As an example, the output gap correlation between Austria and Portugal is negative, while it is positive and quite high between Austria and Luxembourg. Nevertheless, Austria and Portugal belong to the same cluster, while Luxembourg is in a different group. This is due to the fact that, on average, the business cycles of the countries in the first cluster are relatively more similar to each other than to the business cycles of the countries in the other clusters, although the bilateral output gap correlations are lower for some individual country pairs.

Table 20. Correlations between output gaps of OECD countries

	Aut	Bel	Nld	Fra	Esp	Hun	Deu	Ita	Che	Nor	Grc	Prt	Fin	Swe	Aus	Nzl	Pol	Gbr	Slo	Ire	Cze	Jap	Lux	Den	Isl	Usa	Can	Kor	Mex	Tur
Aut	1.00																													
Bel	0.55	1.00																												
Nld	0.82	0.69	1.00																											
Fra	0.61	0.86	0.67	1.00																										
Esp	0.49	0.80	0.48	0.80	1.00																									
Hun	0.28	0.64	0.22	0.62	0.67	1.00																								
Deu	0.52	0.75	0.72	0.67	0.71	0.29	1.00																							
Ita	0.28	0.80	0.55	0.80	0.72	0.32	0.82	1.00																						
Che	0.55	0.68	0.73	0.71	0.56	0.40	0.76	0.70	1.00																					
Nor	0.24	0.25	0.42	0.12	0.08	0.14	0.31	0.14	0.58	1.00																				
Grc	0.18	0.49	0.26	0.47	0.58	0.15	0.64	0.65	0.24	-0.11	1.00																			
Prt	-0.12	0.41	0.03	0.49	0.54	0.28	0.31	0.58	0.18	-0.16	0.54	1.00																		
Fin	0.13	0.76	0.30	0.70	0.75	0.57	0.63	0.88	0.60	0.03	0.67	0.53	1.00																	
Swe	0.61	0.84	0.62	0.92	0.85	0.54	0.73	0.80	0.67	0.02	0.59	0.49	0.74	1.00																
Aus	0.01	0.14	-0.05	0.26	0.02	0.10	-0.05	0.16	0.14	-0.09	0.16	0.02	0.30	0.37	1.00															
Nzl	-0.08	0.48	0.01	0.32	0.50	0.31	0.18	0.40	0.15	-0.01	0.32	0.29	0.59	0.48	0.49	1.00														
Pol	0.36	0.59	0.47	0.60	0.44	0.15	0.47	0.66	0.57	0.30	0.36	0.17	0.55	0.60	0.44	0.46	1.00													
Gbr	0.25	0.59	0.47	0.66	0.40	0.25	0.53	0.68	0.62	0.12	0.51	0.20	0.73	0.68	0.66	0.49	0.71	1.00												
Slo	-0.49	-0.29	-0.46	-0.45	-0.08	-0.14	0.03	-0.08	-0.21	0.04	0.15	0.07	0.02	-0.34	-0.18	0.00	-0.20	-0.26	1.00											
Ire	0.35	0.72	0.40	0.48	0.64	0.36	0.61	0.60	0.37	0.09	0.34	0.43	0.46	0.52	-0.29	0.24	0.32	0.04	-0.04	1.00										
Cze	0.26	0.40	0.46	0.43	0.45	-0.22	0.63	0.64	0.32	-0.10	0.51	0.56	0.31	0.47	-0.22	0.08	0.27	0.20	-0.08	0.57	1.00									
Jap	-0.12	0.44	0.12	0.24	0.36	0.06	0.31	0.47	0.10	0.05	0.42	0.65	0.40	0.20	-0.31	0.30	0.22	0.05	0.02	0.66	0.61	1.00								
Lux	0.73	0.38	0.65	0.37	0.11	0.23	0.31	0.08	0.57	0.41	-0.07	-0.38	0.06	0.42	0.34	-0.05	0.32	0.38	-0.55	0.07	-0.12	-0.35	1.00							
Den	0.69	0.68	0.81	0.66	0.50	0.35	0.75	0.51	0.70	0.29	0.38	0.08	0.40	0.66	0.07	0.03	0.22	0.52	-0.44	0.35	0.41	0.08	0.66	1.00						
Isl	0.42	0.14	0.39	0.30	0.06	0.31	-0.02	-0.08	0.37	0.20	-0.21	-0.20	0.04	0.13	-0.06	-0.22	-0.14	0.16	-0.64	-0.23	-0.17	-0.21	0.49	0.50	1.00					
Usa	0.57	0.27	0.51	0.29	-0.07	0.23	-0.02	-0.14	0.31	0.31	-0.26	-0.45	-0.10	0.18	0.32	-0.05	0.25	0.33	-0.72	-0.12	-0.30	-0.28	0.82	0.49	0.61	1.00				
Can	0.51	0.64	0.63	0.67	0.35	0.38	0.44	0.48	0.66	0.15	0.13	-0.08	0.49	0.67	0.54	0.36	0.45	0.78	-0.58	0.11	0.07	-0.17	0.69	0.73	0.48	0.69	1.00			
Kor	0.04	0.56	0.38	0.33	0.40	-0.07	0.51	0.61	0.29	0.15	0.42	0.47	0.42	0.44	0.03	0.59	0.39	0.34	-0.10	0.58	0.69	0.69	-0.02	0.35	-0.26	-0.14	0.25	1.00		
Mex	0.34	0.15	0.27	-0.03	-0.12	0.31	-0.01	-0.30	0.22	0.49	-0.27	-0.54	-0.10	-0.16	-0.11	-0.19	-0.05	0.00	-0.15	-0.05	-0.45	-0.14	0.52	0.33	0.52	0.67	0.25	-0.27	1.00	
Tur	-0.13	-0.25	-0.28	-0.38	-0.37	-0.16	-0.35	-0.39	-0.21	0.14	-0.52	-0.42	-0.42	-0.45	-0.35	-0.30	-0.12	-0.56	0.09	0.21	-0.19	0.20	-0.08	-0.43	-0.18	0.04	-0.43	-0.20	0.23	1.00

Notes: Output gaps have been calculated by applying the full-sample Christiano-Fitzgerald filter to quarterly GDP. Sample period is from 1970Q1 to 2007Q3, contingent on data availability.

3.9 Synchronisation and Convergence Within the US

We provide our own up-to-date statistics of cyclical synchronisation and convergence for the US states. In order to facilitate comparison between the stylised facts for the United States and those for the euro area countries, we repeated the descriptive exercises from section 2.5, using our data for the United States. Annual data for the US Gross State Product (GSP) is provided by the Bureau of Economic Analysis (BEA). However, there is a serious discontinuity in the GSP series for the United States, resulting from a switch in source data and estimation methodology in 1997. Therefore, the quarterly state personal income series, also provided by the BEA, was chosen as a suitable substitute. Such data has been used in previous research by de Haan et al. (2002) and Barro and Sala-i-Martin (1991). It is the only proxy for GSP that is available over longer periods and for higher frequencies. Following de Haan et al. (2002) and Forni and Reichlin (1997), the data measured in current dollars are deflated using the US implicit GDP deflator. Naturally, because GDP and personal income are two different measures, it is advisable to use caution when comparing the results for the euro area countries with those for the United States. For instance, if there is risk sharing, i.e. if there are interstate fiscal and market institutions that help smooth income between states (e.g. through taxes, transfers and capital income) we expect personal income cycles to be more correlated across states than GDP cycles would be. Kalemli-Ozcan et al. (2005) indeed find that risk sharing between the US states is significant and that asymmetry of personal income across US states is substantially lower than asymmetry of output. However, the same authors also demonstrate that in the European Union income is more asymmetric than GDP in spite of positive risk sharing in the 1990s.

The figures 25 and 26 are the counterparts to figures 2 and 3 of section 3.4. They display in solid the mean of bilateral correlations in cyclical state personal income rolling over a 6-year window and in dotted the average of the bilateral correlations for non-overlapping periods of equal lengths. Two features are worth noting. First, the averages of the bilateral correlations seem to suggest at first glance that business cycles of the United States are on average more synchronised than the cycles of the euro area countries – an observation which would be in line with previous studies. This difference in synchronisation levels is especially pronounced for the cycles generated by the MA and TIM methods. However, the averages of the bilateral correlations of the HP, BK and CF cycles are not much different from the average correlations of the euro area cycles generated by these methods, suggesting that business cycle synchronisation is similar and high in both the euro area and the United States. Furthermore, if we follow the risk-sharing argument mentioned above, the tendency of the United States' business cycles being on average more synchronised than the cycles of the euro area countries could be at least partly attributed to the possibility that personal income cycles are more correlated across states than GDP cycles. Thus, we conclude that there is a filtering-method-sensitive tendency for the cycles of the United States to be on average more synchronised than the cycles of the euro area countries. In addition, because the cycles of the United States are personal income cycles and the euro area cycles are GDP cycles, higher average correlations of the United States' cycles may be attributed to the different type of data used in the analysis.

Fig. 25. Mean of correlations in the US

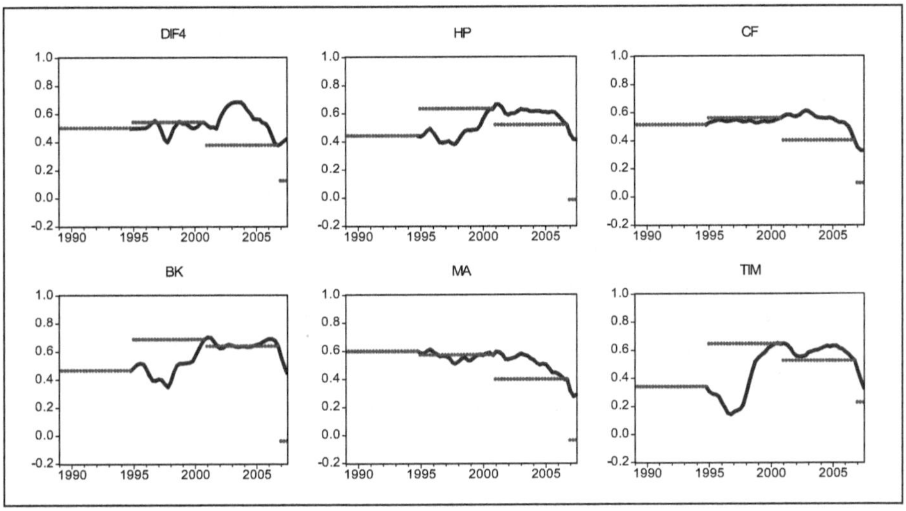

Notes: 6 year rolling window (solid line) and a fixed period of 6 years (dotted line).

Fig. 26. Variance of correlations in the US

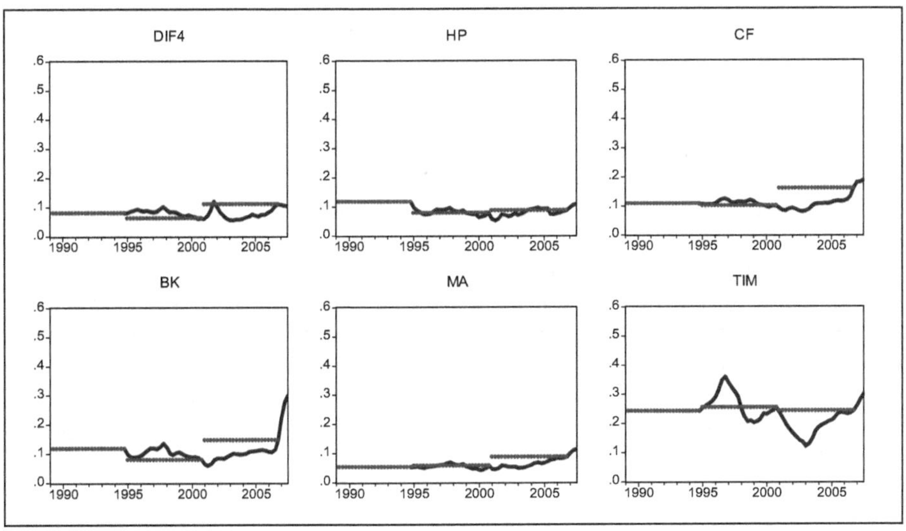

Notes: 6 year rolling window (solid line) and a fixed period of 6 years (dotted line).

Interestingly, the patterns of the rolling window correlations bear remarkable similarities to the patterns of the euro area. A drop in correlation around 1997, which coincides with the Asian emerging market crisis, is visible in both the mean correlations computed for the US states and the euro area countries (recall figure 2 and figure 3 on page 41). A decline in mean correlation since 2005 also emerges among both the euro countries and the US states. Changing the length of the rolling window to 4 years seems to only further confirm the above-stated qualitative observations, therefore allowing us to omit the corresponding figure. The variance estimates of the cross-correlations (figure 26) demonstrate that periods with an increase in mean correlation are accompanied by an increase in the dispersion of correlations. In particular, at the end of the sample period, the variances rise for most filtering methods, again pointing to a de-coupling of business cycles across the US states. In section 3.4, we report the same finding for the euro area.

We also examined the individual states' cycles in order to ascertain the degree of heterogeneity across regions in the US. Figure 27 shows the bilateral correlations of state-cycles and the reference cycle, which is the personal income cycle for the United States as a whole. Similar to some euro area countries, which had cycles that have uncoupled from the euro area cycle, states such as Alaska (2), Louisiana (22), North and South Dakota (38 and 46), Montana (30) and Nebraska (31) seem to have cycles that show very low or no synchronisation with the rest of the country.

To summarise, our results suggest that the time periods of de-coupling and re-coupling are similar among US states and euro area countries. Global events seem to have a greater influence on the (sometimes temporary) changes in synchronisation than currency-union-specific factors. Our descriptive picture of regional synchronisation in the US implies that risk sharing, which is reflected in the personal income cycles of the US, does not seem to completely prevent business cycle de-coupling in eras that are marked by adverse economic events. Cross-correlations of US states versus the aggregate cycle show that the US is not an economic region that is perfectly synchronised over time and over states. In the United States, regional economic specialisation is more pronounced than in Europe. While some states rely heavily on agriculture, other states are dependent on mineral processing or the service industry. Yet the US is widely regarded as a successful monetary union, a conviction that has only be strengthened by the effective monetary policy and macroeconomic conditions of the 1990s, despite the varying degrees of cyclical symmetry during that period. In this regard, a comparison of business cycle synchronisation between the euro area and US may lend support for the optimistic view that the degree of cyclical similarity in the euro area is sufficiently high for the successful sharing of a common currency. This is certainly welcome news, since a further rise in European economic integration and risk sharing is expected to take place.

Fig. 27. Correlations of US states vis-à-vis the US aggregate

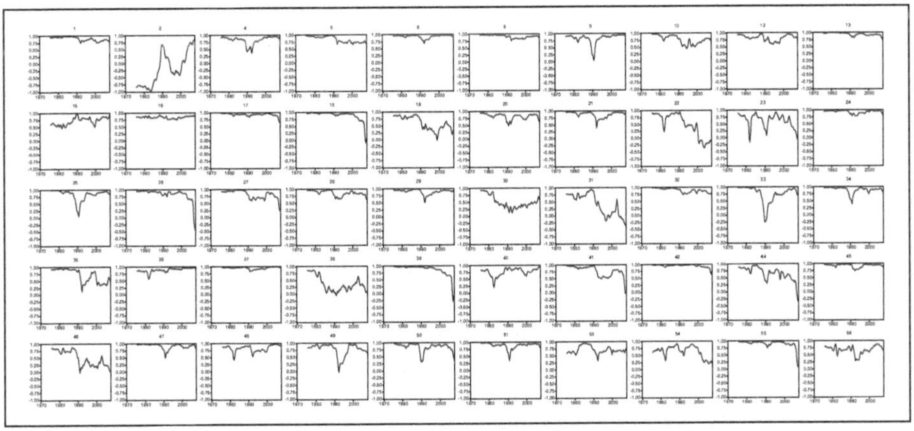

Notes: 6 years rolling window. Alabama (1), Alaska (2), Arizona (4), Arkansas (5), California (6), Colorado (8), Connecticut (9), Delaware (10), Florida (12), Georgia (13), Hawaii (15), Idaho (16), Illinois (17), Indiana (18), Iowa (19), Kansas (20), Kentucky (21), Louisiana (22), Maine (23), Maryland (24), Massachusetts (25), Michigan (26), Minnesota (27), Mississippi (28), Missouri (29), Montana (30), Nebraska (31), Nevada (32), New Hampshire (33), New Jersey (34), New Mexico (35), New York (36), North Carolina (37), North Dakota (38), Ohio (39), Oklahoma (40), Oregon (41), Pennsylvania (42) Rhode Island (44), South Carolina (45), South Dakota (46), Tennessee (47), Texas (48), Utah (49), Vermont (50), Virginia (51), Washington (53), West Virginia (54), Wisconsin (55), Wyoming (56).

3.10 Concluding Remarks

After reviewing the relevant literature in the first part of the study, we analysed business cycle volatility and synchronisation of a possible enlarged euro area with an updated dataset. The group of non euro-12 EU 27 countries and a group of non-EU countries were analysed with respect to business cycle synchronisation with the euro area. The inclusion of these non-euro countries was regarded as being important and it was seen that the prospect of joining the euro is important for countries that are increasingly integrated by trade and capital flows with the euro area. In addition, it was shown that a global pattern of business cycle volatility and synchronisation with the global business cycle play an important role for the euro area. This implies that the dynamics of the business cycle of the euro area can be analysed more accurately by taking into account both internal euro area and global factors.

It was seen that business cycle synchronisation in the euro area is high, without any clear trend towards increasing or decreasing. On average, countries outside the euro area are clearly synchronised to a lower degree than current members but the synchronisation of some of these countries has risen considerably in recent years. Business cycle volatility has declined somewhat in practically all cases, probably reflecting a global process of lower business cycle volatility. In the euro area specifically, increasing intra-euro area trade and financial flows and lower volatility from monetary and fiscal policy shocks as well as structural and institutional convergence may be playing a role, too. However, the small upward trend in fiscal divergence since the introduction of the euro contrasts with the dispersion of output gaps, inflation rates and real interest rates that have all remained constant since then. The introduction of the euro has been conducive to low and stable output and inflation dispersion but perhaps at the cost of some increase in fiscal dispersion.

It is very difficult to disentangle changes in business cycle volatility and business cycle synchronisation in the euro area from the equivalents in the global business cycle, particularly if both are trending in the same direction, as is often the case. Given this difficulty, there is a clear risk of wrongly attributing developments in the euro area to, say, the introduction of the euro, when they are instead a manifestation of global developments such as globally increasing synchronisation.

Against this backdrop, two issues are of particular importance in the remainder of this study: in chapter 4 we analyse the determinants of business cycle synchronisation in the euro area with a particular focus on financial market integration and structural reforms, and in chapter 5 we look at the transmission of country-specific and international shocks and business cycle convergence.

4 Determinants of Business Cycle Synchronisation

By Jonas Keil and Andreas Sachs

The analysis of the determinants of business cycle synchronisation has been a major topic in research on business cycle synchronisation. At the core of this strand of literature is the effort to identify the underlying factors that shape the symmetry or asymmetry of business cycles across countries. Understanding these factors is crucial for the design of currency areas such as the euro area and for conducting a common monetary policy. Building on the literature review in chapter 2, in this chapter a comprehensive empirical study of the determinants of business cycle synchronization is conducted. To this end, recent available data for the euro area and beyond are analysed. In addition to the overall analysis of these determinants, this study focuses on three particular questions: First, have the determinants of synchronisation in the euro area changed since the introduction of the common currency? While much of the literature on business cycle synchronisation has dealt with the phase leading up to the introduction of the euro, analyses of the time period after its introduction are relatively scarce in comparison. In this connection, data from the first decade of the euro are used to answer this question. Second, what is the effect of the increasing integration of financial markets? These two questions are addressed in the first part of this chapter (section 4.1). Third, what is the influence of similarities in institutional conditions and structural reforms on the degree of business cycle synchronisation? Mainly due to data-related problems, the latter two factors have been neglected in the literature as potential determinants of synchronisation. In order to correctly identify their effects, a broad range of indicators are analysed in this study. This question is addressed in the second part of this chapter (section 4.2).

4.1 Financial Market Integration and Synchronisation

In section 2.2 of this book, a broad overview of theoretical and empirical literature on the determinants of business cycle synchronisation was presented. As has been argued in sub-section 2.2.5, among all potential determinants the integration of financial markets can be considered to have received the least attention in the literature, mainly due to methodological problems. This section aims to fill this gap in the literature by providing a comprehensive analysis of the effects of financial integration on business cycle synchronisation. Following a discussion on how to correctly measure financial integration in empirical studies, a broad range of financial variables will be employed.

However, isolated analyses covering only financial integration as a determinant of synchronisation are not adequate. Instead, all relevant determinants need to be included to yield unbiased and meaningful results. Therefore, this section uses the opportunity to conduct an up-to-date and comprehensive analysis of the determinants that have been discussed in section 2.2 of this book. As it has been just over a decade since the introduction of the euro as a common currency, it is possible to analyse and document changes in empirical findings regarding the different determinants of synchronisation and their relative importance.

The contribution of this section therefore is twofold: The main focus lies on analysing the effects of financial integration as a determinant factor. Additionally, this section provides an updated analysis of the different determinants of business cycle synchronisation both for a longer time horizon and sub-periods before and after the introduction of the euro. Section 4.1.1 begins with a discussion of the different available methods of measuring financial integration in the context of this study and section 4.1.2 presents the empirical strategy and models applied here. Results are presented in section 4.1.3 and some conclusions are drawn in section 4.1.4.

4.1.1 Measuring Financial Integration

In contrast to the heavy attention that trade integration and other determinants have received in the literature, the effects of financial integration have only played a minor role in research on factors that influence synchronisation. At least partially, this can be attributed to numerous methodological problems encountered when empirically studying the effects of financial integration. Trade integration, for instance, can be measured relatively easily. International trade flows can be directly observed and appropriate variables that capture international trade integration can be calculated on the basis of such data.

Financial integration, however, is a much blurrier concept than trade integration, making it harder to measure adequately. The term "financial integration" can refer to the international integration of different financial markets such as money markets, banking markets, bond markets, stock markets or markets for other forms of international investment. This suggests that depending on the specific financial market observed, there might be differing degrees of international integration. An empirical study by Baele et al. (2004) corroborates this notion. Consequently, it would be misleading to rely on one single measure of financial integration that refers to only one of these markets. Instead, one has to explicitly take into account various financial markets when analysing the general degree of financial integration between countries. The few studies that have analysed financial integration as a possible determinant of business cycle synchronisation typically have concentrated only on one variable that reflects integration in one type of financial market. The analysis carried out in this chapter improves on the existing literature by analysing a broad range of financial indicators, unified in a single framework, that cover several financial markets.

An additional problem is that it is not possible a priori to identify the concept of financial integration that should be applied in an empirical study of the determinants of bilateral business cycle synchronisation. In a very broad definition, Baele et al. (2004) define an integrated financial market as a market to which all agents have equal access, and in which all of them face a single set of rules and are treated equally. This definition of financial integration thus refers to the harmonisation of the legal, regulatory and institutional framework of international financial markets, a dimension can be captured by binary variables such as the indicators published in the IMF's Annual Report on Exchange Arrangements and Exchange Restrictions (AREAER) or extensions thereof, such as the indicator by Chinn and Ito (2008).

However, such a *de jure* definition of financial integration is not very tractable in empirical studies. Moreover, it does not necessarily capture the effective (or *de facto*) degree of international integration observed in different financial markets. Indeed, the effective degree of integration is better reflected by the prices and volumes observed on financial markets. Accordingly, measures of effective integration can be divided into quantity-based and price-based measures (cf. Baele et al., 2004). Quantity-based measures directly measure effective integration by looking at observable market trading volumes. The assumption is that larger volumes of international financial transactions mean a higher degree of effective integration. Depending of the specific type of data used, such measures can be applied to single countries, country pairs or whole groups of countries. Typically, in the context of country-pair based studies of business cycle synchronisation, bilateral data (e.g. data on financial flows between two countries) are used.

Price-based measures follow a different approach. These measures are based on the idea that in fully integrated international markets the law of one price must hold for financial assets with the same characteristics. Any deviation in prices between countries thus can be regarded as an indication of imperfect market integration (cf. Baele et al., 2004, for a more detailed discussion). For example, when taking equity and debt markets into account, return spreads are commonly used as a price-based measure. However, price-based measures of effective integration suffer from the fact that in empirical applications not all potentially relevant factors determining the prices of financial assets in different countries can be included. In the case of return spreads, divergence could simply be driven by idiosyncratic economic factors rather than by low arbitrage opportunities due to a low degree of market integration. Keeping this caveat in mind, price-based measures should not be used as the only measure of effective integration as they can only be regarded as rough indicators.

Against this background, the use of quantity-based measures of effective integration in several financial markets seems to be the best way of capturing the true degree of financial integration. Imbs (2006) summarises several postulates for the adequate choice of measures of financial integration in the context of country-pair based studies on the determinants of synchronisation. According to Imbs, superior measures of financial integration are measures that are "(i) directly observable, (ii) bilateral rather than aggregated across countries, and (iii) capturing stocks rather than flows" (Imbs, 2006, p. 300). All of these considerations guide the choice of data and variables used in order to map financial integration in this study. As main variables, four quantity-based measures as well as four price-based measures are employed. The construction of these variables is explained in detail in section 4.1.2.2 below.

As argued in section 2.2.5, both the theoretical predictions and the existing empirical results regarding the effects of financial integration on the synchronisation of business cycles are mixed. On the theoretical side, there are several contradicting predictions regarding direct and indirect effects. Empirically, there have been some studies documenting a positive overall effect, while other studies find contradictory results. One aim of the present study is thus to use the insights achieved in empirical studies about the appropriate measurement of financial integration in order to contribute to our understanding of the effects of financial integration.

4.1.2 Empirical Method

In the following, the hypotheses about the determinants of business cycle synchronisation in general and the effects of financial integration in particular will be assessed empirically. Before presenting the results of the estimations in section 4.1.3, the following sections 4.1.2.1 and 4.1.2.2 provide an overview of the empirical models, estimation strategy and data employed here.

4.1.2.1 Empirical Models and Estimation Strategy

In accordance with the literature in the tradition of Frankel and Rose (1998), the statistical units underlying the following analyses will not be single countries, but all possible two-country pairs in the respective sample of countries. As a basic principle, all variables used in the analyses are thus constructed in a bilateral fashion and symmetrically for each country pair. In this way, for a group of n countries, $N = n(n-1)/2$ country pairs are obtained. This study focuses mainly on the twelve original members of the euro area as of 2001, i.e. Austria, Belgium, Finland, France, Germany, Greece, Ireland, Italy, Luxembourg, the Netherlands, Spain and Portugal. This so-called Euro-12 sample yields 66 country pairs. Additionally, a larger sample is constructed in order to compare the Euro-12 results with results obtained from a larger group of industrialised countries. This large sample consists of 25 OECD countries (see appendix for details) and it is largely defined by the availability of data used in the study. This sample of 25 countries yields 300 country pairs at most.

In addition to these main determinants of synchronisation, other determinants have sometimes been proposed in the literature. These are usually indicators that focus on other policy fields such as the exchange rate regime, which obviously is not relevant for the euro area (see section 2.2 of this book for an overview of other determinants analysed in the literature). However, since those potential determinants were mainly not found to be of major importance, in the following, the focus will be on the determinants depicted in figure 28. As indicators of structural features such as union density or international competitiveness have not been analysed in existing literature so far, this topic will be discussed in greater detail in section 4.2.

Fig. 28. Interdependencies between the main determinants

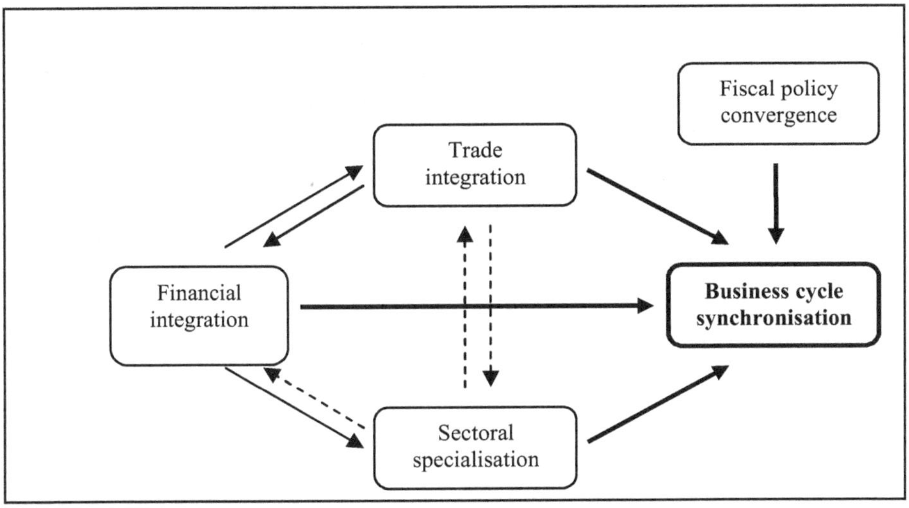

Source: Extended illustration based on Imbs (2004, p. 724, Figure 1)

The general econometric model and estimation framework of the following estimations have previously been used in many of the studies reviewed in section 2.2, most notably in the seminal contribution by Frankel and Rose (1998), which was the first study to employ this framework to quantitatively analyse trade integration as a determinant of business cycle synchronisation. In the literature, this general model has been employed in two different forms: a single-equation model and a simultaneous-equations model. The general formulation of the single-equation model is the regression equation

$$\rho_{ijt} = \alpha_0 + \alpha_1 T_{ijt} + \alpha_2 S_{ijt} + \alpha_3 F_{ijt} + \alpha_4 X^{\rho}_{ijt} + \varepsilon^{\rho}_{ijt} \tag{6}$$

where ρ_{ijt} is a measure of business cycle synchronisation between country i and country j in period t, T_{ijt} is a measure of trade integration, S_{ijt} is a measure of differences between the production structures of countries i and j, F_{ijt} is a measure of financial integration, X^{ρ}_{ijt} is a vector of other relevant regressor variables, and ε^{ρ}_{ijt} is an error term summing up all other influences on the degree of synchronisation not explicitly captured by the model. Estimates for the coefficients α_1, α_2 and α_3 thus capture the individual effects of each determinant on the level of synchronisation. Regarding figure 28, only the direct effect depicted by the bold arrows are included here while the interdependencies depicted by the regular and the dashed arrows are not.

However, this single-equation model can only account for the total (or net) effect, but not for both the direct and indirect effects as depicted in figure 28. Several authors, including Imbs (2001, 2004 and 2006), Akin (2007) and Inklaar, Jong-A-Pin and de Haan (2008), have proposed an extended version of model (6) designed to disentangle the direct and indirect effects of the endogenous determinants. Depending on the specific focus of these studies, each has presented a slightly different version of this model. The general formulation corresponding to figure 28 is the following simultaneous-equations model which includes all of the potential interdependencies:

$$\begin{aligned} \rho_{ijt} &= \alpha_0 + \alpha_1 T_{ijt} + \alpha_2 S_{ijt} + \alpha_3 F_{ijt} + \alpha_4 X^{\rho}_{ijt} + \varepsilon^{\rho}_{ijt} \\ T_{ijt} &= \beta_0 + \beta_1 S_{ijt} + \beta_2 F_{ijt} + \beta_3 X^{T}_{ijt} + \varepsilon^{T}_{ijt} \\ S_{ijt} &= \gamma_0 + \gamma_1 T_{ijt} + \gamma_2 F_{ijt} + \gamma_3 X^{S}_{ijt} + \varepsilon^{S}_{ijt} \\ F_{ijt} &= \delta_0 + \delta_1 T_{ijt} + \delta_2 S_{ijt} + \delta_3 X^{F}_{ijt} + \varepsilon^{F}_{ijt} \end{aligned} \tag{7}$$

In addition to the main equation, which captures the direct effects of the determinants on synchronisation, three new equations are introduced which explicitly model the interdependencies of the endogenous variables T_{ijt}, S_{ijt} and F_{ijt}. In terms of figure 28, all of the depicted interrelations are included in this model. The vectors X^{T}_{ijt}, X^{S}_{ijt} and X^{F}_{ijt} contain sets of exogenous regressors for each of these equations. Model (7) enables the explicit assessment of the mutual relations of the endogenous determinants by inspection of the coefficients β_1, β_2, γ_1, γ_2, δ_1 and δ_2. Additionally, it allows the calculation of the indirect effects of the determinants on synchronisation by multiplying the respective coefficients. For example, any indirect effect of specialisation on synchronisation working via affecting trade patterns is captured by the product $\beta_1 \cdot \alpha_1$. In sub-section 4.1.3.3, which focuses particularly on the effects of multiple measures of financial integration, the following reduced version of model (7) is estimated:

$$\begin{aligned} \rho_{ijt} &= \alpha_0 + \alpha_1 T_{ijt} + \alpha_2 S_{ijt} + \alpha_3 F_{ijt} + \alpha_4 X^{\rho}_{ijt} + \varepsilon^{\rho}_{ijt} \\ T_{ijt} &= \beta_0 + \beta_2 F_{ijt} + \beta_3 X^{T}_{ijt} + \varepsilon^{T}_{ijt} \\ S_{ijt} &= \gamma_0 + \gamma_2 F_{ijt} + \gamma_3 X^{S}_{ijt} + \varepsilon^{S}_{ijt} \\ F_{ijt} &= \delta_0 + \delta_1 T_{ijt} + \delta_3 X^{F}_{ijt} + \varepsilon^{F}_{ijt} \end{aligned} \tag{8}$$

Of the possible interrelations of the determinants, in this model only the mutual effects of trade and finance and the unidirectional effect of finance on specialisation are considered. Referring to figure 28, the relations depicted by dashed arrows are not considered here. This model has previously been employed by Imbs (2006) to study the effects of financial integration. It improves on model (7) by increasing the degrees of freedom due to the smaller number of coefficients to be estimated as well as by potentially strengthening the identification of the three additional equations in the model. Especially when restricting the analysis to the Euro-12 sample and 66 observations at most, the gain in degrees of freedom can result in more accurate estimates.

Due to the potential violation of the basic assumptions of the linear regression model, a regular ordinary least squares (OLS) estimation of model (6) is most likely not appropriate. As portrayed in figure 28, the mutual interdependencies of the main determinants of synchronisation render them endogenous. In this case, the regressors are correlated with the error term, which results in inconsistency of the OLS estimator due to a simultaneity bias. Frankel and Rose (1998) have proposed accounting for this bias by using instrumental variables (IV) estimation, which since has become the standard approach in this strand of the literature. The two-stage least squares (2SLS) approach applied here requires exogenous variables to be used as instruments for the endogenous variables in order to correctly identify the effects of these variables. The previous literature has come up with a comprehensive list of variables that can be used as instruments. They will be discussed below.

Estimation of a system of simultaneous equations as in models (7) and (8) is feasible only under certain restrictive conditions. This is due to the well-known identification problem associated with structural form simultaneous-equation models. Which variables should be used as exogenous regressors? Since the set of instrumental variables is chosen to contain the relevant exogenous variables that exert an influence on the endogenous variables, meeting the identification conditions is ensured by the use of these instrumental variables as exogenous variables in the vectors X_{ijt}^{T}, X_{ijt}^{S} and X_{ijt}^{F}.

As has been pointed out in the literature, while equation-by-equation IV estimation of an identified simultaneous-equations model is possible, this would disregard the contemporaneous correlation structure of the error terms of the equations. Consequently, the three-stage least squares (3SLS) estimation procedure of Zellner and Theil (1962) is proposed by Imbs (2001, 2004 and 2006), Akin (2007) and Inklaar, Jong-A-Pin and de Haan (2008). This procedure estimates the covariance matrix of the full simultaneous-equations model which then is used for an efficient simultaneous estimation based on the generalised least squares approach. Thus, the 3SLS framework achieves both "consistency through instrumentation, and efficiency through appropriate weighting in the variance-covariance matrix" (Imbs, 2004, p. 729).

An important feature of the estimation methods in this section and, in general, of most empirical studies in the tradition of Frankel and Rose (1998), is that they represent "between" estimation, i.e. the annual observations of each time-varying variable in the models are averaged over the respective time period and only the cross-sectional variation between the statistical units (country pairs) is captured in the estimations. The use of "within" estimation methods such as panel fixed effects methods would be desirable for a number of reasons. However, this is essentially prevented by the unavailability of several important variables needed as instrumental variables, such as the gravity variables (see below). In this sense, there is a trade-off between explicitly taking into account the time-dimension and adequately identifying "causal" relationships between the variables; this study seeks to do the latter. An additional advantage of this "between" estimation approach is that missing observations for single years do not matter much since the time-average of the respective variable can still be calculated using the remaining available annual observations. However, an implicit assumption of such "between" estimations is the stability of the interrelations between the variables being analysed over the whole sample period. To account for possible shifts in these interrelations, additional analyses of shorter sub-periods are performed later in section 4.1.3.2.

4.1.2.2 Data and Variables

The measure of *business cycle synchronisation*, ρ_{ijt}, is the correlation coefficient of the cyclical component of GDP between countries *i* and *j* over period *t*. Cyclical GDP components are obtained using the Baxter-King band-pass filter with a frequency band between two and eight years, which covers the typical length of a business cycle. Since the correlation coefficients are by construction calculated for a period of time, they do not need to be averaged over the respective time period like the other time-varying variables in this study. Annual GDP data are taken from the OECD National Accounts database for the OECD countries and from the World Economic Outlook database of the International Monetary Fund (IMF) for the remaining countries in the large sample. GDP forecasts of the IMF are included to circumvent the problem of losing observations at the end of the series due to the use of the BK filter. As emphasized by Otto, Voss and Willard (2001), the correlation coefficients are bounded by the interval $[-1,1]$, which renders the assumption of a normally distributed error term ε_{ij}^{ρ} unreasonable. To correct for this violation of the basic assumptions of the linear regression model, the authors suggest using the transformation $\tilde{\rho}_{ij} = 1/2 \cdot ln((1+\rho_{ij})/(1-\rho_{ij}))$. This transformation maps the correlation coefficients to the interval $[-\infty,\infty]$ and produces variables which asymptotically are normally distributed. Kernel estimations by Inklaar, Jong-A-Pin and de Haan (2008, p. 652) show that this transformation is indeed needed to justify the normality assumption. Apart from this transformation, all other variables except the different dummy variables enter the regression equation as natural logarithms, as is standard procedure in the related literature. Due to these transformations of the variables, the absolute values of the estimated coefficients are hard to interpret directly, such that our interest lies in the sign and the relative size of the estimates.

Against the background of the discussion of section 4.1.1, in the following the construction of the set of variables used to capture *financial market integration* will be explained. As previously stated, our main focus lies on bilateral quantity-based measures of effective integration. The first quantity-based measure of financial integration is the degree of bilateral *foreign direct investment* intensity. Following Otto, Voss and Willard (2003), this is defined as

$$FDI_{ijt} = \frac{FI_{ijt} + FO_{ijt}}{Y_{it} + Y_{jt}} \tag{9}$$

Here, FI_{ijt} denotes the FDI inward position of country i with respect to country j, i.e. the stock of FDI in reporting country i held by partner country j. FO_{ijt} correspondingly denotes the outward position of investment of country i held in country j. The FDI data are taken from the OECD International Direct Investment Statistics database that includes FDI data from 1981 to 2005 with some gaps in availability. Due to its relatively strong comprehensiveness in terms of time periods and countries covered, this database will constitute the basic measure of financial integration used in the analysis.

The second quantity-based measure that uses real bilateral data is *portfolio investment* intensity. The IMF has recently made available the Coordinated Portfolio Investment Survey (CPIS) database that contains data on bilateral portfolio investment holdings for the years 2001 to 2006. This data is used to calculate

$$PI_{ijt} = \frac{I_{ijt} + I_{jit}}{Y_{it} + Y_{jt}} \tag{10}$$

where I_{ijt} denotes the outward investment position of i relative to j. Imbs (2006) is the only other study thus far that has employed CPIS data to examine business cycle synchronisation.

The third quantity-based measure is a variable for *banking integration*. More specifically, this variable captures the bilateral intensity of foreign asset holdings of the banking sector, which is calculated as

$$BI_{ijt} = \frac{B_{ijt} + B_{jit}}{Y_{it} + Y_{jt}} \tag{11}$$

Here, B_{ijt} denotes the value of foreign claims of the banking sector of country i on both the banking and non-banking sectors of country j. Data is taken from the Consolidated Banking Statistics of the Bank for International Settlements (BIS), as reported in BIS (2008). Bilateral data are only available for all countries in the sample from 1999 to 2006 in most cases. A related measure is used by Böwer and Guillemineau (2006), although they use a measure incorporating bilateral bank flows that is calculated based on changes in the foreign claim holdings of banks. Here, however, we opt to construct a measure based on stocks rather than flows since the former are considered to be superior.

The fourth quantity-based variable is a measure of *global financial openness* proposed by Akin (2007). The ratio of gross private capital flows GPF_{it} of country i to its GDP is used to calculate

$$GFO_{ijt} = \frac{GPF_{it}}{Y_{it}} + \frac{GPF_{jt}}{Y_{jt}} \tag{12}$$

These gross private capital flows refer to the sum of all inward and outward flows of foreign direct investment, portfolio investment and other investment of a single country. Note that since GFO_{ij} is not calculated using bilateral data, it does not necessarily indicate financial integration between the country pair i and j. Nevertheless, the degree of global financial openness of the two countries is to a certain extent a proxy for financial integration between the pair, although presumably less so than the truly bilateral variables are. The ratios of gross private capital flows to GDP are taken from the WDI database and are available from 1980 to 2005 for most countries in the sample.

In addition to these four quantity-based measures, two price-based measures of financial integration suggested by Otto, Voss and Willard (2003) will also be considered, namely the return spreads of equity markets and bond markets. Here, the underlying idea is that the law of one price should hold in internationally integrated financial markets (Baele et al., 2004) and that returns of comparable assets should therefore be equal. These two measures suffer from the same shortcoming as the global financial openness measures presented above because they are not based on real bilateral data. Furthermore, return spreads arguably are not very accurate measures of financial integration. Even if financial markets are perfectly integrated, not all relevant economic and financial factors affecting financial asset risk and returns can be appropriately controlled for when comparing asset returns. Nevertheless, highly integrated financial markets can be expected to exhibit similar return patterns over a period of time (Otto, Voss and Willard 2003).

The degree of *equity market integration* is measured as the return spread of the stock markets of countries i and j. These returns are calculated using representative stock market index trends for each country, as based on Eurostat data for nearly all countries in the large sample from the mid-1990s to 2007. Since it is not clear from the outset whether nominal or real return spreads better capture the degree of equity market integration, both measures will be included in the analysis. In addition to these measures, nominal and real return spreads of long term bonds will be considered as a measure of *bond market integration*. Long term interest rates – mostly of 10 year government bonds – are taken from the OECD Economic Outlook database.

All of the above measures of financial integration aim at capturing effective financial linkages by looking at quantities or prices actually observed in financial markets. In addition, there are other measures that capture *de jure* financial integration, including indices of restrictions on international financial transactions such as capital controls. These variables are mainly based on the indices published by the IMF in the Annual Report on Exchange Arrangements and Exchange Restrictions (AREAER). Because they are set by economic policy and thus exogenously affect the de facto degree of integration, these variables are natural candidates for use as instruments to measure financial integration. Therefore, the first set of instruments used here are the bilateral sums and absolute differences of the Chinn-Ito index of two countries. This index, constructed by Chinn and Ito (2008) using the AREAER indices, indicates the degree of de jure financial openness. Its bilateral sums and differences thus capture differential effects of institutional features on de facto bilateral integration. Furthermore, following the approach of Imbs (2004 and 2006), the second set of instruments are indices indicating institutional differences between financial markets in terms of legal structures. La Porta et al. (1998) and related contributions such as Cecchetti (1999) have established that certain features of legal institutions such as the origin of the legal system or the degrees of creditor and shareholder rights protection directly influence financial structures. One example is the predominance of external financing through banks in financial markets of countries with German legal origin as opposed to the predominance of equity financing in countries with British legal origins. Since similar financial structures can reasonably be expected to be conducive to financial integration, bilateral sums and absolute differences of the creditor rights and the shareholder rights indices provided by La Porta et al. (1998) as well as a dummy indicating common legal origins are used as additional instruments to measure financial integration.

The remaining variables used in this study are relatively straightforward and commonly used in the literature and therefore do no not require much discussion. The variables capturing trade integration and sectoral specialisation will also be employed in the accompanying study in section 4.2.

Following Frankel and Rose (1998), in order to capture the intensity of bilateral *trade integration*, the measure

$$T_{ijt} = \frac{X_{ijt} + M_{ijt}}{X_{it} + M_{it} + X_{jt} + M_{jt}} \qquad (13)$$

is calculated, whereby X_{ijt} are the exports from country i to country j and M_{ijt} are the imports of country i originating from country j. X_{it} and M_{it} correspondingly denote total exports and imports of country i, respectively. Annual bilateral and total trade data are taken from IMF's Direction of Trade Statistics database and GDP data are taken from the World Development Indicators 2007 database of the World Bank. Data are measured in US currency and current year prices. As a robustness check, all estimations were carried out using a similar measure that normalises bilateral trade by GDP. As the resulting estimates largely do not differ from those using the above measure, they will not be reported here.

However, as discussed above, not only total trade volumes but also the composition of trade matters. Therefore, a second variable designed to specifically capture intra-industry trade is introduced following Gruben, Koo and Millis (2002). According to Grubel and Lloyd (1975), the share of *intra-industry trade* in bilateral trade can be measured by the weighted Grubel-Lloyd index

$$GL_{ijt} = \sum_{s=1}^{S} \left(1 - \frac{\left| X_{sijt} - M_{sijt} \right|}{X_{sijt} + M_{sijt}} \right) \cdot \left(\frac{X_{sijt} + M_{sijt}}{X_{ijt} + M_{ijt}} \right) \tag{14}$$

Here, $s = 1,...,S$ is the index of the sectors or industries considered, while X_{sijt} and M_{sijt} are the bilateral exports and imports of goods of a particular sector s. Conceptually, intra-industry trade takes place if two countries exchange goods of the same sector, i.e. if both X_{sijt} and M_{sijt} are strictly positive for a given sector s. If either X_{sijt} or M_{sijt} is equal to 0, there is no intra-industry trade. As can be easily verified, the first bracket term of equation (14) is equal to 0 if there is no intra-industry trade in a given sector and the equation is equal to 1 if all trade in a given sector comprises intra-industry trade, i.e. if $X_{sijt} = M_{sijt}$. The second bracket term is a weight indicating the importance of each sector in total trade. A large value for GL_{ijt} thus indicates a high overall share of intra-industry trade in total bilateral trade. Using the weighted Grubel-Lloyd index, the measure $T_{ijt} \cdot GL_{ijt}$ can be calculated. This measure indicates the degree of intra-industry trade integration and is used as an alternative trade variable in this study. Sectoral trade data is taken from the Trade, Production, and Protection Database maintained by the World Bank. As described in Nicita and Olarreaga (2007), this database provides bilateral data on exports and imports for 28 different sectors at the three-digit level of the International Standard Industrial Classification (ISIC) system for the period 1976–2004. Drawing on this database, the Grubel-Lloyd index thus gives a very detailed picture of the sectoral trade structure.

The set of instrumental variables for the trade variables is standard. Gravity variables are truly exogenous explanatory variables for international trade patterns. Therefore, following Frankel and Rose (1998), the distance between the main economic areas of the two countries as well as two dummy variables indicating a common language and a common border, respectively, will be used as instrumental variables. Additionally, following Imbs (2006), bilateral sums and products of the population sizes of the two countries are included in order to capture trade effects of the relative size of the two economies.

There are a number of ways to measure *differences in the sectoral structures* of two economies. Several such measures are applied by Belke and Heine (2006). Here, however, only one will be employed. As in Imbs (2004), differences in sectoral specialisation will be measured by

$$S_{ijt} = \sum_{s=1}^{S} \left| VA_{sit} - VA_{sjt} \right| \tag{15}$$

where VA_{sit} denotes the share of value-added of sector s in the total value-added of country i. Larger values of S_{ijt} indicate less similar sectoral structures, with S_{ijt} being equal to 0 for identical and equal to 2 for completely disparate structures. This measure is a modification of the one applied by Krugman (1991), who uses sectoral employment rather than sectoral value-added data. Data for sectoral value-added are taken from the 60-Industry Database maintained by the Groningen Growth and Development Centre. This database provides annual data for nearly 60 sectors covering all OECD countries in the period 1979-2003. The sectors included in the database cover the whole economy and are disaggregated at two-digit and three-digit ISIC levels. Thus, a very detailed and disaggregated analysis of sectoral differences is possible. Apart from Inklaar, Jong-A-Pin and de Haan (2008), most existing studies do not make use of this database but rather of other less detailed ones. Therefore, the use of such data is an improvement compared to studies such as Böwer and Guillemineau (2006), who use data for only six broad sectors. Instrumental variables for the specialisation variables are constructed following Imbs (2004), who cites evidence indicating that economies tend to exhibit certain patterns of specialisation as income per capita grows: initial diversification is followed by a process of re-specialisation at a certain level of development. Thus, the argument goes, bilateral sums and absolute differences in GDP per capita are to a certain extent able to exogenously account for differences in specialisation. Even if these exogenous variables might be of less explanatory power in the context of developed countries, due to the lack of better alternatives these two variables are employed as instruments here as well. For calculation, GDP per capita data adjusted by purchasing power parity is taken from the World Development Indicators database.

Two additional control variables are used in the analysis: First, a measure of *fiscal policy similarity* following Darvas, Rose and Szapáry (2005). This measure captures differences in the budget balances and is calculated as

$$FP_{ijt} = \left| \frac{GB_{it}}{Y_{it}} - \frac{GB_{jt}}{Y_{jt}} \right| \tag{16}$$

where GB_{it} refers to the balance of the central government budget. Government balance data is taken from the World Economic Outlook database published by the IMF. To control for the effects of *monetary policy similarity* before the introduction of the euro, the measure

$$MP_{ijt} = \left| SR_{it} - SR_{jt} \right| \tag{17}$$

will initially be included in the analysis. Here, SR_{it} refers to short term interest rates, namely three-month nominal interest rates taken from the OECD Economic Outlook database. For these two measures, higher values indicate lower similarity of fiscal or monetary policy, respectively. Accordingly, negative estimated coefficients are expected for these measures. Since both fiscal policy convergence and monetary policy convergence are regarded as being exogenous in the sense of the empirical model applied in this study, the three measures above do not need to be instrumented in the analysis.

4.1.3 Results

The following sections present the results of the different estimations undertaken for this study. Generally, the estimated intercepts of the equations are omitted, as are the estimated coefficients of the variables used as instruments and as exogenous regressors. Included in parentheses is the p-value corresponding to each estimated coefficient. As usual, one, two and three asterisks are used to indicate coefficients significantly different from 0 at the 10%, 5% or 1% level, respectively. Most estimations are conducted for the Euro-12 sample. Several additional estimations also consider the large country sample. The sample sizes of at most 66 and 703 country pairs, respectively, are often reduced due to missing data, especially for the large sample. All estimations using the large country sample include a Euro-12 dummy as an additional regressor. This dummy variable takes the value 1 for a country pair of two Euro-12 countries and 0 otherwise. In this way, any potential residual intra-Euro-12 synchronisation effects not explained by the determinants included in the model can be captured. Several time periods will be considered in the analyses: a long time period from 1980 to 2006 is considered in order to gain insights on the basic relations of the determinants that can be deemed to be stable over a longer period of time. Additionally, the two sub-periods 1987-96 and 1997-2006 will be considered to take into account possible changes in the absolute and relative effects of the determinants. In section 4.1.3.3, the slightly shorter period 1999-2006 will be considered due to limitations in data availability for earlier years.

4.1.3.1 Baseline Results

Before presenting the main results of the study, a brief statistical test of the general validity of the instrumental variables approach is conducted. Such a test is needed in order to judge whether the notion of the endogeneity of the main determinants also holds from a statistical point of view, since so far it was only derived by economic reasoning. The Hausman test employed here tests whether the estimates of an OLS regression (which are efficient but not consistent under endogeneity) significantly differ from the estimates of an IV regression (which are consistent under endogeneity but less efficient than OLS estimates). The null hypothesis of the test is "OLS estimates are consistent". Since the test statistic follows an asymptotic Chi-square distribution, the test is conducted for the large country sample in order to obtain enough observations. The null hypothesis is rejected if the test statistic is too large depending on the chosen significance level. Table 21 shows the test statistics for the main determinants with corresponding p-values. Exogeneity of the trade integration variable is rejected at the 10% level while exogeneity of the intra-industry trade variable $T_{ijt} \cdot GL_{ijt}$ is rejected at the 1% level. These results strongly suggest endogeneity of trade integration in this context. The specialisation measure and the financial integration measure FDI_{ijt} are also found to be endogenous by the Hausman test, the latter very strongly so. All this is evidence in favour of the general instrumental variables framework employed in this study.

Table 21. Hausman test for endogeneity of the main determinants

	T	T·GL	Structure	FDI
Hausman test statistic	3.03 * (0.082)	17.7 *** (0.000)	3.65 * (0.056)	24.78 *** (0.000)

Notes: Own calculations. See section 4.1.2.2 for data sources.

The results of the first-stage regressions in the following IV estimations are not reported here for sake of brevity. Generally, the first-stage regression fit as measured by R^2 is sufficient, typically ranging between values of 0.7 for S_{ijt} or FDI_{ijt} and values of over 0.9 for the trade integration measure. Therefore, it can be concluded that the both the IV estimation approach and the instrumental variables applied here, especially the gravity variables included to account for patterns of trade integration, are appropriately used to tackle the problem of the endogeneity of the main determinants.

Table 22 and table 23 present the results of the estimated models (6) and (7) over the period 1980-2006 both for the Euro-12 sample and for the large sample, respectively. Each column of table 22 and table 23 contains the results of one particular estimation: columns (A) and (B) contain the results for the single-equation and the simultaneous-equations models used as the trade intensity measure, while columns (C) and (D) contain the corresponding results obtained using the intra-industry trade measure. In columns (B) and (D), which contain the results of the 3SLS estimations of the simultaneous-equations model (7), the estimates of the three additional equations are reported below the main equation. The results of the IV estimations in table 22 show that trade integration is found to be a significant determinant of synchronisation, with positive values, as expected. The significance of the other main determinants varies considerably. Fiscal policy convergence also is found to have the expected negative sign indicating that fiscal policy similarity fosters synchronisation. However, judging from its significance levels, it is of minor importance compared to the other determinants considered. Furthermore, the differences between the estimates of model (6) and of model (7) suggest that indirect effects are exerted by the determinants via interdependencies, as explicitly captured by the simultaneous-equations model. The fact that specialisation has inconclusive and insignificant direct effects in these full-model estimations can at least partially be explained by the negative estimate for β_1 in the specification using T_{ijt} as a trade intensity measure: differences in production structure specialisation decreases total trade volumes and thus in turn results in less synchronisation.

Table 22. System of determinants (Euro-12 sample, 1980-2006)

	Trade measure T		Trade measure T·GL	
Main eq.	(A)	(B)	(C)	(D)
Trade	0.1212 ***	0.1044 ***	0.1354 **	0.1305 **
	(0.001)	(0.005)	(0.033)	(0.040)
Structure	0.0731	0.0093	-0.0257	-0.0814
	(0.697)	(0.960)	(0.888)	(0.653)
FDI	0.0178	0.0230	0.0341 *	0.0321 *
	(0.303)	(0.181)	(0.076)	(0.094)
Fiscal policy	-0.0904	-0.1084 **	-0.1035 *	-0.0922
	(0.101)	(0.047)	(0.099)	(0.136)
Trade eq.				
Structure		-0.7761 ***		0.2171
		(0.010)		(0.222)
FDI		0.2335 ***		0.0969 ***
		(0.000)		(0.000)
Sectoral structure eq.				
Trade		-0.1750 ***		-0.2299 ***
		(0.000)		(0.000)
FDI		0.0932 ***		0.0635 **
		(0.000)		(0.013)
Finance eq.				
Trade		0.9598 ***		1.5125 ***
		(0.000)		(0.000)
Structure		4.5558 ***		2.7561 **
		(0.000)		(0.024)
Observations	62	62	57	57

Notes: Own calculations. See section 4.1.2.2 for data sources.

However, this effect is surprisingly not picked up by the specification incorporating intra-industry trade volumes. Compared to trade integration, financial integration as measured by FDI intensity seems to be of less direct importance both in terms of the magnitude of its effect and its significance. However, there is a strong mutual reinforcement of trade and financial linkages captured by the estimates for β_2 and δ_1. A further noteworthy detail is that stronger financial integration and higher relative specialisation seem to be mutually conducive, too, as indicated by the estimates for γ_2 and δ_2. This can be seen as evidence for the presence of risk-sharing effects in financial integration: Countries exhibiting a high degree in financial integration can afford to further specialise their production structures since they are insured against sector specific and thus idiosyncratic shocks by financial links with other countries that have a different production structure. However, the negative effects of risk sharing on synchronisation are dominated by the positive indirect effect of trade integration and the residual direct effect of financial integration and thus do not result in a negative net effect.

Comparing these results for the Euro-12 sample with those obtained for the large country sample reported in table 23 reveals several noteworthy patterns. While also positive and clearly significant, the coefficients for trade intensity are smaller in the larger sample. With respect to the total trade volume measure, the coefficients are about half the size as their counterparts for the Euro-12 sample.

This suggests that the trade channel of business cycle synchronisation seems to play a bigger role within the euro area than in a larger area in 1980-2006. For intra-industry trade, the difference in the coefficients of the Euro-12 versus the large country sample is smaller than it is for total trade, but it is still clearly visible. This suggests the notion that intra-industry trade might not be as important in the euro area as it is in other and possibly more heterogeneous country groups. Turning to the specialisation measure, its coefficient in all four specifications is positive, contrary to expectations, but also insignificant.

Nevertheless, a negative indirect impact of specialisation on synchronisation can again be detected in the simultaneous-equations models, where higher degrees of relative specialisation are found to result in less bilateral total trade and less bilateral intra-industry trade. It is further striking that FDI intensity is robustly found to have a positive direct effect on synchronisation. This effect is both higher in value than it is in the Euro-12 estimations and clearly significant. This rather odd result suggests that a direct effect of financial integration on synchronisation is more prevalent in the larger group of industrialised countries than it is in the euro area. On the other hand, there is not much evidence of risk sharing since the estimates are not significant and have different signs in the two specifications of the simultaneous-equations model. Furthermore, contrary to the findings for the Euro-12 sample, differences in fiscal policy are not found to be an important determinant of business cycle synchronisation in the large sample. This is perhaps surprising in light of the fact that in the large sample there are many countries whose scope for discretionary fiscal policy is not bounded by institutions such as the Maastricht criteria.

It should also be noted that even in these models, which incorporate all determinants that are generally deemed to be of importance in the literature, the estimated coefficients of the Euro-12 dummy in the large sample are still consistently found to have a positive and significant value. This means that the higher degree of business cycle synchronisation among euro area countries is only partially explained by the determinants employed in these models.

Table 23. System of determinants (large sample, 1980-2006)

	Trade measure T		Trade measure T·GL	
Main equation	(A)	(B)	(C)	(D)
Trade	0.0617 ***	0.0583 **	0.1112 **	0.1037 **
	(0.010)	(0.014)	(0.018)	(0.026)
Structure	0.0221	0.0230	0.0752	0.1182
	(0.870)	(0.863)	(0.572)	(0.370)
FDI	0.0562 ***	0.0685 ***	0.0707 ***	0.0855 ***
	(0.000)	(0.000)	(0.000)	(0.000)
Fiscal policy	0.0094	0.0232	0.0182	0.0232
	(0.824)	(0.567)	(0.670)	(0.571)
Euro12 dummy	0.3119 ***	0.3056 ***	0.3330 ***	0.3307 ***
	(0.000)	(0.000)	(0.000)	(0.000)
Trade equation				
Structure		-0.7374 ***		-0.4007 ***
		(0.007)		(0.007)
FDI		0.1330 ***		-0.0040
		(0.002)		(0.866)
Sectoral structure equation				
Trade		-0.0998 ***		-0.1538 ***
		(0.000)		(0.000)
FDI		0.0251		-0.0058
		(0.101)		(0.702)
Finance equation				
Trade		0.4452 ***		0.7238 ***
		(0.000)		(0.003)
Structure		0.7004		-0.2931
		(0.281)		(0.664)
Observations	222	222	217	217

Notes: Own calculations. See section 4.1.2.2 for data sources.

If the model applied here fully captured the effects of all relevant determinants, all cross-country differences such as a higher degree of synchronisation within the euro area should be fully explained by differences in the determinants, so that no residual effect could be captured by a dummy variable. However, other studies, such as Akin (2007), obtain similar findings with dummy variables that indicate whether countries belong to the group of Asian or Latin American countries. Thus, the finding of such a positive unexplained residual effect within homogeneous country groups is not particular to the euro area.

To summarise the results of the estimations so far, the following findings stand out: In the 1980-2006 period, both total trade and intra-industry trade are found to be the main determinants of business cycle synchronisation in the euro area. However, the differential effect of intra-industry trade compared to total trade is not as important as expected by theoretical considerations. Furthermore, this differential effect is found to be more prevalent for the larger group of industrialised countries. In addition, there is some weak evidence for positive direct effects of financial integration and fiscal policy convergence, whereas the former determinant is weaker and the latter is stronger in the euro area sample. Finally, we find evidence of strong mutual reinforcement between trade integration and financial integration, on the one hand, and of risk sharing in the specialisation of the production on the other, the latter of which is particular to the euro area.

4.1.3.2 Financial Market Integration: Is There a Euro Effect?

Since the findings of the previous section are based on a rather long period of 27 years, some of these effects and relationships are likely to have slightly evolved or even completely changed over time. In order to account for such dynamic effects and to analyse whether a shift in the workings of the determinants can be detected after the introduction of the euro, two sub-periods will be considered in this section. To obtain meaningful results, the sub-periods should not be too short. Here, the two sub-periods analysed are 1987-96 and 1997-2006. By choosing ten-year periods, it is ensured that each country in the sample experienced at least one full business cycle. In order to obtain meaningful results, it is important to include in the analysis data from all phases of the business cycle. Appropriately, the euro area aggregate more or less passed through two complete cycles in each of these ten-year periods. The two sub-periods were chosen intentionally for two additional reasons: The first period broadly captures the time of increasing European integration, including the enactment of several institutional milestones (Single European Act of 1987, the Maastricht Treaty of 1993), while the second period can be regarded as the EMU period. Although the EMU was only fully implemented in 1999, Böwer and Guillemineau (2006, p. 16) cite empirical evidence which confirms that 1997 marks the year in which the final implementation of the EMU gained full credibility. This year can thus be seen as the beginning of the convergence process towards the monetary union.

Table 24 presents the 1987-96 results of estimations corresponding to the ones in table 22. The noteworthy results are as follows: Trade is found to be the single-most important determinant of synchronisation in this period. It is highly significant in the three specifications (B) to (D) and marginally significant in specification (A). Furthermore, it has considerably higher coefficients than it does in the long period 1980-2006 and there is a substantial differential effect of intra-industry trade integration, which has coefficients nearly two times as high as total trade has in the respective single- or simultaneous-equations model.

Contrary to expectations, differences in the sectoral structure are found to have positive coefficients throughout, but are not always significant, which adds to the inconclusive results about the effects of specialisation obtained for the long period. Unlike the previous results, financial integration is clearly found not to have any significant direct effect and has negative signs throughout. Similarly, fiscal policy asymmetry is not found to be a significant determinant of synchronisation, although it does have the expected negative sign in all four model specifications. Regarding the indirect effects at work, there still is clear evidence of mutual reinforcement between trade and financial integration as well as of risk-sharing effects in the sectoral specialisation of production structures. The somewhat inconclusive results regarding the direct effects in this sub-period could be caused by a relatively low number of observations that is due to a rather high number of missing values for some of the variables.

Table 24. System of determinants (Euro-12 sample, 1987-1996)

	Trade measure T		Trade measure T·GL	
Main equation	(A)	(B)	(C)	(D)
Trade	0.1949	0.2959 **	0.3790 **	0.5308 ***
	(0.109)	(0.014)	(0.041)	(0.004)
Structure	0.5754	0.9439 **	0.5835	0.9041 **
	(0.176)	(0.023)	(0.131)	(0.016)
FDI	-0.0171	-0.0478	-0.0261	-0.0490
	(0.778)	(0.426)	(0.645)	(0.383)
Fiscal policy	-0.1151	-0.0783	-0.1248	-0.0567
	(0.238)	(0.393)	(0.202)	(0.527)
Trade equation				
Structure		-0.7807 ***		-0.1132
		(0.002)		(0.436)
FDI		0.1634 ***		0.0818 ***
		(0.000)		(0.000)
Sectoral structure equation				
Trade		-0.1616 ***		-0.2367 ***
		(0.000)		(0.001)
FDI		0.0658 ***		0.0583 **
		(0.000)		(0.016)
Finance equation				
Trade		1.4322 ***		2.1672 ***
		(0.000)		(0.000)
Structure		2.0345 *		1.1548
		(0.058)		(0.317)
Observations	40	40	40	40

Notes: Own calculations. See section 4.1.2.2 for data sources.

Turning to table 25, which contains the results for the second sub-period 1997-2006, some very remarkable changes in the workings of the determinants are seen. The coefficients associated with the trade integration measures turn out to be negative and (at least marginally) significant in all four specifications. Beyond this, a higher degree of specialisation now is clearly found to exert a negative influence on synchronisation, while the results related to fiscal policy similarity become completely inconclusive. The counter-intuitive results associated with trade and fiscal policy could be attributable to the fact that financial integration as measured by FDI intensity is for this period found to clearly have a strong direct effect on synchronisation. Taken at face value, these results suggest that financial integration has become the single-most important determinant of business cycle synchronisation since the establishment of the euro. It even clearly overshadows and obscures any positive effect of trade integration, which after all was found to have a strong direct effect over the whole period 1980-2006, as depicted in table 22. In contrast to the changes in direct effects, the indirect effects, as indicated by the interdependencies of the determinants, remain rather stable between the two periods.

Table 25. System of determinants (Euro-12 sample, 1997-2006)

	Trade measure T		Trade measure T·GL	
Main equation	(A)	(B)	(C)	(D)
Trade	-0.2200	-0.5227 ***	-0.4806 ***	-0.7196 ***
	(0.108)	(0.000)	(0.005)	(0.000)
Structure	-1.6929 **	-2.6271 ***	-1.5683 ***	-1.6932 ***
	(0.021)	(0.000)	(0.005)	(0.001)
FDI	0.2209 ***	0.3488 ***	0.2396 ***	0.3335 ***
	(0.000)	(0.000)	(0.000)	(0.000)
Fiscal policy	0.1615	0.0068	0.1826	0.0381
	(0.389)	(0.963)	(0.291)	(0.796)
Trade equation				
Structure		-0.6464 *		0.7255 ***
		(0.078)		(0.001)
FDI		0.2855 ***		0.1323 ***
		(0.000)		(0.000)
Sectoral structure equation				
Trade		-0.2256 ***		-0.1673 **
		(0.000)		(0.049)
FDI		0.0893 **		-0.0111
		(0.021)		(0.773)
Finance equation				
Trade		2.0398 ***		2.4649 ***
		(0.000)		(0.000)
Structure		9.7748 ***		5.9577 ***
		(0.000)		(0.001)
Observations	62	62	57	57

Notes: Own calculations. See section 4.1.2.2 for data sources.

Summing up these results, a euro effect in the sense of changes in the relative importance of the determinants following the introduction of the common currency is clearly found. While trade was found to be the key determinant in the sub-period before the monetary union, a positive trade effect is not detectable afterwards.

This decline in the importance of trade integration as a determinant of synchronisation in the euro area has also been found by Böwer and Guillemineau (2006). In line with the findings of the present study, these authors find that trade actually may have had a negative direct effect in the most recent period. The results obtained here further suggest that the driving factor behind business cycle synchronisation seems to have shifted to financial integration, as measured by FDI intensity, since the introduction of the EMU, which is consistent with the findings of Jansen and Stokman (2004). Of course, within the scope of our study it cannot be judged whether these changes are a causal consequence of monetary union or simply a by-product of general ongoing economic and financial integration. However, the effects of financial market integration will be subjected to some more scrutiny in the next section.

4.1.3.3 Multiple Dimensions of Financial Market Integration

The results obtained above regarding the effects of financial integration compared to the effects of trade integration were rather pronounced yet somewhat surprising. Therefore, it is advisable to conduct further analyses to check whether these results are a robust pattern or maybe just some statistical artefact. As has been argued before, the broad phenomenon of financial integration has more than one dimension and thus cannot be adequately captured by only one measure, such as the FDI intensity employed before. To account for this, all alternative measures of financial integration described above will be considered in the following. It would have been desirable to conduct sub-period estimations such as the ones in table 24 and table 25 for all measures of financial integration to check whether the distinctive shift in the key determinants can be detected for all measures. Unfortunately, limitations in data availability over a longer period of time do not allow us to do so. Therefore, it must suffice to compare the results obtained for the different measures in just one period. Instead of the 1997-2006 period cited above, we use the shorter period of 1999-2006. Data on banking sector asset holdings, stock markets and interest rates for all or most of the countries in the Euro-12 sample could only be obtained for 1999 onward, while data on portfolio investment does not begin before 2001. The 1999-2006 period is thus chosen to achieve consistency and comparability in the data used in the analysis. Being eight years in length, the period is still long enough to ensure meaningful results.

To focus on the effects of financial integration and trade integration, here the reduced version of the simultaneous-equations model will be estimated. The indirect effects of specialisation and the interrelations between trade and specialisation will not be regarded in the following, as these were not found to be of crucial importance before. The results of the estimations are presented in table 26 and 27. For the sake of brevity, only the results of the simultaneous-equations model using variable T_{ijt} as the trade integration measure will be reported here. Table 26 contains the results for the four quantity-based financial integration measures FDI_{ijt}, PI_{ijt}, BI_{ijt} and GFO_{ijt}, while table 27 presents the results for the four price-based measures, namely the nominal and real equity market return spreads (denoted ER^N and ER^R) as well as the nominal and real bond market return spreads (denoted BR^N and BR^R).

Looking at the results of the four specifications in table 26, the first thing that comes to attention is that in all four specifications the financial integration measures are found to have considerable and highly significant positive direct effects on synchronisation. Ranging from 0.37 to 0.46, the coefficients of these four measures are even broadly comparable in value, which indicates that the phenomenon of financial integration seems to be captured quite well by all of these measures and that they produce similar effects on synchronisation. All of this further corroborates the tentative conclusion of the previous section: Financial integration indeed seems to have gained considerably in importance. Interestingly, the results related to trade integration are somewhat equivocal. The trade coefficient is negative in three of four cases, clearly insignificant in one case and large swings in absolute value are present. Therefore, contrary to the results of table 25, trade is not found to have a negative effect throughout, but to have rather ambiguous effects in the different specifications. However, this can be seen as evidence for the dominance of the effect of financial integration over trade integration. Furthermore, differences in specialisation are found to have a clear negative effect on synchronisation, whereas fiscal policy differences do not seem to play a major role.

A possible data-related problem causing the inconclusive trade coefficients here could be multicollinearity. When the observations for two or more regressors are highly correlated, only the total effect of these regressors can be picked up by the estimates, but it becomes hard to disentangle their individual effects since the estimates are very inaccurate.

Table 26. Effects of financial integration (quantity-based measures)

Main equation	FDI	PI	BI	GFO
Trade	-0.0417 **	-0.2058	-0.4257 **	0.0089
	(0.010)	(0.101)	(0.043)	(0.931)
Structure	-1.9787 ***	-1.6805 ***	-2.0373 ***	-2.5121 ***
	(0.008)	(0.006)	(0.003)	(0.000)
Finance	0.3725 ***	0.3889 ***	0.4294 **	0.4648 ***
	(0.000)	(0.000)	(0.014)	(0.000)
Fiscal policy	-0.0547	0.0067	0.2398	-0.0341
	(0.771)	(0.965)	(0.272)	(0.811)
Trade equation				
Finance	0.3477 ***	0.3366 ***	0.3773 ***	0.4503 ***
	(0.000)	(0.000)	(0.000)	(0.002)
Sectoral structure equation				
Finance	-0.0884 ***	-0.2194 ***	-0.1222 ***	0.3167 ***
	(0.001)	(0.000)	(0.000)	(0.000)
Finance equation				
Trade	0.5664 ***	0.0390	0.7820 ***	-0.6311 ***
	(0.003)	(0.759)	(0.000)	(0.000)
Observations	61	66	51	66

Notes: Own calculations. See section 4.1.2.2 for data sources.

The correlation of trade integration and financial integration measures in the estimations of table 26 range between 0.67 for the banking sector integration measure and 0.13 for the portfolio investment intensity variable. There is no set threshold value for detecting multicollinearity, but a value of 0.67 can already be seen as slightly problematic. Indeed, the estimation using the banking sector integration variable results in the strongest negative coefficient for trade of all four specifica-

tions, so multicollinearity might be regarded as being responsible for this. On the whole, however, it does not seem to be a major cause of inaccuracy here.
The price-based measures of financial integration generally produce very insignificant and therefore inconclusive results, as can be seen in table 27. Of all direct effects of the determinants, only the spread of nominal long term interest rates is found to be significant. As expected from theoretical considerations, the interest rate coefficient is negative, which is also true for the two measures of equity market return spreads. The only spread with a positive sign is that of real long term interest rates, which is counterintuitive in light of the other evidence regarding the effects of financial integration. Surprisingly, the trade coefficients are all positive yet insignificant here, contrary to the negative coefficients obtained before. The results regarding the direct effects of specialisation are inconclusive, whereas fiscal policy similarity at least has the expected signs. The indirect effects, however, are mostly found to be significant and have the same signs as found in the previous estimations.

Table 27. Effects of financial integration (price-based measures)

Main equation	ER^N	ER^R	BR^N	BR^R
Trade	0.0813	0.0949	0.0671	0.1028
	(0.625)	(0.577)	(0.509)	(0.381)
Structure	0.0788	0.1217	0.5905	-0.2891
	(0.905)	(0.857)	(0.235)	(0.645)
Finance	-0.1634	-0.1276	-0.3743 ***	0.2950
	(0.615)	(0.692)	(0.000)	(0.274)
Fiscal policy	-0.1364	-0.1430	-0.0179	-0.1039
	(0.451)	(0.421)	(0.900)	(0.514)
Trade equation				
Finance	-0.7374 ***	-0.7537 ***	-0.1105	-0.0546
	(0.000)	(0.000)	(0.164)	(0.727)
Sectoral structure equation				
Finance	0.2798 ***	0.2670 ***	-0.0116	0.3124 ***
	(0.000)	(0.000)	(0.799)	(0.000)
Finance equation				
Trade	-0.2047 ***	-0.2104 ***	-0.3371 ***	-0.1199 **
	(0.000)	(0.000)	(0.000)	(0.020)
Observations	66	66	66	66

Notes: Own calculations. See section 4.1.2.2 for data sources.

The evidence presented here suggests that over the last decade financial market integration gained considerably in importance as a determinant of business cycle synchronisation in the euro area. Indeed, its effect even seems to clearly overshadow any positive effect of trade integration. This tentative conclusion is backed up by similar results obtained by Jansen and Stokman (2004) and Böwer and Guillemineau (2006). The distinct results of this analysis of the effects of financial integration were obtained using bilateral quantity-based data, which are generally thought to provide a superior measure of financial integration compared to price-based measures, which are not bilateral by their nature. Accordingly, these price-based measures only lead to obscured results.

4.1.4 Concluding Remarks

The primary aim of this section was to advance research on the role of financial integration as a determinant of synchronisation and, as a secondary aim, to conduct a comprehensive and up-to-date empirical analysis of all the "traditional" determinants of business cycle synchronisation in the euro area. In order to better understand the causes of prevailing cross-sectional variation at the level of bilateral synchronisation, we analysed whether and to what extent trade integration, differences in sectoral specialisation, financial market integration and fiscal policy convergence matter in determining the degree of synchronisation. All of these potential determinants were investigated in a unified framework. Previous literature shows that trade integration is a prime determinant of business cycle synchronisation and has a relatively robust positive effect on it. Furthermore, to a certain extent, differences in sectoral specialisation and fiscal policy asymmetry have a negative effect. Previous empirical results on financial integration have been somewhat mixed.

The empirical analysis undertaken in this study mostly corroborates previous findings – with, however, some notable exceptions. In general, financial integration is found to have a significant positive effect on cyclical synchronisation. Consistent with some earlier evidence, trade integration is found to have lost importance in the recent post-EMU period, while financial integration has gained considerable importance, such that it now appears to be the driving force behind business cycle synchronisation. This finding is robust under the use of a number of different measures of financial integration.

What do these results imply for economic policymaking in the euro area? They show that the ongoing process of economic integration and globalisation so far seems to have been mostly supportive of synchronisation in the euro area. Assuming that the process of economic and financial integration continues into the future, this is good news for the prospects of the EMU, since this would entail a further increase in business cycle synchronisation, in turn enhancing the viability of a common monetary policy. An additional implication of our findings is that when assessing the suitability of potential entrants to the euro area, a wide array of indicators should be considered, particularly the indicators of economic and financial integration that were the focus of this study. The convergence of fiscal policy, inflation rates and long term interest rates, which are the focus of the current convergence criteria, are not the only relevant parameters for assessing the suitability of a country for euro area accession.

The use of a rich dataset, such as that used in this study, comes at a cost. Limitations in the availability of data prevented separate analyses focusing on the new member states of the European Union. Nevertheless, the results obtained here do point to the possibility that future accessions could be pursued under the aim of endogenously increasing business cycle synchronisation of euro candidates with current member states. While evidence shows that the current level of NMS synchronisation with the EU-12 countries does not qualify the NMS for accession to the euro area, in the future Central and Eastern European countries could perhaps experience a rise in synchronisation due to increasing economic and financial integration, which would raise their prospects of entry. In order to explicitly foster such developments, policy efforts to induce further integration of goods and asset markets seem advised. Furthermore, the results of this study reconfirm the potentially detrimental role of fiscal policy asymmetries, thus underscoring the importance of a sound institutional framework that limits excessive debt levels and discretionary national fiscal policies, not only to foster sustainability and long term growth prospects, but also to reduce short term variation in cyclical activity.

Despite the negative experience of the financial crisis and the subsequent economic and debt crisis in Europe, the results of this study support an optimistic assessment with regard to the effects of increasingly integrated financial markets, as long as these markets are stable. When considering the positive effects of increased financial integration, one should not neglect the potential downsides. In light of the apparent increase in the relevance of financial linkages for real economic activity, it seems likely that not only moderate business cycle fluctuations are transmitted more easily, but also grave economic and financial crises. In this way, increased international linkages through financial markets would thus appear to invariably lead to a greater vulnerability to contagion effects, such as the ones experienced in the most recent financial and economic crisis. As a consequence, it would seem that a sound institutional framework is needed in order to limit the scope of such large-scale financial crises. However, such considerations do not fall within the scope of this study.

Regarding the rather surprising recent surge in the importance of financial integration, it will be important in future research to study whether this proves to be a permanent shift in the system of determinants or just a transitory phase. Also, the notable drop in the importance of trade integration is a matter in need of further enquiry, as this development seems unlikely to be a permanent phenomenon considering the distinct robust role of trade integration in recent decades.

From a methodological perspective, the analysis of this study could be taken further by applying panel-econometric methods that explicitly take into account the time dimension of the underlying panel dataset by using "within" estimations rather than the "between" estimations applied in this study. However, the lack of adequate time-varying instrumental variables has prevented meaningful analyses of this type from being conducted to date. An initial effort has been made by Kalemli-Ozcan, Papaioannou and Peydró (2010), who examine time-varying regulatory frameworks in European financial markets as an instrumental variable for financial integration. It is, however, still unclear whether this identification strategy holds for a broader range of financial variables and the problem of a missing time-varying substitute for gravity variables as instruments for the trade variables remains. Analyses such as the ones presented in this study therefore remain an integral part of research on the determinants of business cycle synchronisation.

4.2 Structural Reforms in the Euro Area

Structural reforms have played an important role in macroeconomic policy debates in recent years. It has been argued that in many EU countries impediments to competition, labour market flexibility and innovation as well as over-regulation have adverse effects on economic activity, employment and productivity. The EU's Lisbon Strategy that was devised to reinvigorate growth in the EU seeks among other things to explicitly coordinate structural reform efforts between Member States.[18] The Lisbon Strategy was enacted first and foremost to enhance the medium-term growth and employment prospects of EU countries. However, it is also likely that structural reforms help to increase the adjustment capabilities of European countries by improving resilience to adverse macroeconomic shocks. In this respect, a coordinated reform agenda may bring Member States' cycles more in sync. In this chapter we thus analyse the effects of structural reforms on business cycle synchronisation in the euro area.

Structural reform policies are also intrinsically linked to the proper function of the euro area, and may contribute to increased economic flexibility, and thus, by extension, to a country's ability to withstand macroeconomic shocks. In this way reforms can partly substitute for the loss of sovereign monetary and exchange rate control inside a monetary union, as emphasised by OCA theory. Not much evidence exists currently on how structural reforms affect resilience to economic shocks and business cycle synchronisation in the euro area, mostly because of data limitations.

Another interesting aspect of structural reforms and monetary union is the possibility that monetary unions contribute to the structural reform efforts of member countries. This argument could imply another manifestation of the "endogenous OCA" hypothesis: if countries that have joined a monetary union find more incentives and opportunities to increase the shock absorbing capacity of their economies, this may compensate for the ex-ante perceived costs of entering. In other words, a monetary union may contribute to reform efforts. This raises the question of whether reform efforts need to be coordinated in a monetary union, similar to fiscal policies, and what the effects of non-coordinated structural reforms in a monetary union are.

Although structural reforms and their effects are of considerable interest, research in this area is to some extent complicated by the fact that it is not very easy to define structural reforms. Furthermore, there are substantial uncertainties about their effects. These difficulties are particularly attributable to the fact that structural reforms are difficult to quantify. Moreover, as countries differ largely in their

---

18 The Lisbon Strategy identifies 102 benchmarks against which individual countries and the EU as a whole are evaluated each spring. These benchmarks cover six areas: general economic background, employment, innovation and research, economic reform, social cohesion and the environment.

institutional arrangements and structural reform policies,[19] it is not easy to compare countries directly in terms of structural reforms and their effects. Nevertheless, if one is willing to accept simplifications, it is possible to obtain insight into reform patterns and their possible macroeconomic effects. Efforts by the OECD and the European Commission in particular have recently led to more systematic measurements and comparisons of structural reforms. This in turn may lead to a better analysis of the scope, speed, timing, sequencing and macro-economic effects of structural reforms. In this chapter we make use of these and traditional measures of reform.

At the theoretical level, it is very difficult to understand or model all effects of structural reforms. Not only are the effects of reforms not a priori certain, there is an additional problem of large implementation lags: a considerable amount of time may pass between the implementation of reforms and the moment when their effects fully materialise. Of particular interest are the effects of structural reforms on potential output, economic growth and on structural unemployment. One would expect that structural reforms help to bring these variables closer to their long run equilibrium values because of their effects on goods and labour market flexibility.[20] A related aspect is the effects of structural reforms on structural budget balances: by stimulating economic activity, structural reforms can contribute to an improvement in the structural fiscal balance. Yet this positive effect is most likely to occur in the longer run, while in the short run the fiscal balance could easily deteriorate, e.g. in case of an accompanying tax reform that cuts tax rates. Another interesting question that has been addressed is under which conditions structural reforms are more likely to be undertaken. In this regard political constraints, the role of the initial fiscal position and the stage of the business cycle all play a role.

Broadly categorised, one can distinguish six areas where structural reforms can be undertaken: labour markets, product markets, financial markets, the trade sector, tax systems and pension systems. Structural reforms in the labour market are measured by evaluating changes in various labour market regulations and institutions like employment protection, benefit replacement rates and benefit duration, and wage setting arrangements. Product market reforms can be determined by considering entry barriers, public ownership, market structure, vertical integration and price controls in various sectors. Regulatory reforms in the financial sector

---

19 At the abstract level, North (1990) defines institutions as follow: "*Institutions are the rules of the game in a society or, more formally, are the humanly devised constraints that shape human interaction. In consequence, they structure incentives in human exchange, whether political, social or economic. Institutional change shapes the way societies evolve through time and hence is the key to understanding historical change. That institutions affect the performance of economies is hardly controversial. That the differential performance of economies over time is fundamentally influenced by the way institutions evolve is also not controversial.*" (p.3)

20 A different question is whether structural reforms lead to a permanently higher growth rate by contributing to innovation, technological progress and an increase in human capital formation.

concern controls on credit issuance, interest rates, international financial transactions, and competition, among others. Trade reforms are only of minor importance in the EU as the creation of the Single Market has in principle led to an integrated market for goods, services, labour, and capital. Tax system reforms may aim at reducing distortions from various taxes that result from either the level of tax rates or the complexity of tax regulations. High taxes rates and the complexity of tax regulations indeed act as a strong impediment to economic activity and employment in the EU. Pension reforms involve changes to the framework and parameters of the pension system (e.g. to address demographic change).

Rather than look solely at whether reforms take place during a period, it is also useful to analyse the initial level of institutional restrictions/impediments and the cumulative reform efforts that have been undertaken during that period. This enables one to treat structural reforms as a "stock-flow" process and to analyse the dynamics of the reform process and its effects. In this way, one can analyse the different effects of incremental reforms and compare them with more comprehensive reform strategies.

This analytical approach could be important since structural reforms are always subject to political constraints during their implementation. These constraints result from the fact that the costs of reforms typically fall in the short run on a clearly defined constituency, whereas the benefits are likely to occur in the long run and are dispersed over a broader group. Accordingly, it would appear that political systems tend to produce a short-run, status quo bias that reduces the probability of introducing radical reforms. This applies in practice in particular to labour market reforms, as structural reforms in this area are very controversial and raise the most protests. This, however, could mean that important complementary effects between different types of reforms will not be attained as the achieved reforms are not comprehensive enough. Labour and product market reforms, for example, are thought to be conducive to strong positive interactions (see e.g. Nicoletti and Scarpetta, 2003). Even worse, a status quo bias may lead to reform cycles whereby past reforms are reversed by a new government and perhaps followed by alternative reforms, leading to stop-and-go policies.

Due to the presence of structural reform spillovers between individual countries, there is a clear case for the coordination of structural reform policies in the EU. In a recent study, Neck and Haber (2007) analyse the spillover effects from structural reforms and fiscal consolidation in Germany, France, Italy and the EU as a whole and compare outcomes in a coordinated and a non-coordinated setting. The authors find that coordinated structural reforms and fiscal consolidation in the entire EU produce the best outcomes.

While the design of structural reforms and the external conditions under which they have been implemented have varied a great deal, a few lessons can already be drawn. Firstly, structural reforms can create their own momentum as reforms in one area highlight the need for reforms in other areas. In addition, the adequate combination and sequencing of reforms can increase their political acceptability. Secondly, international spillovers play an important role. Reforms in one country may in various ways affect the domestic economy of neighbouring countries as well. In addition, reforms in neighbouring countries can provide insights concerning the effects of reforms (i.e. learning effects) as well as draw public attention to reform needs. International institutions like the EU can strengthen the hand of policymakers seeking to carry out reform measures by pressing for adherence to agreements such as the Lisbon Agenda (in the case of structural reforms) and the Stability and Growth Pact (in the case of fiscal consolidation). Thirdly, when undertaking structural reforms, fiscal flexibility is very important. Flexibility is needed to cover any short-run additional government spending needs or changes in tax revenues that may accompany a structural reform. This suggests that it is easier to carry out structural reforms from a sound fiscal position. Fourthly, although the need for structural reforms may be more clearly felt in times of recessions, it is easier to implement reforms under more advantageous macroeconomic conditions, especially during an economic recovery after a recession. In an economic downturn, structural reforms may lack political support.

The topic of structural reforms currently has a prominent place in policy debates across the EU. Considerable efforts have been made to delineate and quantify structural reforms and to estimate and model the effects of structural reforms on economic growth and business cycles. In the Lisbon Strategy, the European Union laid out an extensive reform and innovation agenda. The first results can now be evaluated and confronted with the research question posed here: Have structural reforms contributed to business cycle convergence in the euro area?

4.2.1 Empirical Evidence

This part of the book conducts an econometric analysis to determine whether institutional conditions and structural reforms have a significant impact on business cycle synchronisation by reducing differences in the nature and speed of adjustment mechanisms.

Policies or institutions that increase wage or price stickiness can be expected to result in smaller but more persistent output reactions to shocks. The reason is that (nominal) rigidities worsen the inflation-output variability trade-off, since they flatten the Phillips Curve and thus increase the sacrifice ratio. In addition to many other ramifications, structural reforms may also contribute to business cycle convergence by providing the euro area Member States with more resilience against macroeconomics shocks: in such a case, the amplitude and persistence of the adjustments induced by exogenous shocks will be reduced. This could foster business cycle convergence in the euro area.

Structural policies are likely to affect resilience to shocks given that they may change the impact and/or persistence of the effects induced by exogenous shocks. Macroeconomic stabilisation policies will also play an important role for resilience, but their effectiveness is therefore conditional on structural and policy settings. For example, structural reforms may affect the strength of monetary or fiscal policy transmission mechanisms. Duval et al. (2007) use a pooled regression analysis across 20 OECD countries over the period from 1982 to 2003 to estimate the effect of institutional characteristics on resilience to shocks. Countries are found to differ in resilience and it is shown that the countries seen as more resilient also appear to be the ones that have made most progress on structural reforms over the past two decades. They find that employment protection legislation increases the persistence of output gaps, while product market regulation dampens the initial output gap effect of shocks. Other institutional indicators don't exert an influence on business cycle characteristics. The use of a synthetic overall product and labour market indicator instead of detailed indicators provides clear evidence that more regulation dampens the initial impact of exogenous shocks on the output gap, but makes the shock more persistent.

The existing empirical literature, however, finds little evidence that labour and product market characteristics or the cross-country differences exert a significant effect on business cycle *convergence*. Böwer and Guillemineau (2006) find no significant effect of cross-country differentials in trade union density or employment protection legislation on business cycle synchronisation in the euro area over the period from 1980 to 2004. For a panel of 11 countries over the period from 1970 to 2003, Artis and Claeys (2007) cannot find a robust and significant effect from the NAWRU (non-accelerating wage rate of unemployment), employment protection legislation, union density, the tax wedge, the benefit replacement rate or different indicators of product market regulation on business cycle synchronisation as measured by the bilateral cross-correlation of output gaps in 5-year rolling windows. In both studies, bilateral trade flows – measuring *trade integration* – are found to be the dominant factor driving the synchronisation of business cycles.

Similar to the arguments above, it can be argued that the ongoing process of *fiscal convergence* in the euro area, as originally laid out in the Maastricht and Amsterdam Treaties, may contribute significantly to business cycle convergence: the objective of ensuring fiscal discipline and sustainability has contributed to fiscal convergence as well as a longer run perspective in the formulation of fiscal policy. Yet the risk remains – and this is also true of the common monetary policy – that in the short-run the fiscal framework may not be appropriate for all countries, and may not provide sufficient room for manoeuvre when countries face idiosyncratic shocks and/or business cycle adjustments. In such a case, the fiscal framework could even contribute to reduced business cycle convergence since this would imply inadequate fiscal management from a business cycle perspective. Countries might be forced to run overly restrictive fiscal policies while experiencing a recession. Similarly, there is a risk of overly expansionary policies during times of growth.

Both trade and fiscal policy as well as sectoral structures and monetary policy have been examined in earlier studies dealing with the identification of the determinants of business cycle convergence. In line with these studies, we also implement these variables as controls in our analysis. Yet in addition to these variables, there are other possible factors that influence business cycles which have not been analysed adequately. For example, one would think that real interest rate differences may drive business cycle convergence by boosting resilience to asymmetric shocks. However, since this variable has not been convincingly identified as a determinant of synchronisation, it is not included as a control variable but rather as a potential factor having an impact on business cycle correlations.

The analysis in this chapter is organised as follows. First of all, a descriptive analysis of indicators of institutional arrangements in 20 OECD countries will be carried out. A description of the required transformations which are conducted in order to generate bilateral measures of institutional conditions and structural shifts (i.e. structural reforms) follows. This part will be expanded on with a discussion of sources, data ranges and the necessary transformations for all variables which appear in the empirical estimations. In particular, a connection to the existing literature on business cycle determinants is made by taking into account those variables which have been identified as significant in earlier studies. The empirical approach is explained, focusing on the exact model specification as well as on how to respond to econometric issues. Since only a few studies exist that address business cycle convergence in a panel data framework, this is a rather challenging task. Nevertheless, a method is developed which appears capable of generating robust and reasonable outcomes. The results concentrate mainly on the role institutional conditions and structural reforms play in the process of business cycle convergence. Also considered, however, are long-term interest rates and the Economic Freedom of the World Index as two alternative factors influencing business cycle convergence. Additionally, a sensitivity analysis is carried out in order to cross-check the results for alternative dependent variables, due to the unobservability of the business cycles. Finally, the findings are summarised and interpreted.

4.2.2 Data and Definition of Variables

4.2.2.1 Description of Institutional Structures

The Nickell-Nunziata database delivers eight different indicators of institutional structures for the period from 1960 to 2006 for 20 OECD countries. The indicators measure *employment protection*, *union density and coverage*, *bargaining coordination and centralisation*, *replacement rates*, *working hours*, *active labour market policies*, *regulation* and *taxes*. They are divided into 36 sub-indicators. Some of them will be displayed to give a short overview of the data structure. A detailed description of this database is given by Nickell and Nunziata (2001) and Nickell (2006). In the appendix, we describe the institutional indicators that are relevant for our own investigation.

According to our definition, if an indicator changes from one period to the next, a reform has taken place. Multiple year periods are presented to take into account that institutional reforms are conducted rather infrequently. Each graph shows the data for three time periods in order to provide a picture of the development of institutional conditions in the OECD countries. The period range is the same as in the empirical analysis. Therefore, the first displayed period ranges from 1990 to 1994, the second from 1995 to 1999 and the third from 2000 to 2006.

The union density and coverage indicator in figure 29, called udnet, shows the fraction of the employed who are members of a trade union.

Fig. 29. Union density indicator for OECD countries

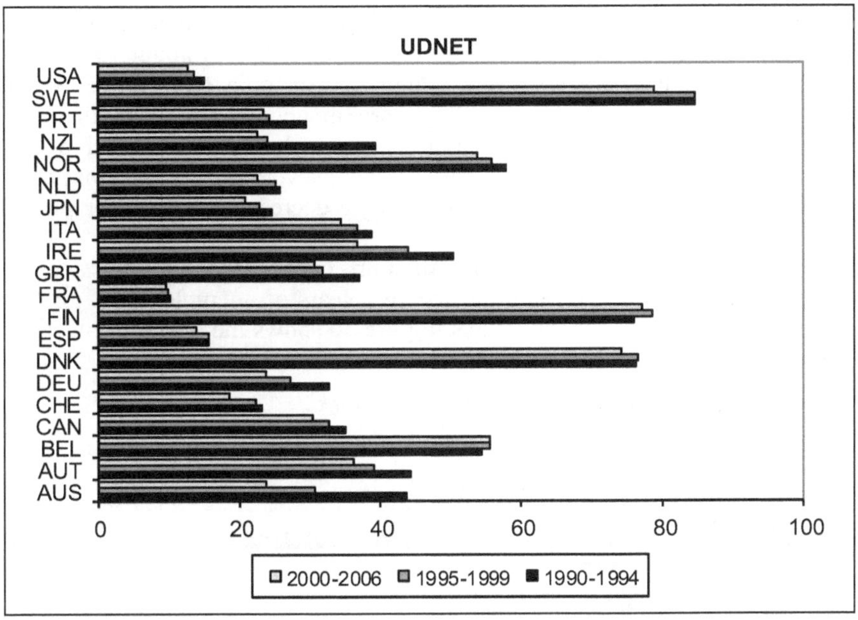

Fig. 30. Replacement rates indicator for OECD countries

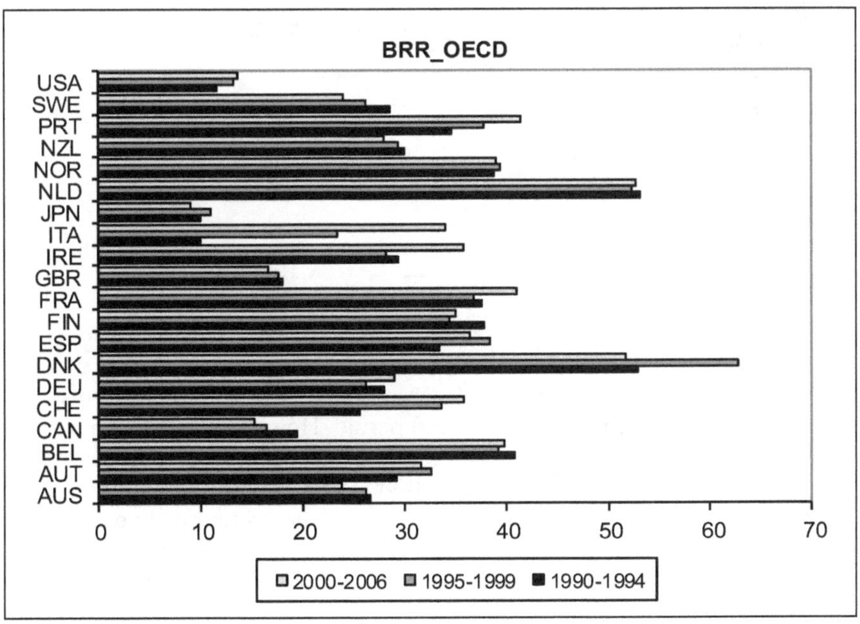

The highest rates of union membership are found in Sweden, Finland and Denmark. During the last 18 years, about 80% of all employees in the Scandinavian countries belonged to a union. The United States, France and Spain form the group with the lowest union participation, registering a rate of about 15%. Only few remarkable changes are observed, mainly in Australia and New Zealand, where union membership rates decrease by approximately 20% over the three periods. The low fluctuations are not surprising since trade union membership generally adjusts slowly to political or social changes. Nevertheless unions in nearly all countries, except Belgium and Finland, show a decreasing trend in employee participation during the displayed period.

The measure for replacement rates is called brr_oecd and displays the average percentage replacement rate during the first five years of unemployment for two income levels and three family situations. Figure 30 shows the average values for each period.

Fig. 31. Employment tax rate indicator for OECD countries

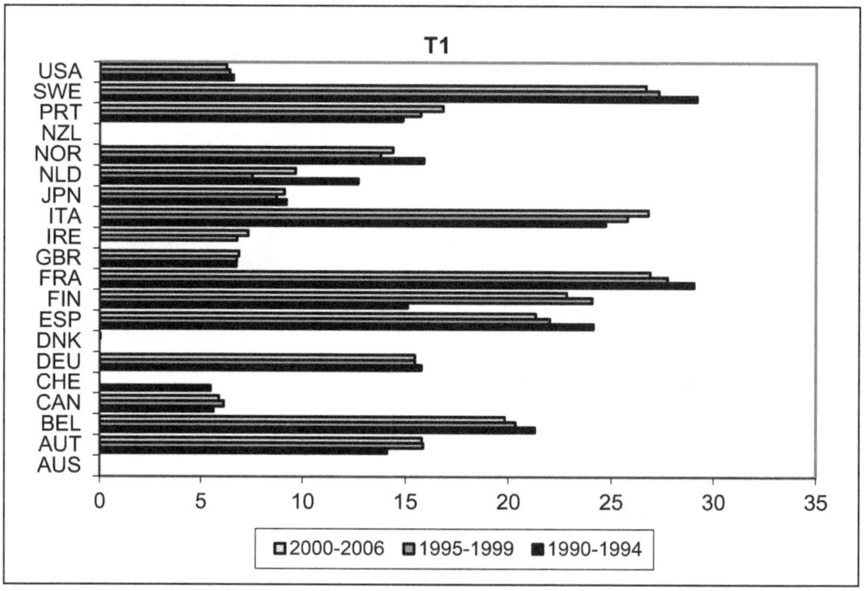

At first glance, it appears replacement rates alter infrequently and only marginally. It is thus all the more surprising that each country conducted reforms concerning replacement rates during the covered period. However, there is no explicit common pattern in reform intensity. The most significant change is observed for Italy. The value of the third period from 2000 to 2006 is about three times larger than the value of the first period from 1990 to 1994. Some countries like Australia, Canada, the UK, New Zealand and Sweden lowered their replacement rates considerably. Others like Austria, Portugal and the United States exhibit increasing replacement rates. Moreover, the cross-country differences in the data are relatively large. Japan, Canada and the United States have replacement rates of about 10%, whereas the Netherlands and Denmark have values of approximately 50%

The countries' employment tax rates, which are shown in figure 31, are measured as a fraction of the employer social security contribution divided by employee total compensation minus the employer social security contribution. Unfortunately, no data are available for New Zealand, Denmark and Austria.

The data show a heterogeneous structure. Especially in Finland and the Netherlands, sizable reforms were carried out in the first two periods. In contrast, changes in Germany, the UK and the United States are quite small.

Again, the graph shows considerable differences in tax rates across the included countries. The employer social security contribution relative to employee compensation is rather low in the United States, Canada and the UK, especially in relation to Sweden, Italy and France, which exhibit high employment tax rates.

Fig. 32. Employment protection indicator for OECD countries

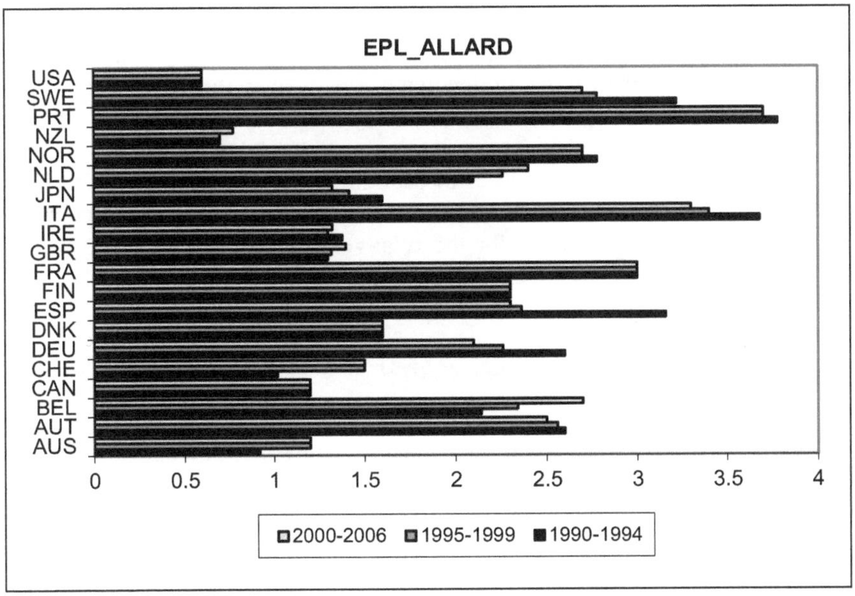

The measure for employment protection shows a higher value in countries with stricter labour regulations in terms of employment and dismissal protections as well as labour contracts. This measure is displayed in figure 32, and shows a rather low variation over the three periods.

Some countries like the United States, Canada and Denmark did not undergo any reforms, while employment protection in Sweden, Spain, Belgium and Germany was substantially restructured over the last two decades. Italy, Portugal, France and Sweden exhibit the highest values, indicating very strict employment protections.

4.2.2.2 Measuring Institutional Similarity and Change

Both a measure for *institutional similarity* as well as for *institutional change* are considered in order to analyse whether institutions (and changes thereto) have an influence on business cycle synchronisation. This analysis yields insights into the effects of both the institutional status quo and the dynamics of structural reforms.

First of all, appropriate bilateral measures of institutional similarity and institutional change are required. In the following, the above mentioned indicators are denoted as P^k. The index k ranges from 1 to 36, thus numbering the different indicators. Our measures of institutional similarity reflect the absolute differences between countries in the levels of the particular indicators P^k, such that

$$X^k_{dis,ijt} = \left| P^k_{it} - P^k_{jt} \right| \tag{18}$$

where P^k_{it} is defined as the level of the particular indicator P^k of country i at time t. In doing so we get 36 different bilateral indicators for institutional similarity between the countries, in the following denoted as *distance*, with a lower (or higher) value of $X^k_{dis,ijt}$ displaying more (or less) similarity between the countries i and j.

To measure institutional change, some more preparatory work has to be done. First, for each country the growth rates of each indicator P^k are calculated. Then the absolute differences between countries in the growth rates of the particular indicators P^k represent the measure for the relative similarity (or dissimilarity) of institutional change. This relationship can be seen in the following definition

$$X^k_{dir,ijt} = -\left(\left| g^k_{Pit} - g^k_{Pjt} \right| \right) \tag{19}$$

where g^k_{Pit} and g^k_{Pjt} describe the growth rates of the particular indicator P^k of countries i and j at time t. The resulting measure $X^k_{dir,ijt}$ is a bilateral variable measuring the relation between an institutional change conducted in countries i and j. The multiplication with (-1) is executed to receive higher (or smaller) values of $X^k_{dir,ijt}$ linked to a stronger (or weaker) similarity between the reforms of countries i and j with respect to indicator P^k. Henceforth, this measure of institutional change will be called *direction*, for which the values of $X^k_{dir,ijt}$ lie between $-\infty$ and 0. Note that taking the absolute value of the difference prevents us from making any statement about the direction of the countries' reforms. This means if countries i and j undergo reforms in the same direction, one does not know whether these reforms raise or reduce the value of the particular indicator. However this does not have an impact on the empirical results since we are interested in the similarity of reforms and their influence on bilateral cycle correlations, and not in the influence of reforms on the individual countries' business cycles.

4.2.2.3 Business Cycle Synchronisation

Due to the fact that business cycles are not directly observable and measurable, an appropriate methodology to model them is required. On the basis of the available real GDP series of the OECD from 1960 to 2005 for all 20 countries, the cycles can be calculated by filtering the GDP series. As described in section 3.1, there are quite a few possibilities for measuring the business cycle. De Haan, Inklaar and Jong-a-Pin (2005) give a short insight into the differences between alternative filtering methods. They conclude that "studies that use standard filters such as the HP, BK and CF filters are likely to yield similar results". Here, the commonly used Hodrick-Prescott (HP) filter with a λ of 100 is applied in order to obtain the output gap as a measure of the stage in the business cycle. A sensitivity analysis with alternative filtering methods is also conducted to check for the reliability of the results. The connection between the business cycles of two countries is made by calculating the correlations over a 5-year interval starting in 1960. The correlation of the last available period is therefore calculated using data from 2000 to 2005. For the sensitivity analysis, two further de-trending methods are selected. The cycles measured by using the Cristiano-Fitzgerald (CF) filter and the year-on-year differences (DIF4) are introduced as substitutes for the HP-filtered series, serving as a robustness test for the results obtained with the HP filter. The cycle component extraction for all three alternatives is described in section 3.1 and the correlations are calculated in the same way as for the HP filter. In the following, the variables included in addition to the structural reform indicators will be described.

4.2.2.4 Control Variables

In section 2.2, trade is mentioned as the major transmission channel for business cycles. To account for this, we use an indicator of bilateral trade intensity, following the approach of Frankel and Rose (1998), who define a variable measuring the share of the two countries' bilateral trade flows T_{ijt} in the total volume of their trade flows with all partner countries. This is formally expressed in equation (13) of sub-section 4.1.2.2. Differences in the sectoral specialisation of the production structure of two countries are measured by the variable S_{ijt} following the definition of equation (15) in sub-section 4.1.2.2.

Primary government net lending, measured as a percentage of GDP based on OECD data (which are available from 1970 to 2006), serves as an indicator of fiscal policy FP_{ijt}. Taking the absolute differences between countries *i* and *j*, the net lending value delivers a measure for the similarity of the countries' fiscal policies. This is formally displayed in equation (16) of sub-section 4.1.2.2.

In order to model a currency union, a dummy variable is used that takes the value 1 if two countries are in the same currency union at the same time and 0 if not. Obviously this is true for the members of the euro area. As 5-year periods are used in the empirical analysis, the dummy value is 0 for all country pairs until the penultimate period. It changes to 1 for all euro area member pairs in the last period from 2000 to 2005.

4.2.2.5 Additional Determinants of Synchronisation

The European Commission's Ameco database delivers comprehensive data on real long-term interest rates from 1960 to 2007 for 17 countries that are included in the empirical analysis. There are no data available for Australia, Canada and New Zealand. The bilateral measure will be defined as the absolute difference between countries i and j at time t, following the approach introduced for the distance measure calculations of the structural indicators.

In addition to the indicators of labour market reforms that have already been presented, the role of an overall index of *labour and product market regulation* is analysed: the Economic Freedom of the World Index, which is maintained by the Fraser Institute for 123 countries from 1970 to 2005. The index includes five different areas[21] and takes into account different aspects of the institutional situation in each country.[22] Clearly, it is not as easy to interpret as the structural indicators of Nickell and Nunziata, but it is worth including in order to take into account another potential source of synchronisation linked to the institutional framework of countries.

Again, the absolute differences of the values of countries i and j at time t are taken, to obtain a bilateral measure. It is important to mention that the index is only available each fifth year from 1970 to 2000, beginning in 1970. It is published annually for the period from 2000 to 2005. Since the empirical analysis is built upon 5-year averaged data, the series is interpolated and the 5-year mean of the resulting values is calculated for the period from 1970 to 2000.

4.2.3 Empirical Strategy

As described in the introduction to this section and in detail in section 2.2, many studies have been published on the "traditional" determinants of business cycle synchronisation, but only few focus on the role that institutional similarity and change play in this process. Böwer and Guillemineau (2006) analyse the influence of trade union density and employment protection legislation as two labour market flexibility indicators by running an extreme-bound analysis (EBA) in a cross-section framework over the period from 1980 to 2004. Using bilateral differences for both indicators, the results do not help to explain the role of structural reforms on business cycle convergence. None of the indicators are identified as statistically significant. Similarly, Artis and Claeys (2007) analyse the influence of four labour market variables and a summary indicator of labour market rigidity on business

---

21 Size of government; legal structures and security of property rights; access to sound money; freedom to trade internationally; regulation of credit, labour and business.

22 Further information is available on http://www.freetheworld.com/release.html.

cycle synchronisation, as measured the bilateral cross-correlation of output gaps in rolling 5-year time windows based on panel data of eleven countries over the period from 1970 to 2003. Their study uses a random effects setup with trade integration as the single control variable, complemented by different additional variable combinations, and yields non-significant results with respect to all labour market indicators.

In this book, we basically follow Artis and Claeys (2007) in using a panel data framework, but implement some alterations to the econometric approach as well as to the data structure and institutional changes. Specifically, we use a larger number of structural indicators and control variables as well as a fixed effects model instead of random effects. Additionally, there are some differences in the determination of the dependent variable. Artis and Claeys (2007) calculate the correlations for 6 periods over a 5-year rolling window by averaging the correlations and using band pass filtered deviation cycles, while we employ HP filtered business cycles to generate correlations over 9 initially defined 5-year periods.

We pay specific attention to the determination of the period length in order to remove biasing short-term cyclical movements. Five-year periods meet this condition and are also suitable to exploit the time dimension of our data as well as to compute correlations with sufficient time observations. Hence, five-year averages of our measures for institutional similarity and change are constructed by generating the arithmetic mean for each period and variable. After this transformation we obtain 9 intervals, the first covering the period from 1960 to 1964, the second from 1965 to 1969 and so on. The last period from 2000 to 2006 comprises a 7-year period as our sample spans 47 years.

The basis of our empirical analysis is a non-structural linear model of the following form:

$$Corr(gap)_{ij\tau} = \alpha_{ij} + \beta_0 T_{ij\tau} + \beta_1 FP_{ij\tau} + \beta_2 S_{ij\tau} + \beta_3 curr_{ij\tau} + \sum_{k=1}^{n} \sum_{l=0}^{p} \gamma_{k,l} X^{k}_{dir,ij(\tau-l)} + \sum_{k=1}^{n} \eta_k X^{k}_{dis,ijr} + \lambda_\tau + \varepsilon_{ij\tau} \qquad (20)$$

$Corr(gap)_{ij\tau}$ represents the (contemporaneous) correlation of the business cycle of countries i and j in period τ. T, FP and S stand for bilateral trade, difference in fiscal policy and degree of specialisation between countries i and j in period τ, $curr_{ij\tau}$ is a dummy variable, which is 1 if countries i and j both are members of the euro area and 0 if not. It measures the *euro effect*. The parameters α_{ij} and λ_τ are cross-section and period specific effects, $\varepsilon_{ij\tau}$ is the error term to control for unobserved influences. The effect of institutional similarity on business cycle synchronisation is captured by $\sum_{k=1}^{n} \eta_\kappa X^{\kappa}_{dis,ij\tau}$. The values of k range from 1 to 36, thus numbering the indicators. The influence of similar structural reforms is accounted for by the term $\sum_{k=1}^{n} \sum_{l=0}^{p} \gamma_{k,l} X^{k}_{dir,ij\tau-l}$ with the coefficient $\gamma_{k,l}$ reflecting the effect of absolute differences of institutional change and their lags. Again, k is the index of the indicators, running from 1 to 36. The second sum accounts for lagged values of the indicators such that p is one if the introduced indicator enters the equation with a lag of one period.

When working with panel data we have to determine whether random or fixed cross-section effects better suit our model and data. Fixed effects estimation means that an individual constant is calculated for each cross-section, suggesting that there are different unobservable, time-invariant conditions influencing the dependant variable. A random effects setup does not explicitly calculate the individual constants but rather puts them into the error term, and as a result the constants only show a randomised variation. Therefore, it is important to come to a conclusion as to whether the unobserved effect, denoted as α_{ij}, and the explanatory variables are correlated. The random effects estimator only provides consistent coefficients if there is no correlation between the random effect and the explanatory variables, while the fixed effects estimator is less efficient but always computes consistent estimates, even if the unobserved effect and the explanatory variables are correlated. The standard way to deal with the unobserved effects problem is to run a Hausman-Test comparing the random effects and fixed effects estimators. As the fixed effects estimator is definitely consistent, a statistically significant deviation of the coefficients computed by the random effects estimator provides clear evidence of its inconsistency. The test is carried out on the basis of the introduced model, i.e. including trade, specialisation, fiscal policy and the euro area dummy as well as time and cross-section-specific effects, but without any institutional indicators. Henceforth, we will refer to this model as the *basic model.*

Our results demonstrate that the hypothesis of no correlation between the cross-section unobserved effect and the explanatory variables has to be strongly rejected. This implies that a cross-section fixed effects model specification fits the data best. The time specific effect λ_τ has to be fixed since our data structure does not allow for balanced data estimation. Furthermore, a redundant fixed effect test proves our assumption that the chosen model specification with cross-section and period specific effects is correct. The hypothesis that the fixed effects are redundant has to be rejected, implying that our chosen standard model with a fixed effect specification is appropriate.

Given that we have 36 different indicators for institutional similarity as well as for institutional change, there are various possible combinations of the above model. Therefore it is important to define a strategy to deal with the enormous amount of data. Our first step is to look at the availability of the bilateral values in order to select at least one significant sub-indicator for each structural group. It is important to note that some indicator groups do not have sub-indicators with sufficient data points for all countries and periods. These include variables such as working hours, active labour market policy and regulation. Variables that are not identified as significant will be excluded. Sub-indicators for which only limited data are available when compared to other sub-indicators of the same group will not be incorporated in the following estimations in order to avoid excluding too much observable data. Subsequently, for each indicator group, one of the preselected sub-indicators will (in the event of significance) be chosen to serve as part of the model.

4.2.4 Results

4.2.4.1 Contemporaneous Institutional Variables

The remaining sub-indicators are tested for significance in a reduced model specification which always includes the control variables trade, fiscal policy, specialisation and the euro area dummy. Thus, we use a modified version of equation (20) with $n=1$ and $l=0$ such that the contemporaneous distance and direction terms of only one indicator can be included per equation.

For each sub-indicator, we estimate three specifications with different combinations of institutional similarity and change. In specification (1), only a sub-indicator's distance term is introduced in addition to the control variables. Specification (2) adds the direction term to the basic model, leaving out the distance term. Specification (3) includes both the direction and the corresponding distance term of a sub-indicator. The results are shown in table 28. The third column represents the values of specification (1), while the fourth column displays the outcomes of specification (2). The fifth and the sixth columns show the result of specification (3), which includes *both* the distance and the direction term. The entries display the coefficients of each sub-indicator. In doing so, we are able to identify sub-indicators which are likely significant for business cycle synchronisation.

Note that the distance and direction terms of each sub-indicator have been both included twice each. In this way seven distance measures which are significant in specification (1) and (3) as well as four significant direction measures in specifications (2) and (3) can be identified. More precisely, the distance measures of union density and coverage (*udnet*, *udnet_vis*), bargaining coordination and centralisation (*cow*, *cow_int*, *cew*, *cew_int*) and the employment tax rate (t1) as well as direction measures of bargaining coordination and centralisation (*co_oecd*, *ce_oecd*), replacement rates (*brr_oecd*) and the employment tax rate (t1) are significant at this stage.

However it is still useful to continue reducing the data by dropping significant indicators that are simply different measures of the same institutional dimension such as cow and cow_int, both of which are indicators for bargaining coordination. In this case, the sub-indicator with fewer observations is dropped. Alongside the employment tax rates (t1), the union density and coverage indicator is represented by udnet, while cow and cew are used as distance measures for bargaining coordination and centralisation, respectively. In this regard, the first indicator represents coordination while the latter represents the centralisation factor. The particular coordination and centralisation indicators are likely correlated, as both refer to the process of wage negotiations. Nevertheless, regarding both aspects as independent has the clear advantage of making the full range of available data on wage bargaining exploitable. If both aspects are jointly estimated, it might lead to a deterioration of the sensitivity of the particular coefficients. Yet, we suspect that this effect does not influence our results substantially. Our preferred measures of structural reforms will be the direction terms of bargaining coordination and centralisation (co_oecd, ce_oecd), replacement rates (brr_oecd) and the employment tax rate (t1). As described above, bargaining coordination (co_oecd) as well as bargaining centralisation (ce_oecd) are considered in the following analysis.

The eight significant bilateral measures for distance and direction mentioned above are tested for robustness in a model similar to equation (3). Since we want to find out whether the assumption of significance for the eight selected measures holds for different combinations of the sub-indicators, we now allow for two as well as three different indicators in the same equation. According to equation (3), two specifications are defined. The first accounts for two different sub-indicators in the same equation (n=2), while the latter brings three different sub-indicators together (n=3). Both specifications also include the control variables trade, specialisation, fiscal policy and the currency union dummy. The equations are still estimated without lagged direction terms, indicated by (l=0) in equation (3).

It is important to mention that in the following equations the distance and direction measures of the same indicator always appear together even though some of them might be insignificant. The reason for including possible non-significant counterparts as control variables is that the exact relation and interaction between the distance and direction measures is not clear-cut. Leaving out one of them due to insignificance is thus not advised.

The first specification (n=2) accounts for every possible combination of pairs within the eight selected sub-indicators, while the second specification (n=3) allows for every possible combination of three selected sub-indicators. In this vein, a total of 56 equations are estimated in order to cross-check the reliability of the results of table 28.

Table 29 displays the coefficients of the sub-indicators' distance terms, while table 30 shows the direction term coefficients. The sub-indicators' names are reported in the first row, while the first column shows the number of jointly estimated sub-indicators per equation. Each single estimation with combinations of 2 (n=2) and 3 (n=3) sub-indicators calculates both the coefficients of the sub-indicator's distance and direction term. As an example, the column titled as udnet in table 29 shows the resulting distance coefficient values of those equations in which the union density and coverage sub-indicator has been included. Table 30 presents the corresponding direction term coefficients of the union density and coverage sub-indicator. Since every possible combination of 2 and 3 sub-indicators is tested, we obtain 21 results for the distance as well as for the direction term of each selected sub-indicator.

The distance measures for union density and coverage (udnet) and for bargaining coordination (cow) as well as the direction measures for replacement rates (brr_oecd) and the employment tax rate (t1) are highly significant in all estimated equations. The relevance of the distance measures for bargaining centralisation (ce_oecd) and the employment tax rate (t1) as well as of the direction measures for bargaining coordination (co_oecd) is not clear as these variables show insignificant coefficients in some equations. Nevertheless, we will refer to the aforementioned seven distance and direction measures as additional control variables in the following estimations as they are likely to influence business cycle correlations.

Table 28. Direction and distance measures, identification test

Indicator	Sub-Indicator	Model Specification			
		(1)	(2)	(3)	
Employment Protection		distance	direction	distance	direction
	epl	-0.07	0.72	-0.08	0.74
	epl_allard	-0.03	0.09	-0.03	0.09
Union Density and Coverage					
	udnet	0.01**	-0.35	0.01**	-0.34
	udnet_vis	0.01**	-0.24	0.01**	-0.26
Bargaining Coordination and Centralisation					
	co_oecd	0.00	0.91**	0.01	0.92**
	co_oecd_int	0.02	0.60	0.01	0.61
	cow	-0.22**	0.57	-0.22**	0.60
	cow_int	-0.24**	0.52	-0.25**	0.84
	ce_oecd	-0.03	0.78*	-0.03	0.79*
	ce_oecd_int	-0.05	0.05	-0.05	0.08
	cew	-0.16**	0.17	-0.16**	0.14
	cew_int	-0.20**	-0.89	-0.19**	-0.70
Replacement Rates					
	brr1	0.02	-0.20	0.02	-0.15
	brr_oecd	-0.00	-0.74**	0.00	-0.80**
	nrw	0.00	-0.17	0.00	-0.15
Taxes					
	t1	0.02**	1.14**	0.02*	1.09**
	t2	0.01	0.49	0.02*	0.47
	t3	-0.01	0.74	-0.01	0.73
	tw	0.00	2.63	0.01	2.81*

Notes: Entries display the coefficient values of the distance and direction terms. Two asterisks next to the value of the particular indicator mean significance at the 1% level, one asterisk indicates significance at the 5% level. The correlation of business cycles of each country pair for 5-year intervals is the dependent variable. Explanatory variables are bilateral measures of trade, fiscal policy, specialisation and a currency union dummy, together with the distance and/or direction term of a sub-indicator. Time and period specific constants as well as the coefficients of the control variables are estimated, but not reported. Specifications (1) and (2) estimate the coefficients of each sub-indicator's distance and direction term separately. Specification (3) estimates the coefficients of each sub-indicator's distance and direction term jointly. Data for a maximum of (20*19)/2=190 country pairs over 9 periods are used.

Table 29. Distance measure, robustness check

	udnet	co_oecd	cow	ce_oecd	cew	brr_oecd	t1
	0.01**	-0.01	-0.21**	-0.03**	-0.13	0.00	0.01
	0.01**	0.01**	-0.31**	-0.03**	-0.18	0.00	0.01*
n=2	0.01**	0.02	-0.23**	0.01*	-0.11	0.00	0.02*
	0.01**	0.03	-0.17**	0.05**	-0.22	0.00	0.01*
	0.01**	0.01	-0.22**	-0.02**	-0.14	0.00	0.02*
	0.01**	0.01	-0.27**	-0.06**	-0.28	0.00	0.02*
	0.01**	0.06*	-0.28**	-0.02**	-0.14	0.00	0.01
	0.01**	0.00	-0.22**	0.00	-0.07	0.00	0.01
	0.01**	0.01	-0.18**	0.03**	-0.17	0.00	0.01
	0.01**	0.00	-0.21**	-0.03*	-0.11	0.00	0.01
	0.01**	0.00	-0.26**	-0.06**	-0.23	0.01	0.01
	0.01**	0.08**	-0.31**	-0.02*	-0.12	0.00	0.01*
	0.01**	0.08**	-0.27**	0.05**	-0.22	0.00	0.01
n=3	0.01**	0.08**	-0.32**	-0.02**	-0.16	0.00	0.02*
	0.01**	0.09**	-0.36**	-0.08**	-0.29	0.01	0.02*
	0.01**	0.27	-0.19**	0.06**	-0.18	0.00	0.02*
	0.01**	0.02	-0.24**	0.01	-0.08	0.00	0.02*
	0.01**	0.42	-0.26**	-0.03**	-0.23	0.01	0.02**
	0.01**	0.03	-0.19**	0.05**	-0.20	0.00	0.02*
	0.01**	0.05	-0.20**	0.09**	-0.37	0.01	0.02*
	0.01**	0.02	-0.27**	-0.02**	-0.26	0.01	0.02*

Notes: Entries display the coefficient values of the distance terms. Two asterisks next to the value of the particular indicator imply significance at the 1% level, one asterisk indicates significance at the 5% level. The correlation of business cycles of each country pair for 5-year intervals is the dependent variable. Explanatory variables are bilateral measures of trade, fiscal policy, specialisation and a currency union dummy, together with the distance and direction terms of two and three sub-indicators. The entries referring to *n=2* present the coefficients of the distance terms estimated by including every possible combination of two sub-indicators (both the distance and the direction term). The entries referring to *n=3* show the coefficients of the distance terms estimated by including every possible combination of 3 sub-indicators (distance and direction term). Time and period specific constants as well as the coefficients of the control variables and the direction terms of the sub-indicators are estimated, but not reported. Data for a maximum of (20*19)/2=190 country pairs over 9 periods are used.

In contrast, the distance measure for bargaining coordination (co_oecd) and the direction measure for bargaining centralisation (ce_oecd) are probably irrelevant determinants, as indicated by the small number of significant coefficients.

Table 30. Direction measure, robustness check

	udnet	co_oed	cow	ce_oed	cew	brr_oecd	tl
	-0.38	0.84**	0.45	0.57	0.33	-0.74**	0.78*
	-0.65	1.56**	-0.83	0.20	-0.45	-0.88**	1.07**
	-0.35	0.80	0.22	0.89*	-0.13	-0.85**	1.06**
n=2	-0.59	1.05**	0.68	1.25**	-0.61	-0.81**	1.12**
	-0.12	1.04**	0.71	0.86*	0.10	-0.67**	1.23**
	0.03	0.58	0.51	0.51	0.60	-0.80**	1.10**
	-0.86	1.46**	-0.84	-0.15	-0.21	-0.80**	0.77*
	-0.37	0.91*	0.16	0.69	0.23	-0.79**	0.73*
	-0.59	0.91**	0.36	0.81	-0.15	-0.74**	0.79*
	-0.14	0.94**	0.56	0.59	0.26	-0.64**	0.90**
	0.00	0.47	0.28	0.11	0.82	-0.73**	0.79**
	-0.70	1.35**	-0.81	0.35	-0.23	-0.96**	0.98**
	-0.75	1.53**	-0.68	0.75	-0.71	-0.87**	1.09**
n=3	-0.44	1.70**	-0.83	0.09	-0.58	-0.77**	1.20**
	-0.14	1.19*	-0.60	0.28	0.35	-0.87**	1.07**
	-0.65	0.75	0.51	1.27**	-0.79	-0.87**	1.08**
	-0.16	0.98*	0.31	0.96*	-0.23	-0.79**	1.18**
	-0.02	0.37	0.29	0.61	0.57	-0.85**	1.06**
	-0.35	1.20**	0.83	1.30**	-0.66	-0.68**	1.27**
	-0.14	0.46	0.35	0.77	0.24	-0.81**	1.13**
	0.50	0.75*	0.65	-0.06	0.47	-0.57*	1.24**

Notes: Entries display the coefficient values of the direction terms. Two asterisks next to the value of the particular indicator imply significance at the 1% level, one asterisk indicates significance at the 5% level. The correlation of business cycles of each country pair for 5-year intervals is the dependent variable. Explanatory variables are bilateral measures of trade, fiscal policy, specialisation and a currency union dummy, together with the distance and direction terms of two and three sub-indicators. The entries referring to *n=2* present the coefficients of the direction terms estimated by including every possible combination of two sub-indicators (both the distance and the direction term). The entries referring to *n=3* show the coefficients of the direction terms estimated by including every possible combination of 3 sub-indicators (distance and direction term). Time and period specific constants as well as the coefficients of the control variables and the distance terms of the sub-indicators are estimated, but not reported. Data for a maximum of (20*19)/2=190 country pairs over 9 periods are used.

4.2.4.2 Lagged Institutional Variables

The use of 5-year panel data enables us to look at the dynamic influence of institutional reforms.

Table 31. Lagged direction measure, identification test

Indicator	Sub-Indicator	Model Specification			
		(1) Direction	(2) Direction	(3) Direction	(4) Direction
Employment Protection					
	epl(-1)	1.37**	1.39**	2.15**	2.11**
	epl_allard(-1)	0.44*	0.46*	0.96**	0.97**
Union Density and Coverage					
	udnet(-1)	0.32	0.64	0.49	0.49
	udnet_vis(-1)	0.32	0.66	0.49	0.47
Bargaining Coordination and Centralisation					
	co_oecd(-1)	-0.31	-0.31	0.61	0.58
	co_oecd_int(-1)	0.29	0.29	1.01*	0.93
	cow(-1)	-0.66	-0.68	-0.03	-0.03
	cow_int(-1)	-0.74	-0.65	-0.28	-0.37
	ce_oecd(-1)	-0.86*	-0.85*	0.98	0.88
	ce_oecd_int(-1)	-0.14	-0.09	0.98	0.93
	cew(-1)	1.56**	1.38**	2.53**	2.53**
	cew_int(-1)	2.89**	2.55**	5.16**	5.23**
Replacement Rates					
	brr1(-1)	0.11	0.09	0.18	0.16
	brr_oecd(-1)	0.71**	0.72**	0.66*	0.79*
	nrw(-1)	-0.40**	-0.40**	-0.44**	-0.44**
Taxes					
	t1(-1)	-0.11	0.09	-0.33	-0.33
	t2(-1)	-0.40	-0.50	-1.92	-1.90
	t3(-1)	0.55	0.59	-0.08	-0.01
	tw(-1)	-0.78	-2.09	-2.52	-2.53

Notes: Entries display the coefficient values of the lagged direction terms. Two asterisks next to the value of the particular indicator mean significance at the 1% level, one asterisk indicates significance at the 5% level. The correlation of business cycles of each country pair for 5-year intervals is the dependent variable. Explanatory variables are bilateral measures of trade, fiscal policy, specialisation and a currency union dummy, together with the lagged direction term of a sub-indicator and in specifications (2) and (4) by the corresponding distance term. Specifications (3) and (4) add the additional control variables of tables 22 and 23 to the list of explanatory variables. Time and period specific constants as well as the coefficients of the control variables and, if included, the additional control variables and distance terms are estimated, but not reported. Data for a maximum of (20*19)/2=190 country pairs over 9 periods are used.

This could be important for our investigation, as more time than five years is probably needed in order for the reform effect to materialise. Hence, the role of one period lagged direction measures is analysed.

Since the dynamic nature of institutional changes is already covered by the direction term, we do not focus on the lagged distance term. The procedure is similar to the approach used for the contemporaneous institutional variables. Again, the first step is to identify likely significant lagged institutional variables. According to equation (3), l is now set to 1 in order to allow for lagged direction terms. The number of n depends on the particular specification. We define four different specifications for the identification test. A sub-indicator's lagged direction term is added to the control variables in specification (1), leading to n=1. In addition, specification (2) includes the corresponding distance term to the lagged direction term. In this way, it can be analysed whether the distance term influences the coefficient of the lagged direction term. Specifications (3) and (4) also include the seven additional contemporaneous control variables that were identified as significant in the previous estimations. Specification (4) is almost identical to specification (3), but it accounts for a sub-indicator's lagged direction term as well as for the corresponding distance term, while specification (3) leaves out the distance term.

Table 31 presents the results of four estimations for identifying significant lagged direction measures. The first and the second column display the indicator names and the corresponding sub-indicators. The remaining columns show the coefficients of the sub-indicator's lagged direction terms in four different specifications. All specifications include the control variables trade, fiscal policy, specialisation and the currency union dummy.

The results suggest taking a closer look at the lagged values of employment protection (*epl_allard*), bargaining coordination and centralisation (*cew_int*) as well as replacement rates (*brr_oecd, nrw*), since these indicators show a possible influence on business cycle synchronisation: all 4 lagged direction measures are significant in all specifications. Similar to the analysis of the contemporaneous distance and direction measures, we run additional estimations as a robustness check for the results in table 31. The significant employment protection sub-indicator (*epl*) is not introduced in the following robustness check since it features fewer observations than the other significant sub-indicator for employment protection (*epl_allard*). *Cew_int* is taken as the relevant sub-indicator for bargaining centralisation, as the other significant sub-indicator (*cew*) shows a slightly lower t-statistic value. We do not exclude either of the 2 significant sub-indicators for replacement rates (*brr_oecd, nrw*), since they exhibit different coefficient signs and therefore are clearly not substitutable.

The first specification estimates every combination of 2 sub-indicators' lagged direction terms in addition to the control variables and the additional control variables of the previous section. This specification is indicated by $n=2$ referring to 2 jointly measured sub-indicator's direction terms. The second specification differs from the first in allowing for the inclusion of an additional direction term. Again, all possible combinations of 3 sub-indicators' lagged direction terms are estimated in each instance and indicated by $n=3$. The distance terms are excluded in the estimations since the results in table 31 report marginal changes in the sub-indicator's direction term coefficient when including the distance term. The outcome is presented in table 32 with the number of jointly estimated sub-indicators in column 1 and the sub-indicator names in the first row. The entries are the coefficients of the sub-indicators in each equation.

Table 32. Lagged direction measure, robustness check

	epl_allard(-1)	cew_int(-1)	brr_oecd(-1)	nrw(-1)
	0.88**	4.95**	0.62*	-0.31*
n=2	0.92**	4.72**	0.57*	-0.42**
	0.89**	4.81**	1.65**	-1.03**
	0.89**	4.81**	1.65**	-1.03**
n=3	0.86**	4.59**	0.55*	-0.30*
	0.83**	4.70**	1.49**	-0.89**

Notes: Entries display the coefficient values of the lagged direction terms. Two asterisks next to the value of the particular indicator mean significance at the 1% level, one asterisk indicates significance at the 5% level. The correlation of business cycles of each country pair for 5-year intervals is the dependent variable. Explanatory variables are bilateral measures of trade, fiscal policy, specialisation and a currency union dummy as well as the additional control variables, together with the direction terms of two and three sub-indicators. The entries referring to *n=2* present the coefficients of the lagged direction terms estimated by including every possible combination of two sub-indicators (only the direction terms). The entries referring to *n=3* show the coefficients of the direction terms estimated by including every possible combination of 3 sub-indicators (only the direction terms). Time and period specific constants as well as the coefficients of the control variables and the additional control variables are estimated, but not reported. Data for a maximum of (20*19)/2=190 country pairs over 9 periods are used.

The results show that the sub-indicators for employment protection (*epl_allard*), bargaining centralisation (*cew_int*) and replacement rates (*brr_oecd*) are significant in every specification while the second sub-indicator for replacement rates (*nrw*) is significant in nearly all specifications.

4.2.4.3 Additional Determinants

Another interesting aspect is whether our findings concerning the influence of the control variables on business cycle synchronisation are in line with the previous results outlined in section 2.2. Trade was identified as a key variable in the determination of business cycle convergence. This hypothesis is confirmed by our results since a positive linkage was discovered between higher trade intensity and converging business cycles. Nevertheless, it should be pointed out that the coefficient of trade intensity was insignificant in several specifications. This supports the findings of Gruben et al. (2002), Calderón et al. (2002) and Imbs (2004), who, in contrast to Frankel and Rose (2002), identify smaller effects of trade on business cycle convergence. By contrast, fiscal convergence seems to have a clear and highly positive connection to greater business cycle correlation, thus supporting the findings of Darvas, Rose and Szapary (2005), who also indentify such a relationship. The role of specialisation, however, is not as clearly defined. The ambiguous results prevent us from drawing a conclusion about the link between similarity of sectoral structures and business cycle convergence. Depending on the model specification, the sign of the specialisation variable changes repeatedly, hence it is impossible to make a statement about the importance of the sectoral structure for the synchronisation process. In the same vein, the impact of a common currency (and, by extension, a common monetary policy) is still unclear. Since the coefficient of the common currency variable in our analysis is non-significant in nearly every estimated specification, we cannot identify a currency union a major determinant of business cycle synchronisation. However, as noted earlier, many effects of the recently established EMU may only materialise over the long term. Thus, while our results indicate that the EMU does not exert a significant influence on business cycle synchronisation, the opposite finding could potentially hold true in a longer time series.

In addition to the usual control variables, we seek to identify further possible sources of business cycle synchronisation. Therefore, long-term real interest rate convergence and the Fraser Institute's Economic Freedom Index are included in the analysis. We use the enhanced standard model to identify the impact of absolute differences in long-term interest rates as well as of the Fraser Index. This means that, in addition to the control variables trade, specialisation, fiscal policy and currency, the significant contemporaneous as well as lagged distance and direction measures are included, leading to a total of 16 explanatory variables. The results are presented in table 33. Specification (1) estimates the effect of the long-term interest rate differential on the business cycle correlation, while specification (2) includes the Fraser index instead of the interest rates. The number of observations shows the amount of included data points in terms of country pairs and time periods. The R^2 is displayed to give an impression of the estimation performance.

The coefficient of the long-term interest rate differential is positive and significant at the 1% level, while the Fraser index coefficient shows insignificance. This suggests that larger real interest rate variability between countries contributes to business cycle synchronisation. An explanation could be that either larger nominal interest rate variability or inflation variability contributes to the stabilisation of asymmetric shocks that countries experience. Most of the structural indicators and fiscal policy are significant in both specifications. The currency union dummy, trade and specialisation as well as some structural indicators are not significant. The large amount of explanatory variables is a possible reason for this. It also has to be kept in mind that a model to explain business cycle synchronisation is a rather fragile construction. Hence, the coefficients are fairly sensitive to any modification. This is also supported by the reported R^2 values. A substitution of the Fraser index by the interest rate differential leads to better performance of specification (1). Nevertheless, the findings of table 33 corroborate our previous results. All coefficients have the expected signs and most are significant.

Table 33. Significance test for long-term interest rates and the Fraser index

Explanatory Variables			Model Specification (1)	(2)
			Coefficients	Coefficients
Control Variables				
		T	7.54	8.70
		FP	-0.11**	-0.07**
		S	0.32	0.06
		curr	0.07	0.13
Structural Reforms				
	distance	udnet	0.01**	0.01*
		cow	-0.13*	-0.19**
		cew	-0.15*	-0.17**
		t1	0.01	0.01
	direction	co_oecd	0.68	0.48
		brr_oecd	-0.63*	-0.57*
		t1	0.89**	0.99**
	direction lagged	epl_allard	0.58*	0.72**
		cew_int	0.84	4.53**
		brr_oecd	1.83**	1.35**
		nrw	-0.98**	-0.83**
Additional Determinants				
		interest rates	0.07**	-
		Fraser index	-	-0.13
Observations			521	675
R^2			0.50	0.37

Notes: Entries display the coefficient values. Two asterisks next to the value of a particular indicator mean significance at the 1% level, one asterisk indicates significance at the 5% level. The correlation of business cycles of each country pair for 5-year intervals is the dependent variable.

4.2.4.4 Sensitivity Analysis

The preceding empirical analysis in this section has been based on business cycles calculated with the Hodrick-Prescott filter (HP). As shown at the beginning of chapter 1, different de-trending methods do not necessarily lead to identical or even similar results, which is due to varying theoretical assumptions in the filter setups. Although the HP filter is commonly used and cited in the business cycle literature, we decided to test the sensitivity of the results of the empirical analysis, using two alternative filtering methods. The band-pass filter of Cristiano-Fitzgerald (CF) as well as the year-on-year difference (DIF4) are applied to the GDP time series in order to obtain alternative measures of the business cycle. The required correlations are calculated in the same way as in the case of the HP-filtered data. The sensitivity analysis comprises three stages. Firstly, the basic model with the control variables trade, specialisation, fiscal policy and currency union is estimated. Then, the second equation is estimated by taking the contemporaneous indicators of structural reforms that were identified as significant in the previous section. Thirdly, the four significant lagged structural reform indicators of the previous section are added to the model. Each equation is estimated three times, only changing in the filtering method of the GDP series. In fact, we find some differences depending on the chosen de-trending method. The distance indicators of union density (*udnet*) and the bargaining centralisation indicator (*cew*) show a change of sign. Furthermore, the significance of the coefficients is no longer retained. Equally, the reform similarity indicators for bargaining coordination (*co_oecd*), bargaining centralisation (*cew_int*) and replacement rates (*brr_oecd*), the last two indicators entering with a lag of one period, exhibit some coefficient changes depending on the de-trending method.

In contrast, the distance measures for bargaining coordination (*cow*) and for the employment tax rate (*t1*) as well as the direction measures for replacement rates (*brr_oecd*), the employment tax rate and the lagged employment protection indicator (*epl_allard*) do not show any sign change, even if the significance of the coefficients alters to some extent.

It should be kept in mind that analysing the influence of institutions on business cycle convergence in a panel data framework gives rise to some possible sources of error. Some of the challenges include measuring structural arrangements and structural reforms, the implementation of an ad-hoc model and the resulting determination of all important explanatory variables as well as the difficulty of using a basically unobservable dependent variable, leaving open the possibility of measurement bias.

Nevertheless, we found that some of the institutional indicators are clearly significant in various specifications, even if they vary in the number and quality of the explanatory variables as well as in the calculation method of the dependent variable. The different results produced by the various filtering methods indeed show a certain sensitivity in several indicators. However, we assume that these results are not a reflection of a weak link between structural reforms and business cycle synchronisation, but are caused by the above described model and data issues.

4.2.5 Concluding Remarks

The purpose of this chapter was to investigate how institutional conditions and structural reforms affect the process of business cycle synchronisation. In this undertaking, one is confronted with some complex issues. Testing hypotheses about the influence of reforms is a challenging task for the full complexity of interactions can hardly be observed, let alone adequately described using econometric techniques. However, if one is willing to accept simplifications, it is possible to obtain insights into reform patterns and their possible effects on business cycles and cyclical synchronisation. There is already a growing literature on the determinants of business cycle synchronisation. Our analysis extends this literature in interesting and important ways. Static cross-section regressions are the prevailing methods used to identify significant factors in business cycle correlation. This limits the possibility of accounting for heterogeneous unobserved effects. Such effects can be better treated with panel data techniques, as pursued in our analysis. In addition, our panel data setup allows us to look at dynamic reform effects, which our results demonstrate to be present and significant in many cases.

In contrast to previous studies, we find that structural settings as well as reforms have an influence on business cycle synchronisation. For the empirical estimations, we first constructed measures of distances between countries' labour market characteristics, as well as of reform efforts in this area.

We find that the distance measures of trade union density, bargaining coordination and centralisation and the employment tax rate, as well as the direction indicators for bargaining coordination and centralisation, replacement rates and the employment tax rate are likely to play a role in explaining business cycle synchronisation. The results indicate that increasing union density participation and employment tax rate differentials as well as diverging structural reforms concerning replacement rates result in more synchronised business cycles. In contrast, similar institutional conditions in the wage bargaining process and homogenous reforms in terms of wage bargaining and employment tax rates lead to converging business cycles. Thus, making institutional arrangements more similar can also have adverse effects on cyclical synchronisation, which is a food for thought in deliberations concerning the nexus between institutions and business cycles.

Furthermore, all tested lagged direction measures, namely employment protection, bargaining coordination and centralisation as well as replacement rates, have a significant effect on business cycle synchronisation in different model specifications. This result corroborates the assumption that adjustments in structural reforms may require a considerable time span until their effects fully materialise. Again, the direction of influence is not distinct since similar reforms in all three mentioned institutional fields yield higher business cycle synchronisation, while similar changes in the second analysed indicator for replacement rates foster business cycle divergence.

Compared to Artis and Claeys (2007) and Böwer and Guillemineau (2006), our results seem more supportive of the notion that similar institutions and institutional changes in countries facilitate convergence in the business cycle. In this regard, some methodological differences potentially underlying the divergent results deserve mention. While both Böwer and Guillemineau and Artis and Claeys focus on differences in structural conditions, an alternative measure for structural reforms was developed for our study. In addition, a larger quantity of data are exploited, leading to more robust and reliable results. Finally, in terms of structural indicators, we analyse a larger number of possible determinants than the aforementioned authors.

In addition to structural conditions, we analyse the influence of long-term interest rates and the Fraser Institute's Economic Freedom of the World Index on business cycle convergence. While the latter factor is insignificant in our specification, the long-term interest rate differential appears to affect business cycle synchronisation. The positive sign of the interest rates coefficient leads to the conclusion that a rising interest rate differential drives business cycle convergence through strengthening resilience to asymmetric shocks.

Furthermore, the effects of the control variables trade, fiscal policy, specialisation and currency union also support the findings of previous studies. Trade intensity clearly influences business cycle convergence, even if it cannot be recognised as the key determinant. In contrast, fiscal policy shows high significance, indicating that fiscal convergence fosters business cycle synchronisation. However, the effects of sectoral structures and a common currency are still unclear since both variables are not significantly involved in the process of business cycle convergence. However, the effects of a currency union cannot be conclusively interpreted at present since a longer time frame may be needed until any effects can be discerned.

All in all, our study delivers rather promising results, as we shed light on the role of structural reforms in the process of business cycle synchronisation. Nevertheless, the presented results have to be taken with some caution. The model is somewhat sensitive to modifications such that the results to some extent depend on the econometric framework as well as the measurement of the included variables.

5 Shock Propagation Mechanisms and Business Cycle Convergence

By Atilim Seymen

This section provides an analysis of shock propagation mechanisms and international business cycles based on structural vector autoregression (SVAR) models. After providing a brief overview of the employed methodology and related literature, results from two different empirical models will be presented. The first empirical model includes the G7 countries, for which relatively long and reliable datasets can be obtained. We examine the properties of output cycles and changes in inflation rates, as well as how these variables are affected by common and structural (supply, demand and nominal) shocks. The second, simpler model covers a shorter sample period and is less theoretical in structure, but deals with more countries than the first model. It allows us to investigate whether gaps in terms of the aforementioned variables between the euro area and its twelve Member States are mainly due to common or country-specific shocks.

5.1 Structural Vector Autoregression Models

Structural vector autoregression (SVAR) models have gained in popularity in macroeconomic analysis since the 1980s. These models allow researchers to estimate structural shocks as well as their dynamic effects on macroeconomic variables by imposing a minimum number of theoretical restrictions on a statistical model. Moreover, SVAR models are not only empirical models; many theoretical models have a structural VAR representation, too. Based on an empirical or theoretical model, a SVAR representation can be employed for the analysis of business cycles. In particular, a structural VAR is well-suited to the modelling approach that views business cycles as a product of exogenous shocks. The propagation mechanisms of the shock thus determine the persistence and amplitude of the business cycle. SVARs allow researchers to examine various aspects of international business cycles:

1. Structural shocks in different countries can be compared.
2. Dynamic responses of macroeconomic variables to a one-standard-deviation structural shock can be compared.

3. Error variance decompositions can be computed for estimating shares of (common and country-specific) shocks in cyclical fluctuations.

In the following, we discuss these three aspects with some examples from the relevant literature and provide an outline of the empirical tools that we employ later for analysis.

5.1.1 Confronting the Estimated Structural Shocks

In a seminal study, Bayoumi and Eichengreen (1992) investigate the coherence of structural shocks across European countries and compare it with US regional data. They estimate bivariate VARs for the output and inflation rates of each European Community (EC) country and US region and identify "supply" and "demand" shocks by employing the identification scheme proposed by Blanchard and Quah (1989). The estimated historical supply and demand shocks for the EC and the United States are plotted and their movements are commented. Moreover, correlations between the anchor country/region (Germany for the European EC and the Mid-East Region for the United States) of these two groups with the other members are reported. Such a correlation analysis is simple and can be very insightful. However, care should be taken not to over interpret the conclusions, since the robustness of the results may not be given; that is, the robustness may change substantially with respect to the choice of the anchor country. The approach used by Bayoumi and Eichengreen also does not distinguish between symmetric and asymmetric (common and country-specific) components of structural shocks; see the critique in Chamie et al. (1994).

Bayoumi and Eichengreen (1992) also take the relative size of estimated shocks into account. Their argument for doing so rests on the postulation that *"the larger the size of the underlying shocks, the more difficult it may be to maintain a fixed exchange rate, and the more compelling may be the case for an independent policy response"*. However, although this argument could be right, it is not possible to compute relative shock sizes, since estimated orthogonal shocks and their dynamic multipliers are identified only up to a certain normalisation and their standard deviations can be changed arbitrarily in the empirical framework.

A simple way to check the convergence (or divergence) between estimated structural shocks is to discern whether the correlation between related shocks is higher (or lower) in later subsamples. A higher correlation in later subsamples may lead to business cycle convergence. Note, however, that strong business cycle synchronisation cannot be taken for granted, even when structural shocks in individual countries consist only of a common component, since it is possible that propagation mechanisms vary between countries due to differing institutions, political preferences or economic structures. We do not report the correlations among possible country pairs in our study due to the sheer abundance of them.[23]

---

[23] For twelve euro area members and the USA, 78 bilateral correlations can be computed.

Chamie et al. (1994) and Xu (2006) follow a two-step approach for estimating structural shocks and their "common" and "country-specific" components. Xu (2006) investigates the common component for country pairs as a share of the overall fluctuation in supply and demand shocks in different subsamples. We modify the approach used by Chamie et al. (1994), who neglect to compute a common component for all possible country pairs in their dataset. We instead calculate a common component for each individual country in order to analyse G7 business cycle dynamics (see section 5.2). We distinguish between components of structural shocks common to every G7 country and country-specific components. If the share of the common component has increased over time, this may be a sign of convergence between economies. This interpretation is valid, however, only under the assumption that the dynamic response of macroeconomic variables to structural shocks is qualitatively and quantitatively similar, as argued above. We find a clear sign of business cycle divergence, on the other hand, if the common component share decreases in later subsamples.

5.1.2 Confronting the Estimated Dynamic Responses to Shocks

Impulse response functions for a specific country provide information on two properties of business cycles: amplitude and persistence. If the variances of all structural shocks are normalised to the same value, as done in our empirical analysis, the magnitude of impulse responses (particularly at the so-called business cycle frequencies) will provide information on the amplitude of the cycle. The shock producing the highest amplitude at business cycle frequencies must be the main driving force behind the business cycle.

A variable either converges gradually to a new long-run value after a one-time shock occurs (if it is non-stationary due to a unit root or if that particular shock is assumed to have a long-run impact on that variable), or the effect of the shock on the variable dies out over time. The length of this convergence process to the new/old long-run value reflects the persistence of the variable response to the particular shock. Shocks with a more persistent effect are likelier to play a bigger role in cyclical fluctuations.

Bayoumi and Eichengreen (1992) investigate the speed of adjustment to supply and demand shocks by comparing impulse response functions. With respect to supply shocks, they report that *"a noticeable feature is the faster speed of adjustment for the US regions despite the lack of the exchange rate instrument within the US currency area. The bulk of the adjustment to supply shocks by US regions occurs within 3 years; for EC countries it typically takes substantially longer"*. This finding, however, is not undisputed. Chamie et al. (1994) report, for example, that *"the adjustment of output in response to a structural shock is slower in the US regions than in the European countries"*.

A numerical unit for measuring the speed of adjustment is suggested by Bayoumi and Eichengreen (1992), namely *"the ratio of the impulse response function in the third year to its long-run level"*. This measure may, however, not be very informative, since the business cycle horizon is typically assumed to be a longer horizon, say from 6 to 32 quarters. A measure related only to the adjustment in the 12th quarter (3rd year) is especially insufficient if the adjustment changes considerably over the total business cycle horizon (which is typically the case). We deal with the speed of adjustment indirectly in our empirical analysis for the euro area by investigating the driving forces of gaps in terms of business cycles between the euro aggregate and individual countries.

Impulse response functions becoming more (or less) similar to each other quantitatively and qualitatively in later subsamples serve as evidence for business cycle convergence (or divergence). Impulse response functions showing increasing similarity over time indicate at the minimum institutional convergence, since similar propagation mechanisms point to similar economic institutions, structures, etc. Yet institutional convergence does not necessarily lead to business cycle convergence, especially when countries are exposed to strong country-specific shocks. Blanchard and Gali (2008) estimate rolling bivariate SVAR models in a recent study in order to assess the changing effects of oil price shocks in the G7 countries over time. We follow a modified version of this strategy in our own empirical work, which uses historical variance decompositions in order to assess the changes in business cycle dynamics in the euro area.

5.1.3 Confronting Shares of Global and Country-Specific Shocks

In general, neither estimating the share of the global component in structural shocks nor estimating impulse response functions alone is sufficient for the analysis of business cycle synchronisation. Therefore, we do not follow these approaches in our own empirical analysis. Characteristics such as amplitude and persistence, which every business cycle possesses, cannot be explained by either the former or the latter method alone. Error variance decomposition is, on the other hand, capable of capturing both of these characteristics. One possibility is to carry out a variance decomposition analysis within individual countries and to check if structural shocks have similar weights in the fluctuations of the same variable. Chamie et al. (1994) follow this strategy in their study, in which they compare US regions with European countries. Their main finding, based on forecast error variance decomposition (FEVD), is that supply shocks have a larger role in cyclical fluctuations in Europe than in the United States. Indeed, carrying out estimations in different subsamples and comparing the findings can bear insightful results.

Another possibility is to estimate common (i.e. common to all countries in the empirical model) and country-specific shocks in an SVAR model and to compute variance decompositions to assess international business cycle convergence. In this line of analysis, an increasing share of common shocks in the fluctuations of output in later subsamples would point to a convergence of business cycles, while a decreasing share of these shocks implies diverging cycles. Constructing a pure SVAR model distinguishing common and country-specific shocks can be an especially challenging task in applied econometrics. We deal with this problem in our first empirical model, which comprises the G7 countries, by employing the empirical methodology proposed by Chamie et al. (1994).

The forecast error variance decomposition is probably the most widely used variance decomposition technique. However, we do not apply this technique in this study due to two main reasons. First, a recent study by Seymen (2008b) has shown that the FEVD is not compatible with conventional business cycle measures. Second, because the model must be then re-estimated for each individual subsample, a subsample analysis is possible with FEVD only to a limited extent. To overcome these two problems, we conduct a historical variance decomposition (HVD) as suggested by Seymen (2008b) based on business cycles measured with the Christiano-Fitzgerald filter for output (in line with our descriptive analysis in chapter 1 and based on the growth rate for inflation). The basic idea behind HVD is that the variable of interest, say x_t, can be decomposed into subcomponents with respect to structural shocks ε_t^i for $i = 1,\dots,N$, where N is the total number of structural shocks in the empirical model, such that

$$x_t = x_{t,\varepsilon_t^1} + \dots + x_{t,\varepsilon_t^N} \tag{21}$$

where x_{t,ε_t^i} is the realisation of x_t had only the i-th structural shock occurred at period t. The variance of x_t is then given by the sum of the covariance of its subcomponents with the total, i.e.

$$var(x_t) = cov(x_t, x_{t,\varepsilon_t^1}) + \dots + cov(x_t, x_{t,\varepsilon_t^N}) \tag{22}$$

Hence, the last term of the equation is the estimated share of the i-th structural shock in the variance of x_t. A negative share, which would imply that the corresponding structural shock has a decreasing effect on the variance of the variable of interest, is not ruled out in this framework.

The structural VAR framework discussed in the foregoing has established itself as a useful device for empirical macroeconomic analyses. It is simple and reproducible, and it can be linked to theoretical models. One of the disadvantages of the framework is its inability to incorporate many variables into the analysis due to the degrees-of-freedom problem. Indeed, adding too many variables/countries to the empirical model will yield a drastic increase in the number of parameters to be estimated. Two approaches can provide a solution to this problem, namely GVAR models and factor models, both of which have already been used for analysing international business cycles and can be seen as extended VAR frameworks. We provide a review of the recent literature on this topic in sub-section 2.1.6 of this book.

We do not employ large global VAR or factor models in our own empirical framework. The technical reason for this is that these models require the painstaking task of collecting a large dataset and the writing of computer codes for estimations that are still not widely used. In addition to the technical difficulties, these models only allow at present a structural analysis to a limited extent. Estimated factors in factor models are typically not given an economic interpretation. The same is valid for the global VAR models, where the analysis of the dynamics is primarily based on generalised impulse response functions, but not from impulse response functions based on shocks that are given a structural macroeconomic interpretation.

Our own empirical work in the next two sections is based on SVAR models. We estimate a model with structural macroeconomic shocks in our first empirical analysis, and then work with a structural VAR model in the second empirical analysis without attributing the estimated shocks a structural economic meaning. The latter model is a simplified version of the factor model suggested by Stock und Watson (2005). The SVAR framework is simple, accessible and easy to interpret. Moreover, the framework is largely sufficient for the empirical analysis we are interested in conducting within this project. The empirical models are explained in the related sub-section in this study.[24] We refer to the related literature for the technicalities, since the applied estimation techniques are rather standard.

We employ SVAR models for the following objectives: i) to estimate structural shocks like supply, demand, etc. and/or their common and country-specific components; ii) to assess the properties of the transmission mechanisms of these shocks; iii) to compute variance decompositions with respect to these shocks; iv) to carry out counterfactual analyses, in which different scenarios are considered by asking questions such as: What would have happened if a certain shock or group of shocks had not occurred in the past? When carrying out these analyses, we also look at changes in subsamples in order to assess changes in business cycle dynamics over time. Unlike the related literature and the previous section of this study, we do not only consider the business cycles measured for a real variable, i.e. output, but also the quarterly changes in inflation rate, i.e. a nominal variable. We think this aspect is important, especially in light of recent increases in food and oil prices and the inflation targeting of the European Central Bank in the euro area.

---

24 Although we had considered proceeding as Fidrmuc and Korhonen (2003) do for identifying euro area-wide structural shocks by estimating a euro area SVAR and comparing it with country-specific SVARs at an earlier stage of our investigation, we have decided not to do so due to the fact that their model based on long-run restrictions contains a lot of uncertainty given the short sample available for many EU members.

5.2 Cycles of G7 Countries

5.2.1 Data and Descriptive Analysis

Our empirical analysis starts with the investigation of output cycle properties and properties of quarterly changes in the inflation rate of the G7 countries. The sample covers the period from 1971Q1 to 2007Q4 (including the initial values used in the estimations) and the data are from the OECD Economic Outlook Database.

Table 34 shows that output cycles of the G7 countries have been positively and highly correlated over the whole sample period, with the three euro area countries being no exception.

Table 34. Correlations of output cycles and inflation growth, G7 countries

	GDP							Inflation						
	can	fra	deu	ita	jpn	gbr	usa	can	fra	deu	ita	jpn	gbr	usa
can	1.00							1.00						
fra	0.44	1.00						-0.19	1.00					
deu	0.32	0.52	1.00					-0.06	0.03	1.00				
ita	0.57	0.73	0.58	1.00				0.19	-0.08	0.25	1.00			
jpn	0.12	0.37	0.59	0.33	1.00			-0.06	-0.05	0.01	0.09	1.00		
gbr	0.45	0.65	0.43	0.41	0.39	1.00		-0.07	0.30	0.11	-0.08	-0.06	1.00	
usa	0.61	0.41	0.54	0.30	0.32	0.55	1.00	0.28	-0.08	0.13	0.03	-0.07	0.06	1.00

Sample: 1972Q2-2007Q4

Japanese output cycles are in general less related to other G7 country cycles excluding Germany. The existence of two cyclically coherent groups – the euro area and English-speaking countries – in terms of GDP cycles, as observed by Stock and Watson (2005) for GDP growth rates, cannot be detected. Inflation cycles show much less coherence, if at all, as can be seen in the table. Whether this is the product of different transmission mechanisms or asymmetric shocks will be discussed below.

Figure 33 shows the mean of correlations in the group of G7 countries over a 6 year rolling window: Output cycles have also invariably shown greater correlation than quarterly changes with the inflation rate. The illustrated mean correlations for the G7 countries are partly in line with the findings for the euro area (cf. figure 6 of section 3.4). In particular, there has been a recent decrease in synchronisation among the G7 countries, as observed for the euro area. This may point to a common global factor behind the recent decreases, such as a decrease in the volatility of common shocks. The mean correlation was rather low in the mid-1990s in both groups and then increased gradually. The euro area cycle mean correlations measured with the Christiano-Filter started, however, to decrease as early as 1999, while the peak for the G7 countries is observed about the year 2004.

Fig. 33. Mean of correlations in the group of G7 countries over a 6 year rolling window

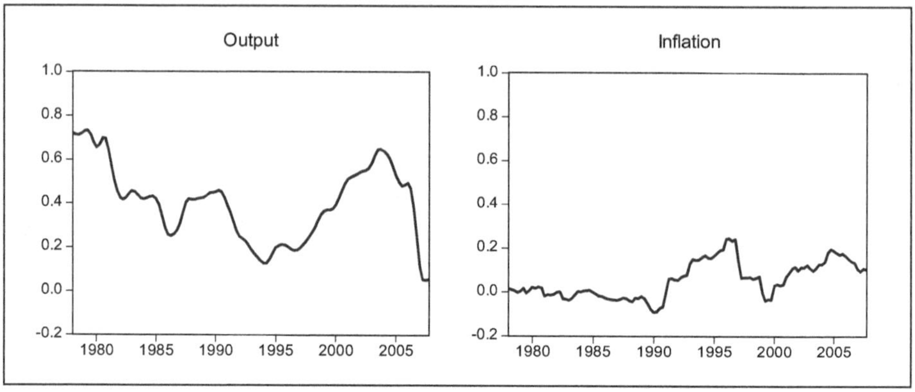

Notes: Output correlations based on Christiano-Fitzgerald filter. Inflaton correlations based on first difference of inflation.

5.2.2 Empirical Model

The estimated model comprises output, the real interest rate and the inflation rate (in this order), i.e. it is an extended version of the bivariate model proposed by Bayoumi and Eichengreen (1992), which contains only output and the inflation rate. Trivariate models of all G7 countries are estimated within a seemingly unrelated regression system in order to increase the estimation efficiency and to connect the country-specific models. The identification scheme developed by Blanchard and Quah (1989) with long-run restrictions is applied to estimate supply, real demand and nominal shocks for every G7 country. The first shock in this system is called a supply shock since this is the only shock that can affect the level of output in the long run. This restriction is consistent with the conventional macroeconomic view that output is solely determined by the supply side of the economy in the long run. The second shock is allowed to affect the real interest rate in the long run along with the supply shock, and is registered as a real demand shock. Changes in the real interest rate can affect the composition of output in the long run, but not its level. The reasoning for this assumption is based on various studies, including King et al. (1991), whose arguments and empirical findings suggest that long-run changes in the real interest rate can affect the consumption/output and investment/output ratios, but not the level of output. The last shock is called a nominal inflation shock, which can only affect the inflation rate in the long-run, leaving output and the real interest rate unaffected. This restriction is also in line with conventional wisdom, according to which money and prices are irrelevant in the long run development of real variables. Although many macroeconomic models do not account for them, we add them to our empirical model for two reasons: i) since we are interested in the dynamics of inflation in the G7 countries; and ii) in order to account for their short-term effects on our single real variable: output.

Any structural VAR strategy may mix supply and demand phenomena within and across countries. Faust and Leeper (1997), for example, compare supply and demand shocks following the models by Blanchard and Quah (1989) and Bayoumi and Eichengreen (1992) for the US economy. Both studies are carried out with bivariate VARs and both comprise output growth. The crucial assumption for the identification of demand shocks is that they cannot affect output in the long run. Furthermore, Blanchard and Quah (1989) include the unemployment rate as the second variable in their model, while Bayoumi and Eichengreen (1992) include the change in the inflation rate. Both approaches can be justified with theoretical arguments; however, as Faust and Leeper (1997) show with an example, the estimated demand shock of one model is highly correlated with the estimated supply shock of the other. The empirical approach that we follow is not vulnerable to such modelling problems as tried and confirmed by different specifications in our analysis; see also Seymen (2008a) on this issue.

Following the methodology of Chamie et al. (1994), common and country-specific components of the structural shocks of individual countries are estimated. The relationship between them can be summarised by

$$\begin{bmatrix} \varepsilon^i_{can,t} \\ \varepsilon^i_{fra,t} \\ \varepsilon^i_{deu,t} \\ \varepsilon^i_{ita,t} \\ \varepsilon^i_{jpn,t} \\ \varepsilon^i_{gbr,t} \\ \varepsilon^i_{usa,t} \end{bmatrix} = \begin{bmatrix} \alpha^i_{can,0} & 1 & 0 & 0 & 0 & 0 & 0 & 0 \\ \alpha^i_{fra,0} & 0 & 1 & 0 & 0 & 0 & 0 & 0 \\ \alpha^i_{deu,0} & 0 & 0 & 1 & 0 & 0 & 0 & 0 \\ \alpha^i_{ita,0} & 0 & 0 & 0 & 1 & 0 & 0 & 0 \\ \alpha^i_{jpn,0} & 0 & 0 & 0 & 0 & 1 & 0 & 0 \\ \alpha^i_{gbr,0} & 0 & 0 & 0 & 0 & 0 & 1 & 0 \\ \alpha^i_{usa,0} & 0 & 0 & 0 & 0 & 0 & 0 & 1 \end{bmatrix} \begin{bmatrix} \xi^i_{0,t} \\ \xi^i_{can,t} \\ \xi^i_{fra,t} \\ \xi^i_{deu,t} \\ \xi^i_{ita,t} \\ \xi^i_{jpn,t} \\ \xi^i_{gbr,t} \\ \xi^i_{usa,t} \end{bmatrix}$$

where $\varepsilon^i_{j,t}$ is the i-th structural shock of the j-th country, $\alpha^i_{j,0}$ is a coefficient related to the common component of the i-th structural shock for the j-th country, $\xi^i_{0,t}$ is the component of the i-th structural shock common to all G7 countries, $\xi^i_{j,t}$ is the country-specific component of the i-th structural shock of the j-th country. After feeding the corresponding entries in this equation back into the country-specific VAR model of the countries, we can compute impulse response functions as well as historical variance decompositions in the standard way. The system of unobservered common and country-specific components is estimated via Maximum Likelihood and the Kalman filter recursion.

5.2.3 Results

Table 35 and 36 show the counterfactual correlations of output cycles and counterfactual correlations of quarterly changes in the inflation rates of the G7 countries that would have taken place if the G7 countries were subject to common shocks only. The high positive counterfactual correlations indicate that the transmission mechanism of shocks in the related countries are very similar. Correlation coefficients close to zero would have indicated completely different transmission mechanisms, while a negative correlation coefficient would have meant that the particular shock leads to a divergence in cycles between the countries. The reported coefficients in table 35 imply that the response of output cycles to supply shocks is highly synchronised in the G7 countries, the lowest correlation coefficient being observed between the cycles of Canada and Italy, with a reading of 0.81. The transmission mechanisms also show important similarities in the face of demand shocks, albeit to a lesser extent than the transmission mechanisms of supply shocks. Germany's relationship to Canada, France and Italy is in this respect somewhat of an exception, with relatively weaker correlations of 0.45, 0.64 and 0.26, respectively. Finally, output cycles also would have been rather highly correlated if the sample period has only contained common nominal shocks. France shows stark contrast in this respect with the other G7 countries, displaying weak correlations with many of them. Common nominal shocks alone even would have led to a divergence between the output cycles of France, Japan and the United Kingdom. The counterfactual correlations reported for inflation growth in table 36 are generally weaker than the correlations reported for output cycles. Although a reason behind this might be that inflation growth is measured by high frequency data whereas output cycles are measured in lower frequencies (i.e. business cycle frequencies, which are in our case assumed to cover periods from 6 to 32 quarters), lower correlations are still obtained if a cyclical component is computed for inflation using the Christiano-Fitzgerald filter, as was done for output.[25] The transmission mechanisms of common supply shocks on inflation growth have been different from country to country according to the reported correlations in table 36. Common demand or nominal shocks alone would have led, however, to generally high positive correlations, implying that the shock propagation mechanisms of the G7 countries are quite similar in this respect. The response of Japanese inflation growth to common demand shocks is an exception. These shocks alone would have led to a divergence of inflation growth between Japan and the rest of the G7 countries. The reported shares in the output cycles of Germany and the United Kingdom have also been driven to an important extent by common shocks to the G7 countries; however, these shocks have played a rather small role in the cycles of the rest of the G7 countries. Table 37 shows that the variance in output cycles in our sample period is explained in every G7 country mainly by supply shocks.

---

25 We do not report results for inflation "cycles", since they hardly vary from the results obtained for inflation growth rates.

Table 35. Counterfactual correlations of output cycles in G7 countries with respect to the common component of structural shocks

	Supply							Demand							Nominal						
	can	fra	deu	Ita	jpn	gbr	usa	can	fra	deu	ita	jpn	gbr	usa	can	fra	deu	ita	jpn	gbr	usa
can	1.00							1.00							1.00						
fra	0.93	1.00						0.96	1.00						0.07	1.00					
deu	0.84	0.97	1.00					0.45	0.64	1.00					0.93	-0.15	1.00				
ita	0.81	0.96	0.97	1.00				0.91	0.88	0.26	1.00				0.86	-0.11	0.81	1.00			
jpn	0.97	0.99	0.94	0.92	1.00			0.90	0.94	0.77	0.70	1.00			0.71	-0.47	0.81	0.90	1.00		
gbr	0.92	1.00	0.98	0.96	0.99	1.00		0.92	0.99	0.72	0.85	0.94	1.00		0.78	-0.54	0.85	0.85	0.94	1.00	
usa	0.98	0.99	0.93	0.90	1.00	0.98	1.00	0.99	0.99	0.54	0.90	0.93	0.96	1.00	0.98	0.27	0.86	0.78	0.57	0.64	1.00

Sample: 1972Q2-2007Q4.

Table 36. Counterfactual correlations of inflation growth in G7 countries with respect to the common component of structural shocks

	Supply							Demand							Nominal						
	can	fra	deu	ita	jpn	gbr	usa	can	fra	deu	ita	jpn	gbr	usa	can	fra	deu	ita	jpn	gbr	usa
can	1.00							1.00							1.00						
fra	0.06	1.00						0.92	1.00						0.99	1.00					
deu	0.44	-0.22	1.00					0.82	0.68	1.00					0.80	0.83	1.00				
ita	0.04	-0.10	0.43	1.00				0.86	0.82	0.85	1.00				0.97	0.97	0.91	1.00			
jpn	0.03	-0.18	-0.05	-0.37	1.00			-0.79	-0.75	-0.79	-0.92	1.00			0.74	0.69	0.35	0.64	1.00		
gbr	0.39	-0.25	0.77	0.11	0.57	1.00		0.97	0.87	0.86	0.90	-0.90	1.00		0.67	0.65	0.35	0.63	0.83	1.00	
usa	-0.28	-0.45	0.31	-0.03	0.74	0.68	1.00	0.67	0.56	0.77	0.61	-0.78	0.77	1.00	0.90	0.90	0.93	0.95	0.60	0.63	1.00

Sample: 1972Q2-2007Q4.

The share of supply shocks is particularly high in the sample period in France, Germany, Japan and the United Kingdom. Italy differs from the other euro area countries in this respect, because output cycles can also partly be attributed to nominal shocks, as in Canada and the US. The US is the only country in which demand shocks contribute, albeit weakly, to output fluctuations. The share of the common component in output cycles is highest in France. The output cycles of Germany and the United Kingdom are also driven to an important extent by common shocks to the G7 countries; however, these shocks play a rather small role in the cycles of the rest of the G7 countries.

Table 37. Share of output fluctuations attributable to shocks in G7 countries

	global	country-specific	supply	demand	nominal
can	0.21	0.79	0.71	0.02	0.26
fra	0.73	0.27	0.97	0.03	0.00
deu	0.30	0.70	0.90	0.03	0.06
ita	0.23	0.77	0.81	0.01	0.19
jpn	0.14	0.86	0.96	0.01	0.03
gbr	0.35	0.65	0.92	0.00	0.08
usa	0.20	0.80	0.67	0.13	0.20

Sample: 1972Q2-2007Q4.

Figure 34 illustrates the shares of output fluctuations attributable to shocks in the G7 countries. Demand and nominal shocks do not play a considerable role in any of the countries throughout the whole sample period.

Table 38. Share of inflation growth fluctuation attributable to shocks in G7 countries

	global	country-specific	supply	demand	nominal
can	0.05	0.95	0.02	0.64	0.33
fra	0.11	0.89	0.05	0.44	0.51
deu	0.18	0.82	0.09	0.44	0.47
ita	0.14	0.87	0.03	0.66	0.31
jpn	0.00	1.00	0.20	0.55	0.25
gbr	0.15	0.85	0.11	0.82	0.07
usa	0.10	0.90	0.09	0.10	0.81

Sample: 1972Q2-2007Q4

There have been, however, episodes in which common supply shocks were an important determinant of output cycles. In particular, French output cycles have largely been driven by common supply shocks, the effect of which has decreased recently. These shocks were also an important driving force of output cycles until the early 1980s in Canada, Germany, Japan and the United Kingdom. The United Kingdom witnessed a significant surge in its share of common supply shocks between 1995 and 2005; the increase of these years disappeared abruptly after 2005, however. Finally, common supply shocks were never an important driving force of output cycles in the US in the sample period. These shocks even had a negative effect on the variance of output cycles in the US in the mid-1990s.

Fig. 34. Share of cyclical GDP fluctuation in G7 countries attributable to global shocks

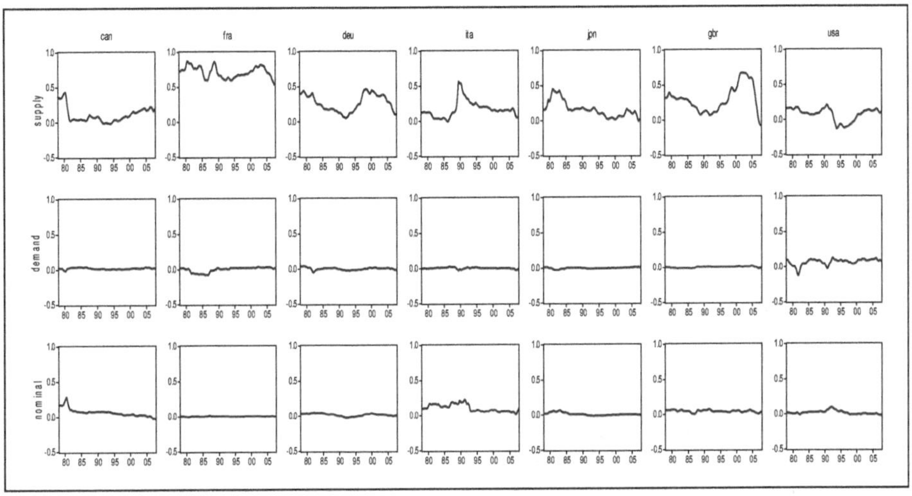

The data in table 38 indicate that inflation dynamics are to a large extent driven by country-specific factors. Japan is the most extreme example here, for the empirical model attributes the whole fluctuation in inflation growth to country-specific shocks. Also, among the G7 countries, Japan's supply shocks make up the largest share (0.20) of fluctuation in inflation growth. Supply shocks have rather insignificant effects in the other G7 countries' inflation growth variance. Country-specific demand and nominal shocks have a rather balanced share in the inflation growth fluctuations of the euro area countries and Canada, while demand shocks are dominant in the United Kingdom, with a share of 0.82, and nominal shocks are dominant in the US, with a share of 0.81.

Figure 35, which shows the share of common shocks in the inflation growth of the G7 countries, is also in line with the above results for the entire sample period: Our calculations indicate common shocks have had negligible effects on this variable in the past. The only exception in this respect is the surge in the share of common demand shocks in inflation growth variance after the year 2000 in the United Kingdom, which, however, reversed itself more recently.

Fig. 35. Share of inflation growth in G7 countries attributable to global shocks

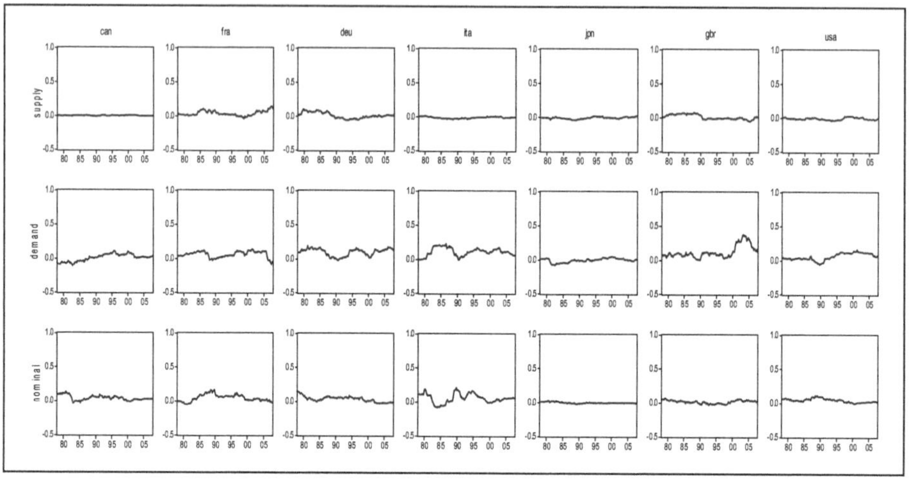

5.3 Heterogeneity of Business Cycles in the EU

5.3.1 Data

We use a modified version of the empirical approach suggested by Giannone and Reichlin (2006), which is itself a simpler version of the strategy followed by Stock and Watson (2005), to investigate the sources of heterogeneity observed in the cyclical fluctuations in (most) EU countries. In contrast to Giannone and Reichlin (2006), who work with annual data, we use quarterly data in our estimations. In this sub-section, we investigate the following: i) the gap between the *cyclical* component of output, ii) the gap between the growth rate of *per capita* output, and iii) the gap between the quarterly change in the inflation rate of individual countries and the euro area. The cyclical component of output is computed with the Christiano-Fitzgerald filter. Inflation is computed as the quarterly rate of change in the Harmonised Consumer Price Index.

Our sample covers the period from 1970Q1 to 2007Q4 for most of the models of output (including the initial values used in the estimations). Austria is the only exception, for which the sample period starts in 1989Q1. The sample covers the period from 1995Q1 to 2007Q3 in most of the inflation rate models (including the initial values used in the estimations). The Irish inflation series starts in 1997Q1. No rolling windows are reported for Greece due to the shortness of its sample, which starts in 2000Q4. A short descriptive analysis of the data is provided along with the counterfactual correlations between the individual countries and the euro area aggregate below.

5.3.2 Empirical Model

Three types of bivariate structural VAR models are estimated in this sub-section. Every model contains the euro area aggregate together with one of the members of the euro area. The identification of the country-specific shock is achieved by assuming that its effect on other countries occurs with a lag. Stock and Watson (2005), for example, write that *"country-specific shocks can lead to spillovers, but those spillovers are assumed to happen with at least a one-quarter lag".* Analogously, in identifying country-specific shocks Giannone and Reichlin (2006) assume that spillover effects occur with at least a one-year lag, since they work with yearly data. Such an assumption is, however, not in line with our empirical findings regarding the lead-lag relationships between the euro area and its Member States, as reported in section 3.4. Therefore, we avoid directly repeating the methods used by Giannone and Reichlin in the following. We argue that working with quarterly data is more in accordance with empirical observations, and we adapt the analysis of Giannone and Reichlin (2006) for output growth with quarterly per capita data.

Our first aim is to discern whether country-specific shocks lead to gaps in output cycles, per capita output growth or inflation growth between a country and the euro area aggregate. Moreover, we hope to identify the driving forces of business cycle dynamics of the euro area countries.

5.3.3 Results

Table 39 reports the true and counterfactual correlations in output cycles between individual members and the euro area. If only euro area shocks had occurred in Member States in the past, their respective output cycles would have shown a very strong correlation with the euro area aggregate; the measured correlation coefficient is larger than 0.95. Among large countries such as Germany, France and Italy, the high correlation coefficient might be explained by a scale effect. Yet small countries such as Austria, Belgium, Luxembourg and the Netherlands also show very high correlation levels. The correlation of the output cycles of Spain, Finland, Greece and Portugal are somewhat less strong in our analysis, but are still 0.80 or higher (had only euro area shocks occurred). This lower correlation level is perhaps due to different propagation mechanisms. Ireland differs significantly from the other countries and shows a correlation of merely 0.32 with the euro area.

Only country-specific shocks also would have led to high correlations in output cycles in many cases. The lowest correlation is between Greece and the euro area at 0.40, which is still moderately high. It is interesting to note that the actual correlation between various countries is lower than would have been the case if only one type of structural shock had occurred. This is possibly due to the fact that in the bivariate model only the euro area and a specific country are considered, while in reality 12 different country-specific shocks occur in every period, and these shocks have mixed effects on the individual countries that cannot be explicitly measured by our simplistic empirical model. Therefore, we interpret the reported high correlations in table 39 as a sign of structural similarity among the Member States of the euro area with respect to the propagation mechanisms of shocks. This interpretation implies that differences among output cycles in individual countries are primarily due to the asymmetry of shocks.

Table 39. True and counterfactual correlations of output cycles

	True	Only euro area shocks	Only country shocks
aut	0.74	0.98	0.95
bel	0.82	0.96	0.96
deu	0.89	0.99	0.76
esp	0.70	0.87	0.96
fin	0.44	0.80	0.51
fra	0.84	0.99	0.96
grc	0.54	0.84	0.40
ire	0.28	0.32	0.60
ita	0.85	0.96	0.94
lux	0.72	0.97	0.88
nld	0.79	0.99	0.74
prt	0.69	0.89	0.99

Sample: 1971Q2-2007Q4. Sample for Austria: 1989Q1-2007Q4

The correlation coefficients reported in table 40, which reflect the similarity of per capita output growth rates, are in general lower than the ones in table 39. This is possibly due to the high frequency nature of the data used for computing these correlations. That the counterfactual correlation with respect to the euro area shock is higher for many countries, Italy and Portugal being an exception, is to a large extent a reflection of the statistical properties of the empirical model, which restricts the response of other Member States to the shock of a specific country in the period that the shock occurs. The true correlation is also lower than both of the counterfactual correlations for almost every country except Luxembourg, possibly due to the reason discussed in the previous paragraph.

The relatively low and partly negative correlation coefficients reported for the quarterly change in inflation, i.e. inflation growth, in table 41 are reflective of the idiosyncratic nature of this variable, either in terms of it being subject to asymmetric shocks or differences in propagation mechanisms related, or both. While the quarterly inflation change in Germany, Spain, Italy and to a lesser extent in Finland and the Netherlands seems to be related to the change in the euro area, the other countries show either virtually no correlation or a negative one. Surprisingly, country-specific shocks only would have led to higher inflation growth correlations than euro area-only shocks.

The variance of gaps between the output cycles in individual countries and the euro area, reported in table 42, can be attributed to country-specific shocks, except in the case of Austria and Spain.

Table 40. True and counterfactual correlations of per capita output growth

	True	Only euro area shocks	Only country shocks
aut	0.51	0.87	0.55
bel	0.53	0.74	0.61
deu	0.85	0.99	1.00
esp	0.59	0.92	0.63
fin	0.36	0.76	0.43
fra	0.65	0.93	0.58
grc	0.25	0.64	0.26
ire	0.23	0.79	0.46
ita	0.45	0.51	0.79
lux	0.31	0.80	0.15
nld	0.49	0.98	0.59
prt	0.37	0.47	0.88

Sample: 1971Q2-2007Q4. Sample for Austria: 1989Q1-2007Q4

Table 41. True and counterfactual correlations of inflation growth

	True	Only euro area shocks	Only country shocks
aut	0.12	-0.33	0.61
bel	-0.36	-0.99	-0.16
deu	0.61	0.68	0.87
esp	0.63	0.75	0.74
fin	0.29	0.36	0.30
fra	0.14	0.30	0.41
grc	-0.29	-0.71	0.66
ire	0.11	-0.28	0.89
ita	0.48	1.00	0.85
lux	0.18	0.26	0.40
nld	0.38	0.50	0.82
prt	0.09	-0.59	0.83

Sample: 1996Q1-2007Q4 (for some countries the last observation is missing). Sample for Greece: 2001Q1-2007Q4. Sample for Ireland: 1998Q1-2007Q4.

This is in line with our interpretation regarding table 39 above, i.e. that the euro area cycles reflect the shocks of 12 Member States, while an individual country is likely to be different than the average of this mixture, although its cycles may be highly correlated with the cycles of many individual countries in the euro area. Euro area shocks seem to be an important driving force of cyclical fluctuations in several Member States, especially in Belgium, Germany, France, Italy, Luxembourg and the Netherlands.

Table 42. Share of output cycle gaps and output fluctuations in Member States attributable to euro area shocks

	Gap		Country variable	
	euro area	country	euro area	country
aut	0.58	0.42	0.14	0.86
bel	0.19	0.81	0.65	0.35
deu	0.01	0.99	0.55	0.45
esp	0.53	0.47	0.21	0.79
fin	0.12	0.88	0.10	0.90
fra	0.26	0.74	0.68	0.32
grc	-0.02	1.02	0.06	0.94
ire	0.30	0.70	0.07	0.93
ita	0.13	0.87	0.40	0.60
lux	0.03	0.97	0.30	0.70
nld	0.09	0.91	0.59	0.41
prt	0.12	0.88	0.15	0.85

Sample: 1971Q2-2007Q4. Sample for Austria: 1989Q1-2007Q4

In contrast, the output cycles of Austria, Spain, Finland, Greece, Ireland and Portugal are mainly driven by their country-specific shocks over the entire sample period. Figure 36 and figure 37 show the share of output cycle gaps and output fluctuations in individual Member States that are attributable to euro area shocks. While the variance of the gap between the euro area cycles and the cycles of Germany and Luxembourg can hardly be traced back to euro area shocks, other Member States' gaps are explained by those in several sub-periods. Euro area shocks even lead to decreases in the variance of the gaps in several countries, including Spain, Finland, Greece and Ireland, in certain sub-periods.

The picture regarding the share of output fluctuation attributable to euro area shocks also differs from country to country. Commonalities that apply to at least a cross-section of euro area countries are hard to find. Euro area shocks are to account for the most part for a positive share of output cycle fluctuations. The picture for Spain and Portugal is especially interesting, as euro area shocks lead to a decrease in the output cycle fluctuations starting roughly in the first half of the 1980s and ending in the first half of the 1990s.

Similar to the case for output cycles, country-specific shocks are a main driving force of output growth fluctuations in Member States.

Figure 38 indicates that the share of output growth rate gaps attributable to euro area shocks has fluctuated considerably in the past. A decrease in the share of these shocks can be observed roughly after the year 2000 in many Member States. Euro area shocks have even contributed to a decrease in Germany's output gap fluctuations in recent years. Greece is the only country in which the share of the gap attributable to euro area shocks was essentially zero for long period time. This share increases slightly after the year 2000, however.

Fig. 36. Euro area shocks as a share of the GDP cycle gaps in individual countries and the euro area over a 6 year rolling window

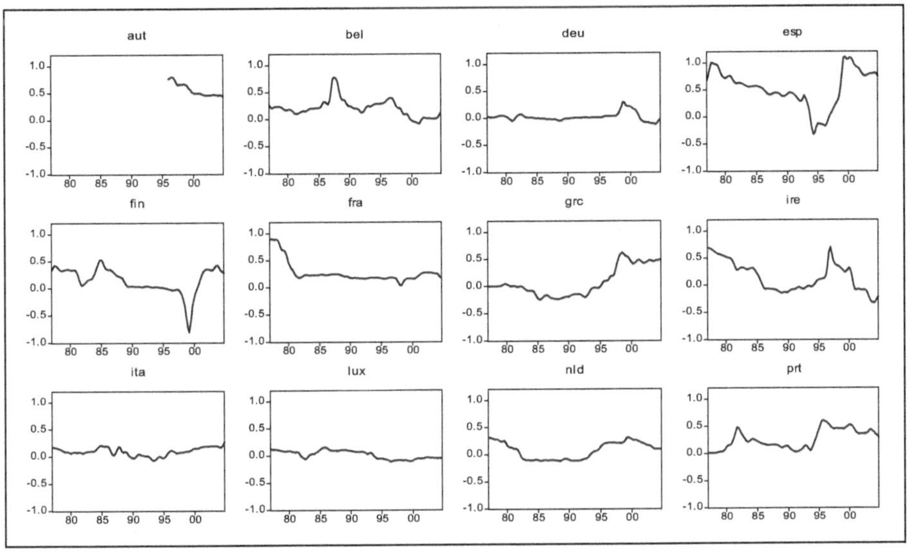

Fig. 37. Euro area shocks as a share of GDP cyclical fluctuations in individual countries over a 6 year rolling window

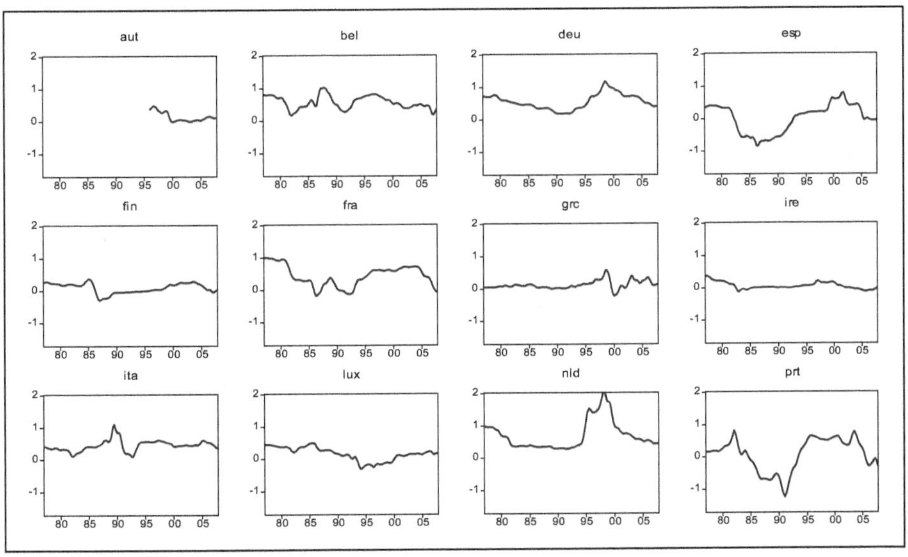

Table 43 shows that the share of euro area shocks in the variance of the output growth gaps of Austria, Belgium, France and Italy has been larger than their country-specific shocks.

Table 43. Euro area shocks as a share of output growth gaps and output variance

	Gap		Country variable	
	euro area	country	euro area	country
aut	0.72	0.28	0.22	0.78
bel	0.60	0.40	0.27	0.73
deu	0.02	0.98	0.15	0.85
esp	0.25	0.75	0.25	0.75
fin	0.14	0.86	0.11	0.89
fra	0.57	0.43	0.32	0.68
grc	0.02	0.98	0.03	0.97
ire	0.13	0.87	0.07	0.93
ita	0.53	0.47	0.14	0.86
lux	0.14	0.86	0.12	0.88
nld	0.04	0.96	0.19	0.81
prt	0.32	0.68	0.05	0.95

Sample: 1971Q2-2007Q4. Sample for Austria: 1989Q1-2007Q4.

Fig. 38. Euro area shocks as a share of the output growth rate gaps of individual countries and the euro area over a 6 year rolling window

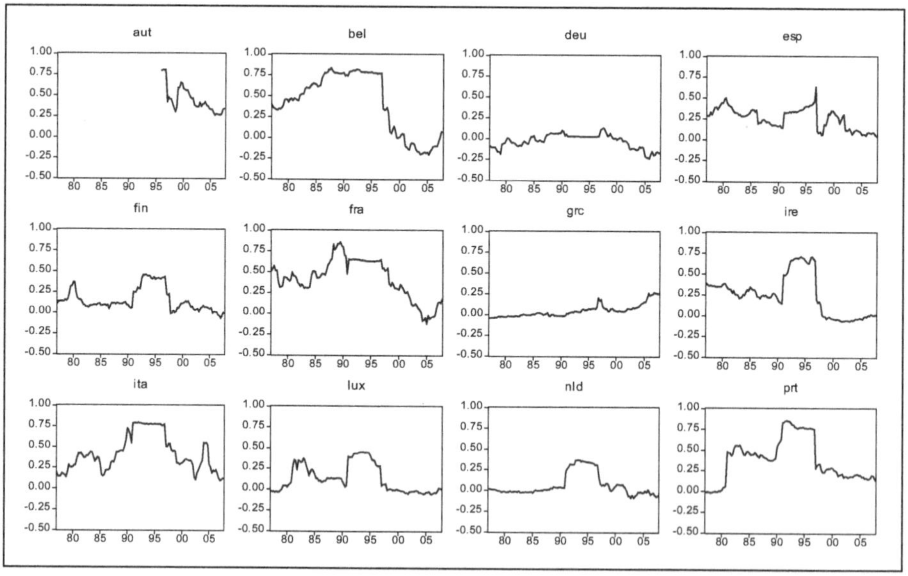

The share of euro area shocks in the output growth rate fluctuations of individual countries has also been rather heterogeneous. However, one common trend is a fall in the output growth rate variance attributable to euro area shocks in the first half of 1990s, as was the case for Germany. At the same time, however, the importance of euro area shocks increased during this period in Belgium, Spain, France, Ireland, Luxembourg, the Netherlands and Portugal.

Fig. 39. Euro area shocks as a share of the output growth rates of individual countries over a 6 year rolling window

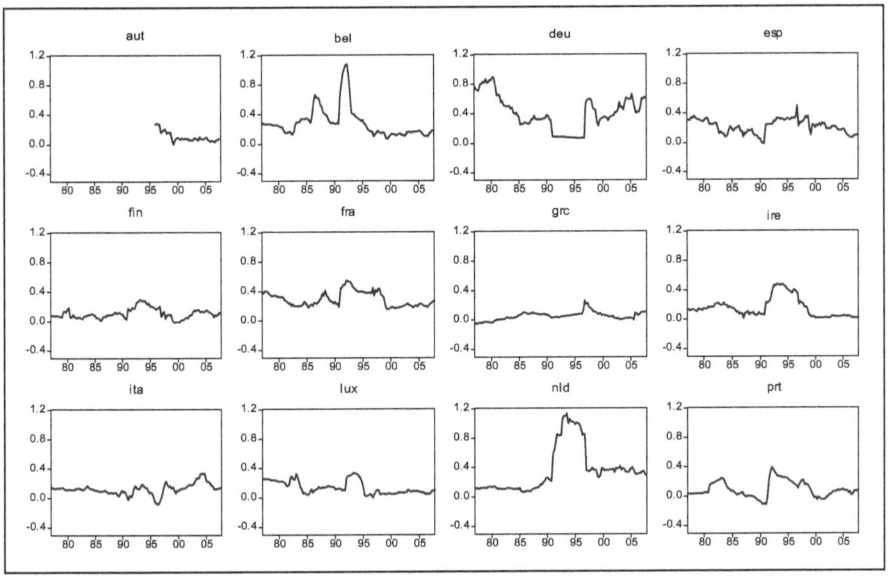

Country-specific shocks account for a large share of the variance in the gap between inflation growth in Austria, Belgium, Germany, France, Greece, Ireland and Portugal. The gaps of Spain, Finland, Italy, Luxembourg and the Netherlands are dominated by their own country-specific shocks; see table 44. The inflation growth of individual countries is also dominated by country-specific shocks to a large extent according to the same table and is in line with the findings for the G7 countries in the previous section. The only exception in this respect is Greece, where the share of euro area shocks in inflation growth fluctuation is 0.45.

Euro area shocks as a share of the gap in inflation growth fluctuation has decreased steadily in Austria, Belgium, Germany, Spain, France, Italy, the Netherlands and Portugal since the beginning of this decade, as illustrated in figure 40. Moreover, it has typically been low in the gaps of Finland, Ireland and the Netherlands. Both of these observations suggest that ECB inflation rate policy has been successful.

Table 44. Shocks as a share of inflation growth gaps and inflation growth in euro area countries

	Gap		Country variable	
	euro area	country	euro area	country
aut	0.90	0.10	0.00	1.00
bel	0.55	0.45	0.12	0.88
deu	0.49	0.51	0.12	0.88
esp	0.13	0.87	0.23	0.77
fin	0.12	0.89	0.12	0.88
fra	0.80	0.20	0.03	0.97
grc	0.64	0.36	0.45	0.55
ire	0.34	0.66	0.28	0.72
ita	0.09	0.91	0.02	0.98
lux	0.07	0.93	0.07	0.93
nld	0.17	0.83	0.04	0.96
prt	0.32	0.68	0.08	0.92

Fig. 40. Euro area shocks as a share of gaps in the inflation growth rates of individual countries and the euro area over a 6 year rolling window

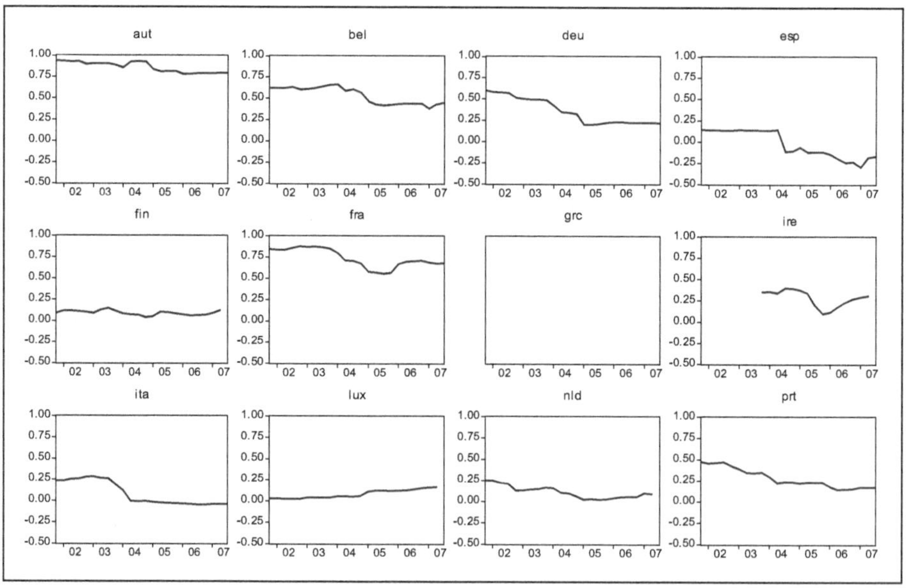

Finally, the share of inflation rate growth attributable to euro area shocks has been close to zero over shorter sub-periods since the year 2000 in almost every Member State; see figure 41. Spain is the only exception in this respect, where euro area shocks have led to a substantial decrease in the variance of inflation growth.

Fig. 41. Euro area shocks as a share of inflation rate growth in individual countries over a 6 year rolling window

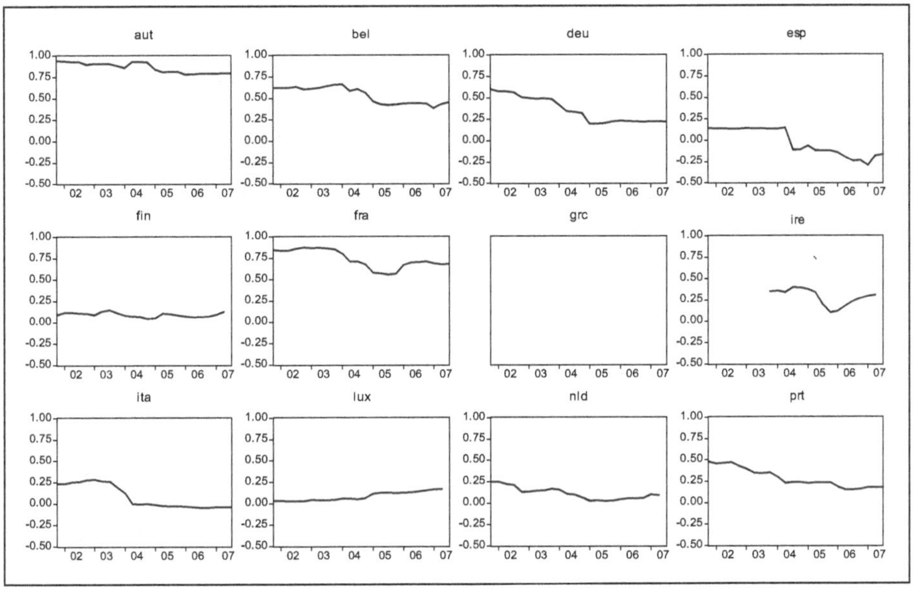

5.4 Concluding Remarks

In this chapter, we first examined the role of structural shocks and the similarity of transmission mechanisms in the G7 countries. Secondly, the heterogeneity of business cycle dynamics within the euro area were analysed. Both analyses were carried out with the aid of structural VAR models, which allow us to estimate structural shocks as well as their dynamic effects on macroeconomic variables by imposing a minimum number of theoretical restrictions.

Our results show that the variance of output cycles is explained in every G7 country mainly by supply shocks. In contrast, demand and nominal shocks seemed to have had only minor influences in the past. Output cycles of G7 countries show different responses to common shocks, which, however, are not that important in explaining the overall observed correlation of output cycles. We computed counterfactual correlations of output cycles and counterfactual correlations of quarterly changes in the inflation rates that would have taken place if the G7 countries were subject to common shocks only. Based on these counterfactuals, we find that the response of output cycles to supply shocks is highly synchronised in the G7 countries. The transmission mechanisms also show important similarities for demand shocks, albeit to a lesser extent than the transmission mechanisms of supply shocks. Furthermore, the output cycles are rather highly correlated when only common nominal shocks are allowed to occur; this correlation declines when countries are exposed to both supply and demand shocks. Transmission mechanisms of shocks to inflation growth are generally less synchronised than shocks to output cycles.

In a further step, we estimated a set of bivariate structural VAR models which contained the euro area aggregate together with one of the Member States. In turns out that the high correlations of euro area business cycles are a reflection of structural similarities with respect to the propagation mechanisms of business cycle shocks. Differences among Member States' output cycles are primarily attributable to shock asymmetry. But we also find common fluctuations to be present and these components have been a relevant driving force for the cycles of Belgium, France, Italy, Luxembourg and the Netherlands in the past. The share of gaps in inflation rate growth that is attributable to euro area shocks has been decreasing steadily in Austria, Belgium, Germany, Spain, France, Italy, the Netherlands and Portugal since the beginning of this decade. Moreover, this share has typically been low in Finland, Ireland and the Netherlands. Again, inflation dynamics seem to rather have their roots in country-specific fluctuations than in common sources.

To summarise, our shock and propagation analyses arrive at diverse findings with regard to the sources of business cycle similarity. Common shocks alone are not capable of explaining the cyclical correlation patterns of the G7 and euro area countries. At the same time, differences in responses to common and idiosyncratic shocks are not very pronounced in the euro area, which can be discerned as a sign of structural similarity.

6 Summary and Policy Implications

Over the decades before the financial crisis, a convergence in business cycles and a decline in output volatility has been witnessed in all major industrialised countries. Hence, it is difficult to identify a specific "euro effect" among the broader business cycle convergence that has occurred. The empirical analyses indicate a high level of business cycle co-movement in the euro area Member States. However, the hypothesis that the introduction of the common currency in 1999 has increased business cycle synchronisation cannot be confirmed. Among the euro area countries, business cycle correlation rose in the run-up to the implementation of Stage 3 of EMU, i.e. in the period from 1993 to 1998. Afterwards, no further increase in co-movement can be seen. Yet at the same time, it is unquestionable that there is also no tendency toward decreasing synchronicity. Consequently, we find no evidence that the implementation of a common currency and monetary policy has had adverse effects on the dispersion of output gaps in Member States.

Our analysis of business cycle volatility and synchronisation of a possible enlarged euro area, comprising the group of non-euro-12 EU-27 countries and a group of non-EU countries, reveals that the global pattern of business cycle volatility and synchronisation with the global business cycle may play an important role for the euro area. This implies that the business cycle dynamics of the euro area can only be accurately analysed by taking both internal euro area and external global factors into account. However, countries outside the euro area exhibit, on average, a lower synchronisation of their business cycles with the euro area on the whole than current euro area members, while only few selected countries have become more synchronised with the euro area over time. This applies particularly to the current EU Member States, especially from Central and Eastern Europe, that have not yet introduced the common currency. Hence, further enlargements of the euro area might lead to more divergence of business cycles, rendering an adequate common monetary policy all the more difficult.

This view is also supported by the results of a cluster analysis. A certain core-periphery pattern is found. On average, the business cycles of the countries located in the centre of the current euro area are more synchronised than the business cycles of the countries located at the periphery. This basic conclusion can be drawn from the descriptive picture that relies on correlation-based measures of cyclical similarity. A drawback is that our broad measures of business cycle congruence hide important sources of synchronicity related to the composition of common and structural shocks. Policies rather than markets should be utilised to bring output back to equilibrium in cases in which business cycle co-movement is largely attributable to common shocks on real economic activity. Differences in the transmission mechanisms of shocks may be related to dissimilarities in economic structures, but they also reflect disparities in the reaction of prices and wages to adjusting supply and demand levels. Market rigidities that inhibit a rapid adjustment of output to its equilibrium level are barriers which prevent an increase in the resilience of an economy, i.e. the degree to which it can absorb the initial impact of a shock and the speed with which it rebounds to trend growth.

We examined the role of structural shocks and the similarity of transmission mechanisms in the G7 countries with the aid of structural VAR models. Our results show that in each G7 country the variance in output cycles is explained mainly by supply shocks, whereas demand and nominal shocks seemed to have had only minor effects in the past. While the output cycles of G7 countries respond differently to common shocks, this is not that important in explaining the overall observed correlation of output cycles. Therefore, business cycle synchronisation among the G7 countries does not seem to be solely driven by common global factors. We do, however, find similarities in the reaction of the G7 countries to shocks. Based on a counterfactual analysis, which is feasible after estimating and identifying the shock components, we find that the response of output cycles to supply shocks is highly synchronised in the G7 countries. The transmission mechanisms also show important similarities in the face of demand shocks, albeit to a lesser extent than the transmission mechanisms of supply shocks. Additionally, if only common nominal shocks occur, the output cycles are usually rather highly correlated, but less strongly than in the case of supply and demand shocks. Transmission mechanisms of shocks to inflation are generally less synchronised than the propagation of shocks to output cycles. This is in line with the observation that output cycles have historically always shown stronger correlation than changes in the inflation rate. In the absence of exchange rates, inflation differentials may be less of concern since they frequently reflect adjustments in competiveness that are taking place between the member countries of the currency union.

We also investigated the heterogeneity of business cycle dynamics within the euro area by estimating a set of bi-variate structural VAR models, each of which contained the euro area aggregate along with one of the Member States. It turns out that the high correlations of euro area business cycles are a reflection of structural similarities with respect to shock propagation mechanisms. Differences between Member States' output cycles are primarily attributable to shock asymmetry, implying that country-specific exogenous sources are important in explaining cyclical variations. But we also find common fluctuations to be present, and these components have been a relevant driving force in the past for the cycles of Belgium, France, Italy, Luxembourg and the Netherlands. The share of euro area shocks to the inflation rate growth gaps has been steadily decreasing for most Member States since the beginning of this decade; for other Member States, it has always been low. Again, inflation dynamics seem to have their roots in country-specific fluctuations rather than in common sources. Taken together, our shock and propagation analyses arrive at diverse findings with regard to the sources of business cycle conformity. Common shocks alone are not capable of explaining the cyclical correlation patterns of the G7 and euro area countries. At the same time, differences in responses to common or idiosyncratic shocks are not very pronounced in the euro area, which can be seen as a sign of structural similarity.

Consistent with some earlier evidence, we find that trade integration has lost importance in the recent post-EMU period, while financial integration has gained considerable importance, such that it now appears to be a relevant driving force behind business cycle synchronisation. This finding is robust under the use of a number of different measures of financial integration and provides evidence that the ongoing process of economic integration and globalisation so far seems to have been mostly supportive of synchronisation in the euro area. Assuming that the process of economic and financial integration continues into the future, this would entail a further increase in business cycle synchronisation, in turn enhancing the viability of a common monetary policy. An additional implication is that when assessing the suitability of potential entrants to the euro area, a wide array of indicators should be considered, particularly the indicators of economic and financial integration that were the focus of this study. The convergence of fiscal policy, inflation rates and long term interest rates, which are the focus of the current convergence criteria, are not the only relevant parameters for assessing the suitability of a country for euro area accession.

The topic of structural reforms currently holds a prominent place in policy debates across the EU. Considerable efforts have been undertaken to delineate and quantify structural reforms and to estimate and model the effects of structural reforms on economic growth and business cycles. In the Lisbon Strategy, the European Union has laid out an extensive reform and innovation agenda. The Lisbon Strategy was devised first and foremost to enhance medium-term growth and employment prospects in EU countries but may also contribute to greater cyclical correlation. In the present study, cross-country similarities between labour and product market institutions as well as reforms thereto are found to support business cycle co-movement. Furthermore, we find that the implementation of structural reforms increases the resilience of economies to exogenous shocks and contributes to reducing the time needed to return to potential growth in the aftermath of shocks.

Structural reforms can create their own momentum as reforms in one area can highlight the need for reforms in other areas. In addition, the adequate combination and sequencing of reforms can increase their political acceptability. International spillovers play an important role, since reforms in one country may affect neighbouring countries in various ways. Reforms can provide neighbouring countries with insights into the effects of reforms (i.e. learning effects), as well as publicly highlight a need for reforms. When undertaking structural reforms, fiscal flexibility is very important. It is needed to cover any short-run additional government spending or changes in tax revenues that may occur. This suggests that it is easier to carry out structural reforms when a country's fiscal position is sound. While the need for structural reforms may be only felt clearly in times of recessions, it is easier to implement them in more advantageous macroeconomic conditions, especially in a period of economic recovery after a recession. This observation follows the reasoning that political support might be difficult to garner in recessionary periods.

7 Appendix

7.1 Data description and sources

Table 45. Countries mnemonics

Euro area		Rest of EU		Other countries	
Id	Country	id	Country	id	Country
Aut	Austria	bul	Bulgaria	aus	Australia
Bel	Belgium	cyp	Cyprus	can	Canada
Deu	Germany	cze	Czech Republic	che	Switzerland
Esp	Spain	dnk	Denmark	isl	Iceland
Fin	Finland	est	Estonia	jpn	Japan
Fra	France	gbr	United Kingdom	kor	Korea
Grc	Greece	hun	Hungary	mex	Mexico
Ire	Ireland	lat	Latvia	nor	Norway
Ita	Italy	lit	Lithuania	nzl	New Zealand
Lux	Luxembourg	mal	Malta	tur	Turkey
Nld	Netherlands	pol	Poland	usa	United States
Prt	Portugal	rom	Romania		
		slo	Slovakia		
		slv	Slovenia		
		swe	Sweden		

Table 46. Variable definitions

Var	Variable name	Unit	Sources[1]
vgdp	Real Gross Domestic Product		1,2
gdp	Nominal Gross Domestic Product	mio. domestic currency , seas. adj.	1,2,3
Et	Total employment	1000	1,2
exch	Exchange rate	euro per local currency	1
Gap	Output gap	%	2

gdpvtr	Potential output, total economy volume	mio. national currency	2
indpro	Industrial production	index	1,2,3
Irl	Interest rate, long-term	%	2
Irs	Interest rate, short-term	%	2
Nlg	Net lending, government	%	2
primnlg	Primary government balance	%	2
debt	Debt level, general government	%	2
canlg	Cyclically adjusted net lending, government	%	2
caprimnlg	Cyclically adjusted primary government balance	%	2
Fow	Freedom of the world, Fraser Institute	Index	
Pcp	Deflator, private consumption	Index	2
pdty	Labour productivity of the total economy	Index	2
Ulc	Unit labour costs	Index	1
Unr	Unemployment rate	%	1,2
Ypg	Current disbursements, government	bln national currency	2
Yrg	Current receipts government	bln national currency	2
Cap	Capacity utilisation ratio	Index	1
Wr	Wage rate (business sector)		2
pgdp	GDP deflator	index	1,2,3
trade	Bilateral trade	current US$	3

[1]: Eurostat (1), OECD Database (2), IMF International Financial Statistics (3).

Table 47. The Nickell-Nunziata database, source: Nickell (2006)

Var	Description	Unit	Range
Ep	Employment protection time varying variable from 1960 to 1995 provided by Blanchard und Wolfers (2000), each observation taken every 5 years. This series was built chaining OECD data with data from Lazear (1990). Note that the OECD data, used from 1985 onward, are constructed on the basis of a more extensive collection of employment protection dimensions compared to the data used by Lazear. This dataset includes an interpolation of the Blanchard and Wolfers series, readjusted in mean. Range is increasing with strictness of employment protection.	index	{0,2}

Epl	Employment protection legislation data from the OECD labour market statistics database using version 1 of the indicator: the strictness of employment protection legislation. This series is extended back as a constant equal to the earliest available observation as long as the above ep index is constant then extended such that the percentage change in ep and epl is the same.	index	{0,2}
Epl_allard	Employment protection legislation series taken from Allard (2005a). This series uses the OECD methodology.	index	{0,5}
udnet	Union density is Union membership/Employment and was calculated using administrative and survey data from the OECD labour market statistics database.	%	
udnet_vis	This series takes udnet and extends it by splicing in data from Visser (2006).	%	
Uc_ochel	Union coverage refers to the number of workers covered by collective agreements normalised on employment. In this case the data were collected by Wolfgang Ochel. Further details may be found in Ochel (2001).	%	
Uc_oecd	Union coverage data taken from the OECD (2004), table 3.3. Where + appears next to a figure, 3 was added.	%	
Uc	This series was constructed as an interpolation of both the uc_Ochel and the uc_oecd data and represents the longest series available.	%	
Co	This index is constructed as an interpolation of OECD data on bargaining coordination. It increases with a higher degree of coordination in the bargaining process on the employers' as well as the unions' side. The resulting series were matched with the data provided by Belot and Van Ours (2000).	index	{1,3}
Co_oecd	This is an index of bargaining coordination taken from OECD (2004). It increases with a higher degree of coordination in the bargaining process on the employers' as well as the unions' side.	index	{0,5}
Co_oecd_int	As co_oecd but interpolated taking the figure given in the table as the middle number of the five year period.	index	{0,5}
cow	This is an index of bargaining coordination taken from Ochel (2000). Based on data reported in OECD (1994), (1997), Traxler and Kittel (2000), Wallerstein (1999), Windmuller et al. (1987) and	index	{1,3}

	Bamber and Lansbury (1998).		
cow_int	As cow but interpolated.	index	{1,3}
ce_oecd	This is an index of bargaining centralisation taken from OECD (2004), table 3.5. It is increasing with a higher degree of centralisation.	index	{0,5}
ce_oecd_int	As ce_oecd but interpolated.	index	{0,5}
cew	This is an index of bargaining centralisation taken from Ochel (2000).	index	{1,3}
cew_int	As cew but interpolated.	index	{1,3}
brr1	Gross benefit replacement rates data are provided by OECD with one observation every two years for each country. In this case the data refer to the first year of unemployment benefits, averaged over three family situations and two earnings levels. The benefits are a percentage of average earnings before tax.	%	
brr23	Gross benefit replacement rates data are provided by OECD with one observation every two years for each country. In this case the data refer to the second and third years of unemployment benefits, averaged over three family situations and two earnings levels. The benefits are a percentage of average earnings before tax.	%	
brr45	Gross benefit replacement rates data are provided by OECD with one observation every two years for each country. In this case the data refer to the fourth and fifth years of unemployment benefits, averaged over three family situations and two earnings levels. The benefits are a percentage of average earnings before tax.	%	
bd	Benefit duration index constructed as bd = 0.6*brr23/brr1 + 0.4*brr45/brr1. This captures the level of benefits available in the later years of unemployment period relative to those available in the first year.	%	
brrl	This index is constructed as brrl = bd*brr1 and captures the benefit replacement rate in later years.	%	
brr_oecd	These are original benefit replacement rates data published by the OECD. It is defined as the average across the first five years of unemployment for three family situations and two money levels taken from www.oecd.org/els/social/workincentives and interpolated.	%	
nrw	Alternative series describing unemployment ben-	%	

	efits by Gayle Allard. The author develops a new indicator for unemployment benefits which combines the amount of the subsidy with their tax treatment, their duration and the prerequisites in order to collect them. See Allard (2005b) for further details.		
hpy	Average actual annual hours worked per person in employment taken from OECD labour market statistics database. The data refer to full year equivalent workers.		
almp	Expenditure on Active Labour Market Policies as a percentage of GDP. Data for 1980, 1989, 1993 and 1998 taken from OECD (2001), table 1.5 and interpolated.	%	
almp_unem	Expenditure on Active Labour Market Policies divided by the Unemployment Rate. This can be rewritten as Expenditure on Active Labour Market Policies per unemployed individual normalised on GDP per member of the labour force.		
regref	The OECD indicators of regulatory reform summarise regulatory provisions in seven non-manufacturing sectors: telecoms, electricity, gas, post, rail, air passenger transport and road freight. The regref indicators have been estimated over the period 1975 to 2003. The regref indicators cover sectors in which anti-competitive regulation tends to be concentrated, given that manufacturing sectors are typically lightly regulated and open to international competition in OECD countries. The range is increasing in regulation.	index	{0,6}
pmr	Overall Product Market Regulation indicator from Conway et al (2005), table 24. The indicator summarises information on 139 economy-wide or industry specific regulatory provisions. It is only available from 1998 to 2003 and interpolated.	index	{0,4}
adminr	Administrative Regulation indicator from Conway et al. (2005), table 24. It is only available from 1998 to 2003 and interpolated.	index	
econr	Economic Regulation indicator from Conway et al. (2005), table 24. It is only available from 1998 to 2003 and interpolated.	index	
t1	The employment tax rate is ESS/(IE-ESS) with ESS equal to the employer social security contributions and IE equal to total compensation for	%	

	employees. ESS is available from the OECD National Accounts detailed tables and IE from OECD Revenue Statistics.	
t2	The direct tax rate is DT/HCR with DT equal to income tax plus employees' social security contributions and HCR equal to household current receipts. Figures for income tax and employee social security contributions were taken from OECD Revenue Statistics. HCR was taken from OECD National Accounts directly for pre-1990 and was calculated as the sum of compensation of employees, property income, social contributions and benefits and other current transfers for post-1990.	%
t3	The indirect tax rate is (TX-SB)/CC with TX equal to indirect taxes, SB equal to subsidies and CC household final expenditures. All three were taken from OECD National Accounts.	%
tw	The Tax Wedge is equal to the sum of the employment tax rate, the direct tax rate and the indirect tax rate.	%
tw_nicol	Average effective tax wedge. Ex-post wedge computed from national accounts taken from Nicoletti institutions data.	%

7.2 Frequency Domain Analyses

The spectral representation or Cramer's representation of a covariance-stationary process y_t is given by

$$Y_t = \int_{-\pi}^{\pi} \theta^{i\omega t}(\varpi)d\varpi \tag{24}$$

in which i is the imaginary unit defined as $i = \sqrt{-i}$, ϖ is the frequency measured in radians over the range from $-\pi$ to π and $z(\varpi)d\varpi$ are complex orthogonal increments with variance $S_y(\varpi)$; the latter is also denoted as the spectrum of the series. The spectral representation says that the process is an infinite sum of waves of different frequencies, each having a random amplitude. The spectrum is computed as follows[26]

26 E.g. Hamilton (1994), Chapter 6.

$$S_y(\varpi) = \frac{1}{2\pi} \sum_{j=-\infty}^{\infty} e^{-i\varpi j} \gamma_y(j) \tag{25}$$

$\{\gamma_y(j)\}_{j=-\infty}^{\infty}$ is a sequence of autocovariances. In the same manner, the *cross-spectrum* of two processes y_t and x_t is defined as

$$S_{x,y}(\varpi) = \frac{1}{2\pi} \sum_{j=-\infty}^{\infty} e^{-i\varpi j} \gamma_{x,y}(j) \tag{26}$$

in which case $\{\gamma_{x,y}(j)\}_{j=-\infty}^{\infty}$ denotes the sequence of cross-covariances between the two variables. The *cross-spectrum* is, in general, complex valued and can be decomposed in a real and an imaginary part

$$S_{x,y}(\varpi) = re(S_{x,y}(\varpi)) + im(S_{x,y}(\varpi)) = CO_{x,y}(\varpi) - i \cdot QU_{x,y}(\varpi) \tag{27}$$

where $CO_{x,y}(\varpi)$ is the *cospectrum* which represents the covariance between the in-phase components of the two variables. $QU_{x,y}(\varpi)$ is called the *quadrature spectrum* and represents the out-of-phase components of the two variables.

Equations (25), (26) and (27) provide us with all the information needed to compute *coherence*, *phase effects* and *dynamic correlation*. *Coherence* is equal to squared *coherency* and defined as

$$H_{x,y}(\varpi) = C_{x,y}^2(\varpi) = \frac{\left|S_{x,y}(\varpi)\right|^2}{S_x(\varpi) S_y(\varpi)} \tag{28}$$

in which $C_{x,y}(\varpi)$ denotes coherency. *Coherence* measures the correlation between the components of two series at different frequencies but disregards the phase effects.

The phase effect $Ph_{x,y}(\varpi)$ can be measured with the aid of the *cospectrum* and the *quadrature spectrum* by the following relation

$$Ph_{x,y}(\omega) = ArcTan\left(\frac{-imag(S_{x,y}(\varpi))}{real(S_{x,y}(\varpi))}\right) = ArcTan\left(\frac{QU_{x,y}(\varpi)}{CO_{x,y}(\varpi)}\right) \tag{29}$$

The phase effect in time units is simply $Ph_{x,y}(\varpi)/\varpi$.

Lastly, *dynamic correlation*, which takes the phase differences of two processes into account, ranges between -1 and 1 and is given by

$$\rho_{x,y}(\omega) = \frac{CO_{x,y}(\varpi)}{\sqrt{S_x(\varpi)S_y(\varpi)}} \tag{30}$$

Since we are not interested in the values of our measures at every frequency, but only on the frequencies that are dominant or that account for the most important fluctuations in the cycle, we follow Azevedo (2002) and compute *mean coherence, mean phase effect* and *mean dynamic correlation.*

Mean coherence is estimated over the frequency band that contains the most dominant frequencies between two cycle series and computed as

$$\bar{\hat{H}}_{x,y} = \frac{\int_{min(\varpi m.x,\varpi m.y)-\Delta}^{max(\varpi m.x,\varpi m.y)+\Delta} \hat{H}_{x,y}(\omega)d\omega}{max(\varpi_{m.x},\varpi_{m.y}) - min(\varpi_{m.x},\varpi_{m.y}) + 2\Delta} \tag{31}$$

in which $\varpi_{m,x}$ and $\varpi_{m,y}$ correspond to frequencies at which the spectrum of the cycles has a peak, $\hat{H}_{x,y}(\varpi)$ is the estimated *coherence* and Δ is the length of a small interval which we set at $\pi/25$. If mean coherence is high, then the major movements in one cycle series are highly correlated with the major movements of the other's cycle series.

In a similar manner, mean phase effects and mean dynamic correlation are computed:

$$\bar{\hat{P}}h_{x,y} = \frac{\int_{min(\varpi m.x,\varpi m.y)-\Delta}^{max(\varpi m.x,\varpi m.y)+\Delta} \hat{P}h_{x,y}(\omega)d\omega}{max(\varpi_{m.x},\varpi_{m.y}) - min(\varpi_{m.x},\varpi_{m.y}) + 2\Delta} \tag{32}$$

and

$$\bar{\hat{\rho}}_{x,y} = \frac{\int_{\Lambda} \hat{C}O_{x,y}(\varpi)d\varpi}{\sqrt{\int_{\Lambda} \hat{f}_x(\varpi)d\varpi \int_{\Lambda} \hat{f}_y(\varpi)d\varpi}} \tag{33}$$

where in the latter case the frequency band is $\Lambda = \left[min(\varpi_{m.x}\varpi_{m.y}) - \Delta, max(\varpi_{m.x}\varpi_{m.y}) + \Delta\right]$.

List of Figures

List of Tables

References

Afonso, A. and Furceri, D. (2007): Business Cycle Synchronisation and Insurance Mechanisms in the EU, ECB Working Paper No. 844.

Akin, C. (2007): Multiple Determinants of Business Cycle Synchronisation, mimeo, George Washington University, Department of Economics, Washington D.C.

Allard, G. (2005a): Measuring Job Security Over Time: In Search of a Historical Indicator, Instituto de Empresa Working Paper, WP05-17.

Allard, G. (2005b): Measuring The Changing Generosity Of Unemployment Benefits: Beyond Existing Indicators, Instituto de Empressa Working Paper, WP05-18.

Angeloni, I. and Dedola, L. (1999): From the ERM to the Euro: New Evidence on Economic and Policy Convergence among EU Countries, ECB Working Paper No. 4.

Artis, M. J. and Claeys, P. (2007): What holds cycles together?, Paper presented at the OECD Workshop on structural reforms and economic resilience: evidence and policy implications, June 2007.

Artis, M. J. and Zhang, W. (1997): On Identifying the Core of EMU: An Exploration of Some Empirical Criteria, CEPR Discussion Paper No. 1689.

Artis, M. J. and Zhang, W. (1997): International Business Cycles and the ERM: Is there a European Business Cycle?, International Journal of Finance and Economics Vol. 2(1), 1-16.

Artis, M. J. and Zhang, W. (1999): Further Evidence on the International Business Cycle and the ERM: Is there a European Business Cycle?, Oxford Economic Papers Vol. 51(1), 120-32.

Asdubrali, P., Sørensen, B. E. and Yosha, O. (1996): Channels of Interstate Risk Sharing: United States 1963-1990, Quarterly Journal of Economics Vol. 111, 1081-1110.

Azevedo, J. V. (2002): Business Cycles: Cyclical Comovement Within the European Union in the Period 1960-1999. A Frequency Domain Approach, Bank of Portugal Working Papers 2002-05, Lisbon.

Babetskii, I. (2005): Trade integration and synchronisation of shocks: Implications for EU enlargement, Economics of Transition Vol. 13(1), 105-138.

Baele, L., Ferrando, A., Hördahl, P., Krylova, E. and Monnet, C. (2004): Measuring Financial Integration in the Euro Area, ECB Occasional Paper No. 14.

Bamber, G. J. and Lansbury, R. D. (1998): Profiles of Union Growth: a Comparative Statistical Portrait of Eight Countries, Basil Blackwell.

Barro, R. J. and Sala-I-Martin, X. (1991): Convergence across States and Regions, Brookings Papers on Economic Activity, No. 1, 107-158.

Baxter, M. and Kouparitsas, M.A. (2005): Determinants of Business Cycle Comovement: A Robust Analysis, Journal of Monetary Economics Vol. 52(1), 113-157.

Bayoumi, T. and Eichengreen, B. (1992): Shocking Aspects of European Monetary Unification, NBER Working Paper No. 3949.

Beffy, P. O., Ollivaud, P., Richardson, P. and Sédillot, F. (2006): New OECD Methods for Supply-Side and Medium-Term Assessments: A Capital Services Approach, OECD Economics Department Working Paper No. 482.

Beine, M. and Coulombe, S. (2003): Regional Perspectives on Dollarization in Canada, Journal of Regional Science Vol. 43(3), 541-569.

Belot, M. and Van Ours, J. (2000): Does the Recent Success of Some OECD Countries in Lowering the Unemployment Rates Lie in the Clever Design of their Labour Market Reforms?, IZA Discussion Paper No. 147.

Bergman, M. U. (2004): How Similar are European Business Cycles?, mimeo, Department of Economics and the Institute of Economic Research, Lund University.

Blanchard, O. J. and Wolfers, J. (2000): The Role of Shocks and Institutions in the Rise of European Unemployment: the Aggregate Evidence, The Economic Journal Vol. 110(462), 1-33.

Blanchard, O. J. and Simon, J. (2001): The long and large decline in U.S. output volatility, Brookings Papers on Economic Activity, No. 1, 135-164.

Blanchard, O. J. and Gali, J. (2008): The Macroeconomic effects of oil shocks: Why are the 2000s so different from the 1970s?, CEPR Discussion Paper No. 6631.

Blanchard, O. J. and Quah, D. (1989): The Dynamic Effects of Aggregate Demand and Supply Disturbances, American Economic Review Vol. 79(4), 655-673.

Bordo, M. D. and Helbling, T. (2003): Have National Business Cycles Become More Synchronized?, NBER Working Paper No. 10130.

Böwer, U. and Guillemineau, C. (2006): Determinants of Business Cycle Synchronisation across Euro Area Countries, ECB Working Paper No. 587.

Buch, C., Doepke, J. and Pierdzioch, C. (2004): Business cycle volatility in Germany, German Economic Review Vol. 5(4), 451-479.

Caldéron, C., Chong, A. and Stein, E. (2002): Trade Intensity and Business Cycle Synchronisation: Are Developing Countries Any Different?, Central Bank of Chile, Working Paper No. 195.

Camacho, M., Pérez-Quirós, G. and Saiz, L. (2005a): Are European Business Cycles Close Enough to be just One?, CEPR Discussion Paper No. 4824.

Camacho, M., Pérez-Quirós, G. and Saiz, L. (2005b): Do European Business Cycles look like one?, Banco de Espana, Documentos de Trabajo, No. 0518.

Canova, F. (1998): Detrending and business cycle facts, Journal of Monetary Economics Vol. 41(3), 475-512.

Chamie, N., DeSerres, A. and Lalonde, R. (1994): Optimum Currency Areas and Shock Asymmetry: A Comparison of Europe and the United States, Bank of Canada Working Paper No. 94(1).

Chinn, M. D. and Ito, H. (2008): A New Measure of Financial Openness, Journal of Comparative Policy Analysis: Research and Practice Vol. 10 (3), 309-322.

Christiano, L. J. and Fitzgerald, T. J. (2003): The Band Pass Filter, International Economic Review Vol. 44(2), 435-465.

Clark, T. E. and Van Wincoop, E. (2001): Borders and Business Cycles, Journal of International Economics Vol. 55(1), 59-85.

Conway, P., Janod, V. and Nicoletti, G. (2005): Product Market Regulation in OECD Countries: 1998 to 2003, OECD Economics Department Working Paper No. 419.

Croux, C., Forni, M. and Reichlin, L. (2001): A Measure of Comovement for Economic Variables: Theory and Empirics, The Review of Economics and Statistics Vol. 83(2), 232-241.

Darvas, Z. and Szapáry, G. (2005): Business Cycle Synchronisation in the Enlarged EU, CEPR Discussion Paper No. 5179.

Darvas, Z., Rose, A. K. and Szapáry, G. (2005): Fiscal Divergence and Business Cycle Synchronisation: Irresponsibility is Idiosyncratic, CEPR Discussion Paper No. 5188.

De Bandt, O. and Mongelli, F. (2000): Convergence of Fiscal Policies in the Euro Area, ECB Working Paper No. 20.

De Haan, J., Inklaar, R. and Sleijpen, O. (2002): Have Business Cycles become more Synchronized?, Journal of Common Market Studies Vol. 40(1), 23-42.

De Haan, J., Inklaar, R. and Jong-A-Pin, R. (2005): Will business cycles in the Euro Area converge: a critical survey of empirical research, CCSO Working Papers 2005/08.

Dees, S., Di Mauro, F., Pesaran, M. H.. and Smith, L. V. (2007): Exploring the International Linkages of the Euro Area: A Global VAR Analysis, Journal of Applied Econometrics Vol. 22(1), 1-38.

Doyle, B. M. and Faust, J. (2002): An Investigation of Co-Movements among the Growth Rates of the G7 Countries, Federal Reserve Bulletin Vol. 88(10), 427-437.

Dubois, E., Hericourt, J. and Mignon, V. (2007): Costs and Benefits of Euro Membership: A Counterfactual Analysis, CEPII Discussion Paper No. 2007-17.

Duval, R., Elmeskov, J. and Vogel, L. (2007): Structural Policies and Economic Resilience to Shocks, OECD Economics Department, Working Paper No. 567.

ECB (2008): 10th anniversary of the ECB, Monthly Bulletin, May 2008.

Eickmeier, S. (2006): Business Cycle Transmission from the US to Germany – A Structural Factor Approach, European Economic Review Vol. 51(3), 521-551.

European Commission (2006): Public finances in EMU, European Economy 2006, No. 3.

European Commission (2007): The reduced volatility of output growth in the euro area, Quarterly Report on the Euro Area Vol. 6(1), 37-46.

European Commission (2008): EMU@10: Successes and challenges after 10 years of Economic and Monetary Union, European Economy No. 2.

Fatás, A. and Mihov, I. (2003): The case for restricting fiscal policy discretion, Quarterly Journal of Economics Vol. 118(4), 1419-1447.

Faust, J. and Leeper, E. (1997): When Do Long-Run Identifying Restrictions Give Reliable Results, Journal of Business and Economic Statistics Vol. 15(3), 345-353.

Fidrmuc, J. and Korhonen, I. (2003): Similarity of supply and demand shocks between the euro area and the CEECs, Economic Systems Vol. 27(3), 313-334.

Fidrmuc, J. and Korhonen, I. (2006): Meta-analysis of the business cycle correlation between the euro area and the CEECs, Journal of Comparative Economics Vol. 34(3), 518-537.

Forni, M. and Reichlin, L. (1997): National Policies and Local Economies: Europe and the United States, CEPR Discussion Paper No. 1632.

Frankel, J. A. and Rose, A. K. (2002): An estimate of the effect of common currencies on trade and income, Quarterly Journal of Economics Vol. 117(2), 437-466.

Frankel, J.A. and Rose, A. K. (1998): The Endogeneity of the Optimum Currency Area Criteria, Economic Journal Vol. 108(449), 1009-1025.

Fritsche, U. and Kuzin, V. (2005): Declining output volatility in Germany: impulses, propagation, and the role of monetary policy, Applied Economics Vol. 37, 2445-2457.

Gali, J. (1999): Technology, Employment and the Business Cycle: Do Technology Shocks Explain Aggregate Fluctuations?, The American Economic Review Vol. 89(1), 249-271.

Gali, J. and Rabanal, P. (2004): Technology Shocks and Aggregate Fluctuations: How Well Does the Real Business Cycle Model Fit Postwar U.S. Data?, IMF Working Paper, WP/04/234.

García Herrero, A. and Ruiz, J. M. (2007): Do Trade and Financial Links foster Business Cycle Synchronisation in a small Economy?, mimeo, Banco de España.

Gayer, C. (2007): A Fresh Look at Business Cycle Synchronisation in the Euro Area, European Economy Economic Papers No. 287.

Gayer, C. and Weiss, P. (2006): Convergence of Business Cycles in the Euro Area: Evidence from Survey Data, Applied Economics Quarterly Vol. 52(3), 193-219.

Giannone, D. and Reichlin, L. (2006): Trends and Cycles in the Euro Area: How Much Heterogeneity and Should We Worry About It?, ECB Working Paper No. 595.

Graff, M. (2006): Internationale Konjunkturverbunde (International Business Cycles), Jahrbücher für Nationalökonomie und Statistik 226/4, 385-417.

Gruben, W. C., Koo, J. and Millis, E. (2002): How Much Does International Trade Affect Business Cycle Synchronisation?, Research Department Working Paper 0203, Federal Reserve Bank of Dallas.

Gwartney, J. and Lawson, R. (2007): Economic Freedom of the World: 2007 Annual Report. With dataset: http://www.freetheworld.com/2007/2007Dataset.xls.

Hansen, H. and Rand, J. (2006): On the Causal Links Between FDI and Growth in Developing Countries, The World Economy Vol. 29(1), 21-41.

Harding, D. and Pagan, A. (2002): Dissecting the cycle: A methodological investigation, Journal of Monetary Economics Vol. 49, 365-81.

Harvey, A. C. (1993): Time Series Models, 2nd edition, MIT Press.

Hoffmeister, A.W. and Roldos, J. E. (2001): The Sources of Macroeconomic Fluctuations in Developing Countries: Brazil and Korea, Journal of Macroeconomics Vol. 23(1), 213-239.

Imbs, J. (2004): Trade, Finance, Specialization and Synchronisation, Review of Economics and Statistics Vol. 86(3), 723-734.

Imbs, J. (2006): The Real Effects of Financial Integration, Journal of International Economics Vol. 68(2), 296-324.

Inklaar, R., Jong-A-Pin, R. and De Haan, J. (2005): Trade and Business Cycle Synchronisation in OECD Countries: A Re-Examination, CESifo Working Paper No. 1546.

Kalemli-Ozcan, S., Papaioannou, E. and Peydró, J. (2010): Financial Regulation, Financial Globalization and the Synchronization of Economic Activity, ECB Working Paper No. 1221.

Kalemli-Ozcan, S., Sørensen, B. E. and Yosha, O. (2001): Economic Integration, Industrial Specialization, and the Asymmetry of Macroeconomic Fluctuations, Journal of International Economics Vol. 55(1), 107-137.

Kalemli-Ozcan, S., Sørensen, B. E. and Yosha, O. (2004): Asymmetric shocks and risk sharing in a monetary union: Updated evidence and policy implications for Europe, mimeo.

Kalemli-Ozcan, S., Sørensen, B. E. and Yosha, O. (2005): Asymmetric Shocks and Risk Sharing in a Monetary Union: Updated Evidence and Policy Implications for Europe, In: The Internationalization of Asset Ownership in Europe, 2005, Hary Huizinga and Lars Yonung (eds.), Cambridge University Press.

King, R. G., Plosser, C. I., Stock, J. H. and Watson, M. W. (1991): Stochastic Trends and Economic Fluctuations, The American Economic Review Vol. 81(4), 819-840.

Kose, M. A., Otrok, C. and Prasad, E. S. (2008): Global business cycles: Converging or decoupling?, IZA Discussion Paper No. 3442.

Kose, M.A., Otrok, C. and Whiteman, C. H. (2003): International Business Cycles: World, Region, and Country-Specific Factors, American Economic Review Vol. 93(4), 1216-1239.

Kose, M.A., Otrok, C. and Whiteman, C.H. (2005): Understanding the Evolution of World Business Cycles, IMF Working Paper, WP/05/211.

Krugman, P. (1979): Increasing Returns, Monopolistic Competition, and International Trade, Journal of International Economics Vol. 9 (4), 469-479.

Krugman, P. (1980), Scale Economies, Product Differentiation and the Pattern of Trade, American Economic Review Vol. 70 (5), 950-959.

Krugman, P. (1991): Geography and Trade, MIT Press.

La Porta, R., Lopez-de-Silanes, F., Shleifer, F. and Vishny, R. W. (1998): Law and Finance, Journal of Political Economy Vol. 106(6), 1113–55.

Lane, P. and Milesi-Ferretti, G. (2001): The External Wealth of Nations: Measures of Foreign Assets and Liabilities for Industrial and Developing Countries, Journal of International Economics Vol. 55(2), 263-294.

Lazear, E. (1990): Job Security Provision and Employment, Quarterly Journal of Economics Vol. 105(3), 699-726.

Lumsdaine, R. L. and Prasad, E. S. (2003): Identifying the common component of international economic fluctuations: A new approach, The Economic Journal Vol. 113(484), 101-127.

Marinheiro, C. (2003): Output smoothing in EMU and OECD: Can we forego government contribution? A risk sharing approach, CESifo Working Paper No.1051.

Massmann, M. and Mitchell, J. (2004): Reconsidering the Evidence: Are Euro Area Business Cycles Converging?, Journal of Business Cycle Measurement and Analysis Vol. 1(3), 275-307.

McKinnon, R. (2001): Optimum currency areas and the European experience, mimeo.

Mink, M., Jacobs, J. and De Haan, J. (2007): Measuring Synchronicity and Co-movement of Business Cycles with an Application to the Euro Area, CESifo Working Paper No. 2112.

Mundell, R. (1963): Optimum Currency Areas, American Economic Review Vol. 53(4), 717-724.

Neck, R. and Haber, G. (2007): Macroeconomic and welfare effects of structural and budgetary policies: spillovers in the MSG3 model, in van Aarle, B., and K. Weyerstrass (eds.), Economic Spillovers, Structural Reforms and Policy Coordination in the Euro Area, Springer Verlag, Contributions to Economics Series.

Nickell, W. (2006): The CEP-OECD Institutions Dataset (1960-2004), CEP Discussion Paper No. 759. With dataset: http://cep.lse.ac.uk/pubs/download/data0759.zip.

Nickell, S. and Nunziata, L. (2001): Labour Market Institutions Database, CEP Discussion Paper No. 502.

Nicoletti, G. and Scarpetta, S. (2003): Regulation, productivity and growth: OECD evidence, Economic Policy Vol. 18(36), 9-72.

North, D. (1990): Institutions, institutional change and economic performance, Cambridge: Cambridge University Press.

Ochel, W. (2000): Collective Bargaining (Centralisation and Coordination), Ifo Institute, mimeo.

Ochel, W. (2001): Collective Bargaining Coverage in the OECD from the 1960s to the 1990s, CESifo Forum, Winter, 62-65.

OECD (1994): Employment Outlook, Paris: OECD.

OECD (1997): Employment Outlook, Paris: OECD.

OECD (2001): Employment Outlook, Paris: OECD.

OECD (2002): Ongoing changes in the business cycle, OECD Economic Outlook, No. 71, 141-156.

OECD (2004): Employment Outlook, Paris: OECD.

Otto, G., Voss, G. and Willard, L. (2001): Understanding OECD Output Correlations, Research Discussion Paper No. 2001-05, Reserve Bank of Australia.

Otto, G., Voss, G. and Willard, L. (2003): A Cross Section Study of the International Transmission of Business Cycles, mimeo, University of Victoria, British Columbia.

Partridge, M. D. and Rickman, D. S. (2005): Regional Cyclical Asymmetries in an Optimal Currency Area: An Analysis Using US State Data, Oxford Economic Papers Vol. 57(3), 373-397.

Pesaran, M. H. and Smith, R. (1995): Estimating long-run relationships from dynamic heterogeneous panels, Journal of Econometrics Vol. 68(1), 79-113.

Pesaran, M.H. and Shin, Y. (1998): Generalized Impulse Response Analysis in Linear Multivariate Models, Economics Letters Vol. 58(1), 17-29.

Pesaran, M.H., Schuermann, T. and Weiner, S. M. (2004): Modeling Regional Interdependencies Using a Global Error-Correcting Macroeconometric Model, Journal of Business & Economic Statistics Vol. 22(2), 129-162.

Rose, A. K. (2000): One Money, One Market: The Effect of Common Currencies on Trade, Economic Policy Vol. 15(30), p.7–33.

Schiavo, S. (2007): Common currencies and FDI flows, Oxford Economic Papers Vol. 59(3), 536–560.

Seymen, A. (2008a): A Comparative Study on the Role of Stochastic Trends in U.S. Macroeconomic Time Series, Centre for European Economic Research Discussion Paper No. 08-007.

Seymen, A. (2008b): A Critical Note on the Forecast Error Variance Decomposition, mimeo Center for Economic Policy Research Discussion Paper.

Sims, C. A. and Zha, T. A. (1998): Does Monetary Policy Generate Recessions?, Federal Reserve Bank of Atlanta, Working Paper 98-12.

Stock, J. H. and Watson, M. W. (2005): Understanding Changes in International Business Cycle Dynamics, Journal of the European Economic Association Vol. 3(5), 968-1006.

Traxler, F. and Kittel, B. (2000): The Bargaining System and Performance: A Comparison of 18 OECD Countries, Comparative Political Studies Vol. 33, 1154-1190.

Van Wincoop, E. (1994): Welfare Gains from International Risk Sharing, Journal of Monetary Economics Vol. 34(2), 175-200.

Visser, J. (2006): Union Membership Statistics in 24 Countries, Monthly Labour Review, January, 38-49.

Wakerly, E., Scott, B. and Nason, J. (2006): Common Trends and Common Cycles in Canada: Who Knew So Much Has Been Going On?, Canadian Journal of Economics Vol. 39(1), 320-347.

Wallerstein, M. (1999): Wage-Setting Institutions and Pay Inequality in Advanced Industrial Society, American Journal of Political Science Vol. 43(3), 649-681.

Windmuller, J. P. (1987): Collective Bargaining in Market Economics: A Reappraisal, Geneva: ILO.

Wynne, M. A. and Koo, J. (2000): Business Cycles under Monetary Union: A Comparison of the EU and US, Economica Vol. 67(3), 347-374.

Xu, X. (2006): A Currency Union for Hong Kong and Mainland China?, Journal of International Money and Finance Vol. 25(6), 894-911.

MIX
Papier | Fördert gute Waldnutzung
FSC® C083411

Kolibri 360 GmbH
Ferdinand-Jühlke-Straße 7
99095 Erfurt, Deutschland
produktsicherheit@kolibri360.de